Theatre and Performance Practices

General Editors: Graham Ley and Jane Milling

Published

Christopher Baugh   *Theatre, Performance and Technology*
Greg Giesekam   *Staging the Screen*
Deirdre Heddon and Jane Milling   *Devising Performance*
Helen Nicholson   *Applied Drama*
Michael Wilson   *Storytelling and Theatre*
Cathy Turner and Synne K. Behrndt   *Dramaturgy and Performance*

Forthcoming

Deirdre Heddon   *Autobiography in Performance*
Philip B. Zarrilli, Jerri Daboo and Rebecca Loukes
   From Stanislavski to Physical Theatre

Staging the Screen

The Use of Film and Video in Theatre

GREG GIESEKAM

palgrave
macmillan

© Greg Giesekam 2007

First published 2007 by
PALGRAVE MACMILLAN

Palgrave Macmillan in the UK is an imprint of Macmillan Publishers Limited, registered in England, company number 785998, of Houndmills, Basingstoke, Hampshire RG21 6XS.

Palgrave Macmillan in the US is a division of St Martin's Press LLC, 175 Fifth Avenue, New York, NY 10010.

Palgrave Macmillan is the global academic imprint of the above companies and has companies and representatives throughout the world.

Palgrave® and Macmillan® are registered trademarks in the United States, the United Kingdom, Europe and other countries.

ISBN 978-1-4039-1698-3 hardback
ISBN 978-1-4039-1699-0 paperback

This book is printed on paper suitable for recycling and made from fully managed and sustained forest sources. Logging, pulping and manufacturing processes are expected to conform to the environmental regulations of the country of origin.

A catalogue record for this book is available from the British Library.

A catalog record for this book is available from the Library of Congress.

Printed in Great Britain by the MPG Books Group, Bodmin and King's Lynn

Contents

List of Figures

General Editors' Preface

This series sets out to explore key performance practices encountered in modern and contemporary theatre. Talking to students and scholars in seminar rooms and studios, and to practitioners in rehearsal, it became clear that there were widely used modes of practice that had received very little critical and analytical attention. In response, we offer these critical, research-based studies that draw on international fieldwork to produce fresh insight into a range of performance processes. Authors, who are specialists in their fields, have set each mode of practice in its social, political and aesthetic context. The series charts both a history of the development of modes of performance process and an assessment of their significance in contemporary culture. Each volume is accessibly written and gives a clear and pithy analysis of the historical and cultural development of a mode of practice. As well as offering readers a sense of the breadth of the field, the authors have also given key examples and performance illustrations. In different ways each book in the series asks readers to look again at processes and practices of theatre-making that seem obvious and self-evident, and to examine why and how they have developed as they have, and what their ideological content is. Ultimately the series aims to ask questions about what are the choices and responsibilities facing performance-makers today?

Graham Ley and Jane Milling

Acknowledgements

I would like to express my gratitude to the following people involved in the companies studied here who talked with me and/or provided me with materials: Václav Janeček and Petr Tošovský (Laterna Magika), Andrea Kunešová (Czech National Theatre); Chris Britton, Tim Britton, Ed Jobling, Penny Saunders and Robin Thorburn (Forkbeard Fantasy); Matt Burman, Tim Etchells, Hugo Glendinning, Terry O'Connor (Forced Entertainment); Claire Hellereau and Marianne Weems (The Builders Association); Clay Hapaz (The Wooster Group); Mark Godber (Station House Opera); Micheline Beaulieu (Ex Machina). I would also like to thank the various photographers who have allowed me to reproduce their work, along with Dagmar Walach of the Institut für Theaterwissenschaft der Freien Universität Berlin (Nachlass Traugott Müller) for the Piscator illustration; Meg Mumford and Benno Plassmann for help with German translation; the Arts and Humanities Research Council for a grant towards travel; my former colleagues Dee Heddon and Minty Donald for reading and responding to some of the material; and the students on my Film and Video in Performance courses at the University of Glasgow over recent years, whose discussions and responses to the work, along with practical experimentation with me, have fed greatly into how I approach the work here. My thanks also to Kate Wallis and Sonya Barker at Palgrave Macmillan and Jane Milling and Graham Ley for their patience as General Editors.

This volume is dedicated to my wife Lalitha Rajan who endured the usual periods of frustration and distraction that accompany any extended piece of research and writing and then read and commented on much of the manuscript; and to my children Bryony and Jannik (who were at least spared reading it).

Introduction: Contamination or Remediation?

Alongside director, designer and producer and the rest, a new credit is becoming common on theatre programmes: 'video designer'.

(Lawson, *Guardian*, 5 April, 2003)

As I began researching this book, a leading media commentator, Mark Lawson, published an article warning of the threat posed to live theatre by the incorporation of video. Noting the use of video designers for recent productions such as Terry Johnson's *Hitchcock Blonde*, the Royal Shakespeare Company's version of Salman Rushdie's *Midnight's Children*, Tom Stoppard's *The Coast of Utopia* trilogy, and the English National Opera production of *The Handmaid's Tale*, Lawson claimed that productions seem to be 'apologising for not being films, like someone changing their appearance to look like a rival in love'. Arguing that performance gains its power from the fact that it 'is created as we watch' and identifying this with the notion of 'liveness', he concluded apocalyptically, 'recent British theatre has suggested not so much a co-existence between stage and screen as the old red velvet theatre curtains being flapped in surrender'.

Despite his melodramatic, doom-laden outlook, Lawson's article provides a useful starting point for this study for several reasons: the commonly found historical amnesia that suggests the use of recorded media in theatre is a recent phenomenon, an amnesia which this book attempts to challenge; his acknowledgement of the proliferation of such work in recent mainstream work, exemplified by its appearance at the RNT, RSC and ENO; his undifferentiating approach to various ways of using media in theatre, which also informs his view of their use as an invasion that needs to be repelled if theatre is to retain a supposedly essential 'liveness' – an outlook which this study will question.

1

It is true that *video* has only become common in theatre in the past 25 years, as diminishing costs, smaller, more flexible equipment, and increasingly sophisticated editing and projection have made its use more attractive. The use of film in theatre, however, extends back a century, to very soon after the invention of cinema. It appears as early as 1904 in France and was regularly used in Germany in the 1920s. While video has certainly extended the range of ways in which recorded media may be deployed, there are many areas of similarity and continuity between such early experiments, other activities in the 1930s to 1960s, and more recent developments. An investigation of these enables a longer-term perspective on current usage.

Lawson correctly notes video's more frequent appearance in recent mainstream theatre work. Even in the 1980s, apart from occasional spectacular scenic use in opera and the international tours of the Czech company Laterna Magika (and other work by its scenographer Josef Svoboda), few mainstream theatres employed film or video. Instead, it was companies such as The Wooster Group in the US, Forced Entertainment and Forkbeard Fantasy in Britain, Robert Lepage's Ex Machina in Canada, and Spain's La Fura dels Baus, along with occasional performance artists and experimental filmmakers who were exploring the interaction between live performers and video material.[1] What is notable about Lawson's more recent list is the range of venues and types of work where video is now found: at the RNT, the RSC and ENO, and in plays such as *Hitchcock Blonde* (a West End hit) and *Midnight's Children* – where the authors scripted in the use of video, as opposed to it resulting from a directorial or design decision, as is more commonly the case.

The list is easily extended. It has almost become *de rigueur* for RNT productions to include video. Nicholas Hytner's 2003 production of Shakespeare's *Henry V* treated Henry's French expedition as a modern media-war, with cameramen and interviewers attending the king, and videos depicted his younger wastrel days with Falstaff at one point. Simon McBurney's production of *Measure for Measure* (2004) employed large-scale projection onto cyclorama and floor for setting purposes. CCTV footage created the atmosphere of a surveillance society, and royal arrivals and pronouncements were again accompanied by camera crews: all this from someone who made his name as an imaginative deviser/director of physical theatre with Théâtre de Complicité, where the focus has always been on the performers' inventiveness.[2] Video also appeared extensively in the RNT production of Philip Pulman's *His Dark Materials* (2003). William Dudley, designer for *The Coast of Utopia* and *Hitchcock Blonde*, subsequently designed Andrew Lloyd Webber's musical *The Woman in White* (2004), using a cyclorama and eight video projectors to create a cinematic feel to the set, as locations shifted between various interiors and sweeping panoramas of the countryside. Towards the end, in a moment recalling early screenings of the brothers Lumière 1895 film *The Arrival of a Train*, a steam train rushed towards the spectators, some of whom ducked, 'so fantastic and realistic' was the effect (Lampert-Gréaux, 2005). The spectacular filmic setting featured in the television advertising campaign for the show, mimicking the sort of trailers normally seen for films.[3]

Throughout Britain well-established companies have employed video in their work: from York Theatre Royal's 2003 Christmas pantomime, *Mother Goose's Silver Jubilee*, to the veteran socialist company Red Ladder's 2004 touring show for young people *Tagged* and Boilerhouse's *Running Girl* (2002). Dealing with the electronic tagging of young offenders, the set of *Tagged* included three monitors built into manoeuvrable pylon-like structures that showed a mix of pre-recorded material and live feed of the onstage performers. *Running Girl* was a promenade performance, advertised as 'cinema made flesh'; the title character ran for 90 minutes on a treadmill mounted on a mobile platform, which was backed by a large projection screen. The platform was shunted about the Glasgow Tramway space, with cityscapes and action projected onto the screen providing a backdrop for her encounters with various figures of urban street-life.

Leading companies in dance and physical theatre, which normally place a premium on the presence and physicality of the live performer, are experimenting with video within their performances, as in DV8's *Just for Show* (2005) and Shobana Jeyasingh's *(h)Interland* (2002). The latter combined pre-recorded film of the backstreets of Bangalore, a projected simultaneous webcast of a dancer performing there, and live performance by two dancers in a London venue. In Belgian choreographer Wim Vandekybus's *Blush* (touring since 2002), a large 'screen' made up of vertical slats of elasticised material allowed performers to move to and fro through it. While the performance focused on the high-energy dance and risk-taking choreography associated with Vandekybus, striking effects were achieved through using the screen to project an underwater scene, into and out of which dancers leap – with stunningly precise synchronisation between their physical disappearance from the stage and their onscreen reappearance swimming underwater.

To these we might add companies who make movies on stage in front of the spectators; for example, the Dutch company Hotel Modern, which toured internationally with *The Great War*, a staging/filming of World War One, in which performers moved toy soldiers around a table-top mock-up of the Western Front made with potting compost, sand, twigs, parsley and so on. Fixed cameras and minicams wielded by the performers relayed events to a screen; spectators saw the making of this animated video of the war and the video itself, yet the impact was as moving as, if not more moving than, that of the big special effects war movies which fill commercial cinemas. The New York company Big Art Group's 2003 production *Flicker* made more camp use of a similar approach; again, performers created a movie on stage, this time a gory horror flick, while their actions were caught on camera, edited and relayed onto three screens running across the front of the stage.

So, everybody's doing it. Moreover, the fact of doing it has become a marketing tool – brochures and flyers are rife now with references to 'exciting multimedia effects', 'fascinating fusions of theatre and video', and so on. In particular, it is believed that such work will appeal to the media-savvy younger audiences which theatres are desperate to attract. Discussing his own turn towards video and computer-generated projected settings, William Dudley suggests that theatre needs to get away from bare-stage performances because younger audiences don't like

> the stillness where you're in one locale for two to three hours ... . They like high visual dynamics and action, all those things people think theatre can't do. ... fine language full of profound thoughts and plays on words pass them by. (Dudley, 2004, 21)

Where early television advertised itself as bringing theatre into your home, it seems now as if theatre advertises itself as bringing television or cinema into your local theatre.[4] Philip Auslander has commented,

> The general response of live performance to the oppression and economic superiority of mediatised forms has been to become as much like them as possible. ... [E]vidence of the incursion of the mediatised into the live event is available across the entire spectrum of performance genres. (1999, 7)

Perhaps predictably, a reaction has set in, seeing it all as just a postmodern fad, theatre succumbing to the rampant dominance of the visual in contemporary culture, or as a last ditch attempt by a threatened industry to attract jaded customers back, when theatre would do far better to go 'back to basics', actors and audience in a shared space, stripped of technological trimmings. As early as 1968, Jerzy Grotowski condemned the 'hybrid-spectacles' of the so-called 'Rich Theatre – rich in flaws', which tried to 'escape the impasse presented by films and television' by chasing after a total theatre. Grotowski described the 'integration of borrowed mechanisms (movie screens onstage, for example)' as 'all nonsense' (1969, 19).

Of course, the binary of a 'poor theatre' which focuses on actor and performance and a theatre which supplements the actors' and writers' efforts with technology has a history stretching back to Aristotle's view that 'the organisation of a tragedy's visual aspect' was a matter for stage technicians, not the playwright, since tragedy should be able to achieve its purposes without recourse to visual effects. And the idea of the theatre being based around 'two planks and a passion' has sur faced in various guises before Grotowski, notably with Jacques Copeau's influential advocacy of the *tréteau nu* (bare stage) in France during the 1920s. The reaction against employing film or video in theatre has been partly shaped by this long-running tension and oscillation between a stripped down theatre and one that enjoys the visually spectacular.

Furthermore, the history of the interactions between theatre, film, television and video has frequently been marked by border disputes between their respective cultural guardians, as each medium has in turn remediated one or more of the others.[5] More recent alarms over theatre remediating film, television and video are ironic, given that these media themselves originally borrowed considerably from theatre, before they developed more distinctive conventions and concerns. As the newer media evolved critics attempted to demarcate their specific qualities and conventions, often rejecting work that seemed too 'theatrical' for failing to acknowledge the distinctiveness of the particular medium – not that there is much agreement amongst critics as to what actually constitutes the 'theatrical' and the 'cinematic'. So, for example, an influential tradition associated with André Bazin privileges film for its supposed capacity to show reality, contrasting this with the 'artificiality' of theatre; others privilege film's capacity to create illusion and fantasy, and theatre is seen as being limited by the spatial and temporal constraints of live performance. Again, some critics argue that theatre is mediated – based on a pre-existent script that is then mediated by any number of different performances to produce different versions of the story and characters; Erwin Panovsky suggested that film is less mediated and that the characters have no aesthetic existence outside the actors. From another point of view, one could ague that on stage we see the real flesh and blood human beings, while on screen we see images of performers that have been mediated by the camera. Reviewing such arguments, Susan Sontag (1966) suggests that what distinguishes theatre from film is the treatment of space – theatre being confined to logical, continuous space, while cinema may access alogical, discontinuous space. A further distinction is, of course, temporal; watching a film, we watch something that has happened in the past, whereas, watching a play, we watch something that unfolds in the time of the performance – even if it represents events from the past.

Some regard such debates as irrelevant, since live theatre has increasingly lost audiences and cultural cachet, while the electronic media of television, video and the internet have apparently established a global domination – to the extent that the idea of contemporary society being a mediatised spectacle has become a commonplace. If Tony Fry's view that television is no longer a medium 'in a context', but *the* context of contemporary life, 'an organic part of the social fabric' (1993, 13), is correct, then it is unsurprising that some theatre practitioners want to engage with it in their work. (A decade on, we might also include the internet along with Fry's television.) In contrast, the idea of theatre or performance art providing a protected zone for the 'live' experience, an oasis for those searching for personal contact in an electronic desert, has seemed attractive to some; but Roger Copeland argues that our perceptions of the world are now so shaped by exposure to media rather than immediate sensory experience that 'to assume that a few hours of "live" theatre will somehow restore a healthy sense of "being there" is naïve and self-deceptive'. For him, 'the idea that theatre's "liveness" is – in and of itself – a virtue, a source of automatic, unearned, moral superiority to film and television, is sheer bourgeois sentimentality' (Copeland, 1990, 42).

Copeland's ire is directed at ahistorical, essentialist views of what theatre or performance should be, which both underestimate the extent to which theatre has often involved a range of mediations and overestimate the oppositional potential of 'liveness' *per se*. Auslander suggests, 'All too often, such analyses take on the air of a melodrama in which virtuous live performance is threatened, encroached upon, dominated, and contaminated by its insidious Other' (1999, 41). That such discussion is steeped in ontology and deontology, as supporters and critics of intermedial work assert what theatre *is* and what theatre *should do*, marks the extent to which the introduction of recorded material into live theatre reorientates many of the ways in which theatre is made and seen.

How, then, does the introduction of electronic media reshape theatre and its reception? Despite the long history and the controversy surrounding it, few general studies of the practice and its implications have appeared, in English at least.[6] Individual practitioners and companies, such as Erwin Piscator, Robert Lepage and The Wooster Group, have been the subject of occasional studies in which their use of film or video has been touched upon. An issue of *Tulane Drama Review* in 1966 made an initial, but limited, foray into discussing what Michael Kirby dubbed 'filmstage'. Subsequently, scholars such as Philip Auslander and Johannes Birringer have explored more fully theoretical issues surrounding the position of theatre in a mediatised society and have commented on some broader characteristics and implications of multimedia work.[7] Occasional articles, such as Marvin Carlson's 2003 discussion of how video extends theatrical space and Steve Dixon's 2005 discussion of how video affects handling of time, provide valuable insights into individual aspects. But there has been little systematic exploration of the variety of ways in which the introduction of film or video into theatre may radically alter approaches to *mise-en-scène*, dramaturgy, performance, modes of production and spectatorship; neither has there been much discussion of the similarities and differences between work with film and work with video.

This book will explore issues such as these through examining in detail the work of a number of practitioners who have contributed significantly to experiment in the field. After Chapter 1's investigation of the historical antecedents of contemporary work, Chapter 2 investigates how Czech scenographer Josef Svoboda, in a career spanning the last half of the 20th century, employed film to develop a more dynamic 'polyscenic' approach to production. Subsequent chapters treat a selection of British and North American practitioners who illustrate different aspects of work with video over the past three decades: The Wooster Group, Forced Entertainment, The Builders Association, Robert Lepage and Station House Opera; Forkbeard Fantasy's idiosyncratic commitment to working with film will also be studied. Before moving on, however, the rest of this chapter will involve some introductory discussion of how the incorporation of film and/or video may challenge common practices and ideas about areas such as *mise-en-scène*, dramaturgy, performance, modes of production and spectatorship, while signalling some of the debates that have arisen from these challenges. It will be useful to begin with consideration of two terms that sometimes appear in discussion of the field: multimedia and intermedia.

Multimedia and intermedia

Apart from its use in discussing computer-related practices, the term 'multimedia' is often applied indiscriminately to any sort of perform-ance event that employs film, video or CGI (computer-generated imagery) alongside live performance. Yet there is surely the world of difference between, say, a production of a Shakespearian text which occasionally uses some video projection to establish its setting or to imply modern parallels with the action, and a newly devised produc-tion in which a significant amount of the actors' performances appears on video, dialogue occurs between onstage and onscreen performers, and live relay regularly focuses attention on particular pieces of busi-ness or parts of a performer's body. In the former type of production, it may be argued that video is employed in a manner analogous to the way in which lighting, set or costumes are used to locate the action and suggest particular interpretative approaches to it; video is one of many apparatuses that collectively support performances that are other-wise built around fairly traditional understandings of the role of text and the creation of character. Such work might be properly described as multimedia. For the second type of production, where more exten-sive interaction between the performers and various media reshapes notions of character and acting, where neither the live material nor the recorded material would make much sense without the other, and where often the interaction between the media substantially modifies how the respective media conventionally function and invites reflec-tion upon their nature and methods, I would suggest the term 'inter-media' is more appropriate.[8] In practice, the divisions are not always as neat as such distinctions would suggest, and it may be more appro-priate to see these as ends of a spectrum. We sometimes encounter work which may be broadly multimedial, but which shifts sometimes towards a more intermedial approach; or we may encounter work which, to the extent that there is a very strong interconnectivity between its onstage delivery and its recorded material, seems interme-dial, but which, on closer inspection, simply employs film or video to vary the mode of performance or audience address, without there being a deeper interaction between the media. Nevertheless, when considering individual practitioners and works, it may be informative to have these distinctions in mind.

I would suggest that the use of film in theatre was initially mostly multimedial, but increasingly complex interactions between theatre and the other media from the 1960s on led to the emergence of genuinely intermedial work. Despite this, much recent technologically sophisticated use of video projection in mainstream theatre reflects more of a multimedial approach; productions such as *Measure for Measure* and *The Woman in White*, for example, are more appropriately described as multimedial. Dudley's collaboration with Terry Johnson on *Hitchcock Blonde* exemplifies work that initially might seem more ambiguous. A clever exploration of desire and the cinematic gaze, it interweaves scenes in which an academic and his female student reconstruct an unknown early Hitchcock film with 'flashback' scenes involving Hitchcock and Janet Leigh's body-double for the shower scene in *Psycho*. Projection is used substantially for setting purposes and for showing reconstructed moments from the film; a couple of times video also briefly conjures up subjective fantasies of the characters. While, in keeping with its themes, the overall atmosphere is cinematic, and the brief film 'reconstructions' persuasively suggest early Hitchcock, there is little active interaction between the stage and projected material and the themes about film are worked through primarily in the action and dialogue. Despite some initial similarity with intermedial work, it ultimately emerges as a multimedial piece.

Although most of the productions that Lawson sees as exemplifying a threat to the stability of boundaries between theatre and film turn out to be multimedial, it might be argued that, at their best, it is intermedial works that pose the greatest challenge to attempts to hold onto clear-cut divisions between theatre and film and video. Often such works challenge our common assumptions about film or video as much as they extend the boundaries of what is conventionally seen as theatre. Although this study traces developments in both multimedia and intermedia, discussion of recent work will focus more on work that tends towards the intermedia end of the spectrum.

Scenography, *mise-en-scène* and dramaturgy

In work that is primarily multimedial, film or video often contributes to scenography or *mise-en-scène* in relatively straightforward ways – even if the technology involved is very complex. In *The Woman in White*, for example, the narrative moves between stately homes, London streets, Cumbrian hills, a lunatic asylum and other locations. In the Victorian theatre, with its penchant for the spectacular,

premise that they are being filmed. Rouse's opera worked with the format of a Jerry Springer style chat-show, with roving cameramen filming the action onstage and in the audience, which could then see itself projected live onto large screens behind the performers.[11] The possibilities of live relay over the internet have now extended this further; the past decade has witnessed increasing experiment in connecting performers and audiences in different locations (see Giannachi, 2004), with Station House Opera's latest work *Play on Earth* (2006) involving performers in São Paolo, Newcastle and Singapore performing for their respective audiences as they interact with live projections of their fellow performers beamed in from the other cities.

While some practitioners, such as Josef Svoboda, have primarily used the available technology to enhance the telling of a central tale, others have adopted a more collagist approach, layering very different orders of story or event against each other, thereby often throwing into question the representational apparatuses employed. Different styles or genres play off against each other, demanding that the spectator bring to bear a range of spectatorial strategies, and challenging conventional notions of how spectators or viewers are positioned by and respond to theatre, film and television. Multiplicity of materials, viewpoints and styles is often also accompanied by a greater degree of simultaneity, more focus on visual imagery, and an increased self-reflexivity than is generally the case in theatre driven more by text, character or narrative.

These aspects also contribute to a somewhat paradoxical effect in much of the work discussed. For all that the productions make use of film and/or video, this study will suggest that, contrary to Lawson's assumptions, many are more overtly 'theatrical' than the quasi-naturalistic text-centred productions that occupy many theatres. Canadian theatremaker Robert Lepage touched on this when he suggested that 'utilising video allows me to be cinematographic, while saying things which are theatrical: my writing belongs more to theatre than cinema' (St-Hilaire, 2000, my trans.). Practitioners such as Lepage, The Wooster Group and Forkbeard Fantasy, all in their different ways, actively play with the theatrical, acknowledging the presence of the audience and the fact of theatre being created out of the interaction between the performers, their technology and the audience. In contrast, quasi-naturalistic dramas that maintain the fourth-wall convention often seem today as though they would be more suited to television than to theatre.

Modes of production

The increased range of source materials in much intermedial work leads towards a tendency to 'assemble' productions, to create 'compositions' of images, sound, light, action and performance, with consequent impacts on how writers, directors, scenographers and performers work. The breakdown in the hierarchies that dominate much mainstream theatrical production, in which design, direction and performance serve a text, often parallels a blurring of hierarchies amongst the co-creators of such work and a diminution in the role of the author (along with the authority invested therein). Marianne Weems of The Builders Association describes how after initial periods of research, discussion and filming, the various collaborators on *Alladeen* (2003) worked in devising sessions over several weeks:

> There's lots of ideas beforehand, but nothing really gets thrashed out or even seriously considered until we get it up on stage. So all the performers were there, and the primary version of the set. All the video was on the sides. Chris Kondek, an amazing video designer, was running up and down the stairs, because he had his computer off in another room. He'd get stuff mixed up, dash down, throw it up ... Dan Dobson, the sound designer was sitting next to me doing the same thing. And Norman Frisch [dramaturg] and I were working, with Martha Baer [writer], and Keith Khan and Ali Zaidi [co-designers], on what the text would be, and constantly cutting, re-editing and re-structuring. It's an almost indiscernible process ... It's sometimes hard to tell if the text leads the video or the video leads the text. (Weems, Interview, 2003)

In Builders Association performances the onstage presence of computer and video operators, and the way they share the performers' curtain call, visually marks this interdisciplinary collaboration. Such collaborative processes, of stopping and starting, experimenting, piecing together the various resources on the rehearsal floor, are common to companies such as Forced Entertainment, The Wooster Group, and Ex Machina.

Weems' account of the symbiotic relationship between the emerging text and the video material also illustrates Johannes Birringer's contention that 'The image/sound technology itself, highly fluid and capable of instant and extensive reprocessing of recorded or generated signals, affords the producers an immediate experience of the constructability of imagery and image relations, and of decision-making and selection processes' (1998, 114). Of course, most creative productions depend upon collaboration and the use of electronically processed materials is hardly a pre-requisite for devising processes that explore the 'constructability of imagery and image relations'; but the presence of such materials, or of cameras and editing facilities that allow the creative team to process ongoing performance explorations, often encourages the creation of work that is more oriented around discovering new relationships between images, texts and performances through open-ended experiment.

Such processes and the intermedial theatre produced inevitably impact on how performers work when performing. It is a commonplace that film acting makes different demands of actors from those made of stage performers. Acting for the cameras without an audience; performing blue-screen sequences without the scenery that will eventually be seen onscreen; playing whole sequences without other participants in the scene actually being present; film performers often function in a way which is more 'virtual' than, say, a stage performer working in a naturalistic production, where the presence of other characters, a representational set and an evolving narrative, all contribute to a very different relationship between performer, character and action.[12] To perform in intermedial theatre is similarly likely to make different demands of performers, as they may shift in one performance between working with variously 'real' and 'virtual' performers and settings, or as their performances may seem to be subsumed within a much more diversified complex of images, sounds, and actions than is often found in more narrative or character-based theatre. Although some of their performances may take place in a similar continuous 'real time' to that of naturalistic theatre performers, and in the presence of an audience, the demands on the performers are often closer to those placed on film performers.

Concerns have been raised about the consequences of the technical demands made of performers. Many productions studied here demand split-second timing, as performers either lip-synch with onscreen images of themselves, engage in dialogue with recorded performers, or move to and fro between stage and screen in a *trompe l'œil* fashion. Performer and performance are to some extent subject to the technology (and without the film-actor's chance to do another take), and the fear is expressed that performers simply become like Edward Gordon Craig's *Übermarionetten*, with hitting their marks and lines exactly preventing them from investing their performance with an in-the-moment vitality and spontaneity. This lies partly behind Lawson's fear that video prevents theatre from 'being created as we watch'. Behind this lie more complex issues concerning presence and liveness which will be addressed later, but for the moment, I would propose that anyone who witnessed the virtuosity with which Wooster Group performer Ron Vawter lip-synched through much of *Frank Dell's The Temptation of Saint Antony*, or has seen the hilarious tightrope act of Chris and Tim Britton as they move in and out of the screen in Forkbeard Fantasy shows while still handling the audience like old-time vaudevillians, will be sceptical of the view that using film and video necessarily inhibits the vitality of the performer/audience relationship. (Moreover, such a concern underestimates the extent to which actors in other types of production are constrained by the technical demands of their productions.)

Doubts are also raised over work involving a lot of live relay, as in the work of companies such as The Builders Association and Ex Machina. With the scale and conventions of stage and screen acting being traditionally different, we might expect performers to experience a conflict between what they see as the demands of performing for the camera, for their fellow performers, and for the audience. Also, for the audience itself, there is the question of whether to watch the live performer or the performance framed on the screen. In practice, performers in such work are generally adept at adopting and discarding different performance modes, and the tensions between the live performance and its framed onscreen presentation often become a significant point of focus or source of spectatorial pleasure.

We will see that such adoption and discarding of performance modes frequently characterises more contemporary work, where, in line with much postmodern cultural production, performances often function in an overtly citational fashion. Often the styles and genres cited are cinematic or televisual, with productions and performers playing off spectatorial familiarity with the conventions of popular film genres, soap opera, reality shows, and so on.[13] In these and other ways we will see contemporary intermedial work illustrating Auslander's contention that

the incursion of mediatisation into live performance is not simply a question of the use of certain equipment in that context. It also has to do with approaches to performance and characterisation, and the mobility and meanings of those within a particular cultural context. (Auslander, 1999, 33)

Spectatorship and demands on the audience

The radical shifts described inevitably impact on how spectators view the work and provoke debates about the demands placed on them and the degree of agency afforded them. In contrast with the camera's eye focus that dominates classic realist cinema, theatre is sometimes seen as allowing spectators a freer rein, as they are able to take in the whole stage picture or any elements of it. In practice, of course, most theatrical productions steer the spectators where the director wishes them to go: blocking, delivery, lighting, and so on, are manipulated to draw attention a certain way. But with intermedial theatre, the practice of presenting multiple, simultaneous images and actions in different media tends to diffuse focus and demand a scanning approach from the spectator. Such work also challenges approaches to theatre that depend upon an audience identifying with actors and their characters. The shifts of medium, genre and style and the approach to performing generally demand a response predicated more on reading the interrelationships between different sources than on empathetic or emotional responses.[14] Such issues and their links with broader debates around liveness and mediation require some detailed discussion.

In some productions potential relationships between the materials may be relatively straightforward. We will see how Piscator, for example, established dialectical relationships between projected materials and onstage performances, and some contemporary work still operates along similar lines. In other work, the relationships may seem more diverse and demand different types of reading by spectators – or may even resist attempts at coherent readings. In The Builders

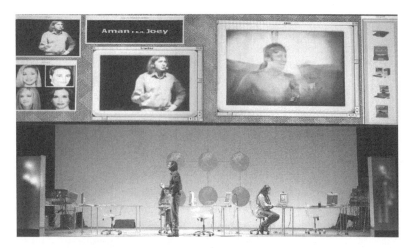

Figure 1   The Builders Association, *Alladeen*

Association's *Alladeen* a wide range of actions, images, information and sounds vie for the spectator's attention as four or five video sources accompany the action. Some supplement onstage action with documentary material or information, some are scenic or atmospheric, some suggest parallels between Aladdin films and the lives of the onstage figures, and some computer-rendered images merge the live performers' faces with those of television performers. Inevitably, comparisons are made with music videos, with multimedia applications for computers, and with the way news programmes show various image boxes and running text displays simultaneously.

Proponents of such multiplicity argue that it reflects contemporary realities and encourages spectators to adopt a more actively productive (and selective) role in responding to the work, as opposed to what they would see as the constraining nature of more 'closed' work. Arguments for the more 'open' productions of postmodern theatre have not gone unchallenged, however. Marco De Marinis, for example, argued that the 'highly indeterminate make-up and loose fixing of reading strategies' of many supposedly 'open' avant-garde performances may in fact be counter-productive, since 'the cooperation asked of an audience … requires a spectator to possess a range of encyclopaedic, intertextual, and ideological competencies which is anything but standard' (De Marinis, 1987, 104). As will be seen in individual production studies, this fear of indeterminacy shapes some of the negative reactions to intermedial work.

The sort of multiplicity and simultaneity being considered, however, is not confined to intermedial theatre, and arguments around these aspects reflect broader cultural debates. Again in the context of computer-based multimedia, Bolter and Grusin use the term 'hypermediacy' to describe such layering of many different sources of information and imagery beside each other. Hypermediacy parallels the prevalence of collage in much postmodern cultural production, but as Bolter and Grusin point out, it is hardly new: 'As an historical counterpart to the desire for immediacy, the fascination with multiplicity can be found in such diverse forms and media as medieval illuminated manuscripts, Renaissance decorated altarpieces, Dutch painting, Baroque cabinets, and modernist collage and photomontage' (1996, 330). Acknowledging that 'the logic of immediacy has perhaps been dominant in Western representation, at least from the Renaissance until the coming of modernism', they suggest,

Sometimes hypermediacy has adopted a playful or subversive attitude, both acknowledging and undercutting the desire for immediacy. At other times, the two logics have coexisted, even when the prevailing readings of art history have made it hard to appreciate their coexistence. At the end of the twentieth century, we are in a position to understand hypermediacy as immediacy's opposite number, an alter ego that has never been suppressed fully or for long periods of time. (Ibid., 330)

There has often been a resistance to hypermediacy, particularly from proponents of supposedly transparent art, art which lays claim to an 'immediate' relation between the viewer and the subject of the artwork. As Ovid's 2,000-years-old assertion 'ars est celare artem' ('it is art to conceal artistry') indicates, the counter-contention that immediacy is actually an *effect* of art, an aspiration rather than a reality, is not as new as theorists sometimes imply. By proliferation and play with different media, hypermediatic work draws attention to the fact that art *always* involves mediation of some sort, contrary to Lawson's imagining that true theatre is 'created as we watch'.[15] Bolter and Grusin suggest this potentially critical role through comparing electronic multimedia with photomontage:

When photomonteurs cut up and recombine 'straight' photographs, they discredit the notion that the photograph is drawn by the 'pencil of nature', as Fox Talbot had suggested. Instead, the photographs themselves become elements that human intervention has selected and arranged for artistic purposes. Photographs pasted beside and on top of each other and in the context of other media such as type, painting, or pencil-drawing create a layered effect that we also find in electronic multimedia. (Ibid., 332)

They suggest that, 'in the logic of hypermediacy the artist (or multimedia programmer or web designer) strives to make the viewer acknowledge the medium as a medium and indeed delight in that acknowledgement' (ibid., 334). Much of the theatre considered in this study, beyond making use of electronic media, does in other ways frequently draw attention to, and indeed delight in playing with, theatre as a medium. Companies such as Forced Entertainment and Forkbeard Fantasy continually play with overt disguise and transformation, working with cheap wigs, exaggerated costuming and obvious gender swapping. The performers often adopt very diverse performance styles and performance personae, thereby drawing attention to the act of performance. As with Bolter and Grusin's photomonteurs, the hypermediacy of such productions is then an extension of a more general subversion of notions of immediacy.

Beyond a spurious clinging to immediacy, however, criticism of the multiplicity of sources is also grounded in a more general resistance to what is seen as an overload of information and images in contemporary society, with television and video often castigated as major culprits. Discussion of both postmodernism and television is pervaded by notions of the society of the spectacle, the simulacrum, the disappearance of the referent of the sign, immersion in and seduction by images, and a waning of affect that arises from the proliferation of depthless pastiches of historical imagery, and so on. Television, for which 'the screen must always be filled, the void is not permitted ... a profusion of images is needed' (Baudrillard, 1993, 148) is portrayed as a key producer of 'the noise and jumbled signals, the unimaginable informational garbage, of the new media society' (Jameson, 1991, 80). This is not just because of its culturally dominant place, but because what Raymond Williams described as the total flow of its programming, as it moves between dramas, news, advertisements, comedy and so on, supposedly contributes to the development of undifferentiating spectatorial habits, with critical distance and memory being lost.[16] Modifying Williams's idea of flow, Margaret Morse argues that 'television discourse typically consists of "stacks" of recursive levels which are usually quite different in look and "flavour" ' (Morse, 1998, 114). Suggesting that television works to elide potential ideological contradictions that might emerge from the co-presence of these different stacks, Morse ties television in with the freeway and the shopping mall as major 'institutions of mobile privatisation' in a culture of distraction, a world of simulations and derealisation (ibid., 118).

In such a technological scene, the sort of dialectical montage associated with a critical Brechtian tradition is seen as giving way to 'reified dramaturgies of montage to be found virtually everywhere in cinematic practices, commercial advertising, television programming, exhibitions, sports events, etc' (Birringer, 1991, 171). The challenge then for theatre practitioners and critics becomes not just whether theatre can provide a counter-site to the limitless seduction of the media, but whether spectators saturated by such reified dramaturgies are able to switch viewing modes when confronted by similar stacks of seemingly incommensurable information and imagery in intermedial work. Is it possible to create work that acknowledges and even exploits the prevalence of electronic media, but does not leave its audience either seduced or overwhelmed, deprived of the capacity for critical thought?

Here we should return to issues surrounding the notion of liveness touched on earlier. Accepting Copeland's sceptical view of live performance functioning *per se* as a vaccination against our exposure to mediatisation, is it possible to argue that live theatre that makes use of media does not just undermine the notion that any theatre is ever 'immediate', but can, through 'staging the screen', also create opportunities to engage with and critique how media such as film and television function? This is not to assert that intermedial work *automatically* adopts such a resistant role or to suggest it is only worthwhile if it does so (which would simply echo ontological ideas about performance which Auslander and Copeland have critiqued), but to recognise that it may sometimes serve to disrupt the flow or draw attention to the way things are stacked up, in a zone of public rather than privatised reception.

Two issues will be considered here: how the co-presence of media and live performers may serve to put into question the practices and underlying assumptions of the media used, and the way different viewing circumstances and different expectations associated with theatre attendance may in themselves affect the ways spectators view media when they appear in the theatre.

Adapting Jacques Derrida's discussion of presence to recent American theatre, Elinor Fuchs argues that Derrida's deconstruction of the notion of presence – the idea that we can ever be fully present to ourselves (or to others), has been matched by theatre practitioners who 'have begun to expose the normally "occulted" textuality behind the phonocentric fabric of performance' (1985, 166). Writing, acting and direction in theatre that lies within broadly naturalistic conventions combine to produce a type of identification-based performance in which performer and character are expected to fuse in a single presence: as we watch, we should feel the character is here before us now, uttering these words and doing these actions (and this reinforces the notion that in daily life coherent self-presence is also a possibility). Fuchs suggests, however, that contemporary experimental theatre practitioners expose the textuality that lies behind the creation of such theatrical performances. Fuchs illustrates different tactics employed for signalling the textual origins of what is done or said, including The Wooster Group's practice in some productions of showing the actors reading from scripts. Such open acknowledgement of textual origins is accompanied by other devices that challenge the performers' presence, amongst them the use of video, whether showing contrasting actions and texts or footage of the performers themselves (when it often shows a split or doubled image). Such practices challenge the authority normally vested in a text.[17]

Similarly, when particular generic conventions and modes of viewing film and television have become so pervasive that they seem 'natural', placing film or video material on the stage often draws attention to the conventions of filming, distribution, presentation and reception that are normally occluded when we watch a film in the cinema or a television programme in our homes. (We should note that most academic discussion of cinema spectatorship tends to assume films are watched in cinemas and most discussions of television viewership tend to assume that it is watched in the privacy of the home, with there being little discussion of how reframing their presentation and viewing may destabilise assumptions about their impact on viewers.) In various ways, companies such as The Wooster Group, Forced Entertainment and Forkbeard Fantasy actively defamiliarise the genres they cite or the mechanisms of screening or projection. We will see, for example, how in *Emanuelle Enchanted* Forced Entertainment works over the news programme format and how Forkbeard Fantasy continually plays with the construction and destruction of various types of screen, a practice that, along with the visible presence of an array of projectors on stage, draws attention to the material nature of film and its projection. Their knowing play with film genres also plays off and subverts their power; in the case of *The Barbers of Surreal*, for example, its film prologue plays with conventions for suturing the spectator into the world of thrillers, but then disrupts the trajectory which would normally follow such an opening.

To suggest that intermedial performance may pose such challenges is not to disregard Auslander's and Copeland's scepticism about conventional ontological oppositions between 'live' and 'mediatised' performances. Auslander accepts that we can 'make phenomenological distinctions between the respective experiences of live and mediatised representations, distinctions concerning their respective positions within cultural economy, and ideological distinctions among performed representations in all media' (1999, 51). He warns, however, that such distinctions 'need to derive from careful consideration of how the relationship between the live and the mediatised is articulated in particular cases' (ibid., 54).

Any suggestion that intermedial theatre that engages with mediatisation may function in a resistant manner needs, then, to take account of such distinctions. Subsequent discussion of individual companies will indeed investigate 'the relationship between the live and mediatised in particular cases'. For the moment, however, it may be useful to return briefly to the issue of the spectator's agency. Although Baudrillardian views of the overwhelming effect of media highlight persuasively the extent to which we are caught up in the circulation of signs that are increasingly without content, leading to the experience of hyperreality, many critics find unconvincing the totally solidifying effect proposed and the evacuation of any possibility of agency that comes from pushing the logic of such a position to the extreme. Here it is useful to consider Elizabeth Klaver's argument that the proliferation of different media and viewing contexts problematises assumptions that have dominated critical discussion of issues such as the television audience or the spectatorial gaze in cinema (Klaver, 1995).

Noting contemporary viewers' exposure to an ever-expanding network of different media, Klaver argues that 'a viewer watching any of the media will be at the crossroads of various media looks and open to a variety of subject positions' and that 'the viewer exerts agency by *performing* in the viewing situation, by bringing a history of media and life experiences to what she is watching' (ibid., 311). She proposes 'a theoretical shift from a passive, monolithic voyeur, who is controlled by the looking structures embedded in a show, to a pluralistic, changing, interactive viewer' (ibid.). In particular, Klaver argues against uncritical application of Laura Mulvey's theories of the male gaze in discussions of cinema and theatre spectatorship and common assumptions about a female televisual viewing situation. Instead of concluding that the increasing cross-fertilisation between different media leads simply to viewers adopting one amorphous, uncritical way of absorbing media representations, Klaver argues that the contemporary spectator has become more critical: 'Given the playful intersections going on among film, theatre and television and the shredding of their boundaries, a viewer not only watches in a variety of media-viewing positions but also sees the deconstructions and alterities of media performing each other' (ibid., 318).

Accepting Klaver's argument for audiences generally possessing more flexible viewing strategies than common monolithic theories suggest, is there also a case for suggesting that the conditions under which spectators encounter the conjunction of electronic media and the 'live' in intermedial performances might also encourage a more active critical viewing than is often deployed in daily encounters with the media? Although it may be a result of cultural conditioning about the relative value of the live and the electronic media or be influenced by a nostalgia for auratic presence (i.e. the meaning and value of 'liveness' is contingent and historical), many spectators do, in practice, place a particular value on attending 'live' performances – even though, as we have seen, they do involve mediation. Most people in highly industrialised countries have ready access to television, videos and sound recordings. In contrast, to see a live performance, of theatre, live art, or even football or political debate, usually involves some sort of planning: we generally make a special effort to attend the live event at a specified time and place; we journey there specially, pay an entrance fee, buy a programme, and so on. Such performances have a sense of being demarcated off from everyday practices and routines. We tend to view them more attentively than we do most of the media performances we casually encounter in daily life. While we may view a favourite television programme more attentively, much television-viewing takes place in a semi-distracted fashion: we are perhaps chatting with others, having a meal, or channel-hopping. I am suggesting, therefore, that even if we reject an ontological distinction between live theatre and the electronic media and acknowledge that so-called live performances involve mediation, in actual practice, we may often adopt more active spectating strategies towards them. If the viewing conditions encourage more focused attention and greater expectations of them, this further supports the argument that intermedial performances may, through staging the media in a context in which they do not normally appear, offer the opportunity to intervene critically in the flow of media. Instead of seeing such work as inevitably overwhelming or seducing audiences, we might recognise its potential for encouraging more active and critical spectatorship.

Aims and structure of this study

At a time when the combination of video with live performance operates in all sorts of contexts, such as rock concerts, business presentations and political conferences, and when developments in computer technology have led to such hybrid activities as virtual reality theatre on the web, it may be seem a little narrow to focus on theatrical productions which incorporate the use of film and/or video. Yet, despite the existence of some broader theoretical discussion of issues surrounding such work, the relative lack of a sense of the history of its development and closer discussion of different companies' particular dramaturgical approaches to incorporating film and/or video has contributed to the way both critics of, and apologists for, such work tend to make sweeping generalisations about its supposed properties, whether these are portrayed as threat or salvation for theatre in the 21st century.

This study is not a manifesto nor does it suggest only this hybrid form holds any future for theatre. It does, however, argue that such work does not signal a defeat of theatre and that it is a futile task to patrol some putative ontological borders between theatre, film and video, driving out supposed invaders of the theatrical space. It accepts that when the media and mediation play such a significant role in our lives, we might expect some theatrical practitioners to acknowledge this in their work, and that the introduction of recorded or recording media into a performance does not automatically render it any less 'created as we watch' than many a long-running theatre production that runs along the same lines night after night. (Neither does it guarantee that the work will be at the cutting edge of thinking about how we might survive and flourish in a world saturated with mediation.)

The book, then, is intended as an introductory (and inevitably incomplete) historical charting of the field, in the course of which vari ous critical issues that arise from particular practices will be touched upon. Chapter 1 traces the early history of how theatre employed film, discussing a range of European experiments that anticipated the activities of Erwin Piscator in the 1920s. It illustrates how the work of Georges Méliès, Jean Painlevé, Sergei Eisenstein and others, along with the more thorough-going practice and theorisation of Piscator, established models for theatre's handling of media that are often broadly applicable to much contemporary work. Three main lines of development emerge in this period. The first is aptly described by Eisenstein's phrase 'theatre of attractions': here film's ability to introduce other characters and places helps create moments of fantasy or transformation, where the collision between the 'real' world of the stage and the 'magic' world of film becomes an attraction in its own right. By contrast, the second approach employs film's apparent capacity to show 'reality' to introduce aspects of the outside world into the 'artificial' world of the stage, often in a didactic manner, as in Piscator's work. The third uses film to suggest something of the subjective experience of onstage characters, as depictions of characters' dreams or fantasies appear or rhetorical devices such as close-ups or flashbacks are employed. Chapter 2's discussion of the work of Czech scenographer Josef Svoboda illustrates how he developed further such approaches in his broader scenographic work for international theatre companies and examines in more detail productions by Laterna Magika, the Prague-based theatre company he founded specifically to create productions that fuse theatre and film. Chapter 3 briefly explores how a combination of technological and artistic innovations in the 1960s laid the foundations for video art and the use of video in intermedial performance art, which in turn influenced how theatre practitioners began to use video.

In contrast with the European and historical focus of the first two chapters, subsequent chapters focus on contemporary North American and British practitioners.[18] With the exception of Forkbeard Fantasy, which has consciously chosen to work with film, most contemporary practitioners work with video. The Wooster Group, under the direction of Elizabeth LeCompte, is often seen as pioneering the regular incorporation of video into theatrical production and has greatly influenced subsequent practice. Chapter 4, therefore, examines in considerable detail the company's path from its relatively simple employment of video in *Route 1 & 9* in 1979 through to its much more complex use in recent productions such as *To You, the Birdie!* (2002), exploring how LeCompte's self-conscious play with the conventions of popular television makes a major contribution to the company's reframing of the classic texts with which it works. The next company studied, in Chapter 5, Britain's Forced Entertainment, was initially influenced by The Wooster Group, but developed its own distinctive approach to working with video in several productions in the late 1980s. While both companies employ devices and tropes found in earlier work with film, it will be seen that the move to video and their use of television monitors accompanies a more self-reflexive handling of the media and exploration of issues to do with representation and mediation. This is developed even further in the work of The Builders Association, founded in 1994 by Marianne Weems and other former associates of The Wooster Group. Chapter 6 illustrates the company's shift from reworking classic texts to devising intermedial spectacles that make striking use of large-scale video projection, including live relay and CGI material, to stage critical investigations of the changing experiences of time, space and identity in an age shaped by the revolutions in communications and information systems over the past half-century. In Chapter 7 film makes a reappearance in the work of Forkbeard Fantasy, whose Surrealist-inspired flights of fancy revivify the 'theatre of attractions' tradition, combining a detailed, yet critical, homage to cinematic history with a satiric take on the ambitions of contemporary science. Science of a different sort, in the shape of quantum theory, seems to have inspired aspects of the work of Station House Opera dealt with in Chapter 8. Taking advantage of the possibilities of life-size projection, like Forkbeard Fantasy, they play a lot with performers moving in and out of the screen, but use the device to create what might be seen as multiple possible worlds, as what seem to be the dreams and fantasies of the performers intersect with their onstage behaviour in a way that undercuts attempts to draw clear distinctions between the material and immaterial, the real and the virtual. Chapter 9 surveys some of the prolific output of Canadian director/performer Robert Lepage, renowned (and sometimes excoriated) for his eclectic use of video and enthusiasm for technical wizardry, which turns the stage into a magic-box of tricks. While sometimes video functions as primarily another tool in the box, it will be seen that certain underlying themes around displacement and transformation often inform the way in which he deploys video and other technologies.

Rather than being structured around such case-studies, this book might have been structured around a series of issues or topics, with illustrations taken from a wider range of examples. I have taken the present route partly because of my experiences teaching this area. I have found my students more interested in exploring the close development of complete productions and seeing how broader critical and theoretical questions inform their understanding of them, rather than primarily theoretical discussion based on 'cherry-picking' brief illustrative moments from diverse work, usually taken out of context and aimed at buttressing an author's theoretical stance. My hope is that through exploring the diverse paths taken by this range of practitioners a greater understanding of different strategies and purposes for working with film and video in theatre will emerge, along with some sense of the key critical issues. Given that there has been little detailed documentation of much of the work, and given that the dramaturgy of the sort of intermedial work on which I mostly focus involves complex interactions between performance, text, scenography and recorded material, the individual case-studies include quite descriptive analyses. These can never, of course, reconstitute the experience of watching the performances, nor do they attempt this. It is hoped, however, that they convey a sufficient sense of the overall productions to gain some fruitful insights into how film or video functions in them, and that these will feed into a more differentiated understanding of the potential range of ways in which these may be employed in theatre more generally.

1 Magic to Realism: European Pioneers

Discussions of the use of film in theatre generally begin with German director Erwin Piscator's politically inspired experiments from the mid-1920s onwards. Closer investigation reveals, however, that within a decade of the Lumière brothers exhibiting the first films in Paris in 1895, theatre practitioners were employing film. This chapter will initially illustrate how experiments that pre-dated Piscator established certain lines of subsequent development, often anticipating tropes which re-emerge in more recent work; we will see how the arguments of an early evangelist for such work, the German stage historian Franz Kranich, anticipate later practitioners. We will then explore how Piscator built on the earlier experiments, and in particular, how the Marxist dialectics that informed his political beliefs lay behind the dialectic he set up between stage and screen, leading to a more dynamic interaction than seen previously.

Georges Méliès

Before the appearance of purpose-built cinemas, films were often shown in music-halls and vaudeville theatres, in mixed programmes that also included comedy turns, magic demonstrations, songs and dances. As films began to treat fictional scenarios rather than documenting real-life events, many key figures in cinema's early development emerged from popular theatre. It is not surprising then that the earliest example I have found of a film specifically created for use in a theatrical production was produced in 1904 by Georges Méliès, a pioneer of cinema, who began making films while running a theatre of illusions and spectacle, the Théâtre Robert-Houdin.[1] Having exhibited

27

his early fantasy films in his theatre since 1896, Méliès was commissioned by the Folies-Bergère to make a film for one of its revues. Ten minutes long, it was subsequently released for cinematic showing, with the title *Le Raid Paris-Monte Carlo en Deux Heures.* The film employed the cast of the Folies-Bergère in a spectacular comic 'road movie', featuring a character based on Leopold II of Belgium, who was notorious for his love of fast cars and women, as well as his penchant for accidents. As the king sets off for Monte Carlo, his car backs over a policeman, flattening him. While the car carries on, the bystanders reinflate the policeman with bicycle pumps – until he explodes. Arriving at the Paris Opéra, the king is met by a crowd including the famous music-hall performer Little Titch. Speeding through the countryside, he causes general mayhem – knocking a postman off his bike, spread-eagling market-traders and their wares, crashing over a cliff and so on, until he finally makes a grand entrance into Monte Carlo. The film is the ancestor of many a comic car journey in subsequent movies.

Although there was continuity of sorts between the performers on film and the stage cast, the film's placement in a revue suggests it probably operated as an independent episode, as opposed to being more closely interwoven with an onstage narrative. Nevertheless, already it illustrates certain motifs that recur in subsequent discussion of the use of film in theatre. An argument quickly emerged for film's capacity to expand theatre's range both spatially and temporally. In the 19th century spectacular theatre an episode such as this as could have been staged, albeit in limited fashion, using a diorama and illusionist acts. Film, even one mostly shot with a fixed camera in a studio with painted backdrops, could transport the spectators more smoothly through a range of landscapes, with editing allowing easy movement from one elaborate crowd scene to another. Moreover, it enabled 'trick' sequences such as the inflation of the flattened policeman or various crashes and explosions to function more seamlessly. Film also more easily compressed the events of the trip into a ten-minute sequence. The idea of driving from Paris to Monte Carlo in two hours was a fantastic *reductio ad absurdum* of the king's passion for speed, and its compression into a ten-minute film underlined the hectic pace even further. The sequence also married two of the latest technologies, which were still sources of fascination for popular audiences: film and the car. Incorporating an episode such as this, the Folies-Bergère was advertising itself as up to date for its popular audience. We will see this urge to reflect the 'contemporary' recurring frequently as motive or justification amongst later practitioners – from Erwin Piscator in the 1920s, through Josef Svoboda in the 1950s, to Marianne Weems and Robert Lepage in the 1990s.

In 1905, Méliès also created a film for *The Pills of the Devil*, a production at the Châtelet Theatre, the theatre for which Jules Verne wrote *Around the World in 80 Days*. It was famous for its *féeries*, fantastic panto-style performances.[2] Much of their attraction lay in the spectacular settings and scenes of transformation and illusion, for which Méliès had previously provided various magic tricks and special effects. *The Pills of the Devil* centred on a Faustian plot that included plentiful comic fantasy scenes featuring a trickster Mephisto who leads his modern Faust, an English scientist named William Crackford, a merry dance. Its twenty scene changes, fifty special effects and countless trick costumes epitomised the house-style.

Méliès created another fantastic journey film to be inserted into this phantasmagoria. A devilish coachman driving an elaborate coach drawn by a skeletal white horse carries Crackford up Mount Vesuvius, from where they are blasted into orbit. They gallop through the heavens, passing stars, comets, the Sun, the Moon, and the planet Saturn (with a little man popping out of it), until they finally run out of heavenly road and take a headlong plunge down to Hell. Coach, horse, and passengers spin vertiginously downwards, although Crackford shows great aplomb in using his umbrella as a parachute.[3] Onstage, Crackford proceeded to sup with the Devil, before being taken off to be roasted. Méliès himself went on to develop this brief insert into a fuller, fifteen-minute treatment of the whole story, distributed under the title *The Merry Frolics of Satan*.[4]

Although it is not recorded exactly how the transition from the end of the film into the subsequent scene was achieved, the production probably provided an early example of a practice seen a few years later in Germany and frequently in subsequent work, whereby a filmic figure emerges on stage as if he has just walked out of the film into the 'live' world.[5] We might imagine Crackford walking on folding up the umbrella that softened his (filmed) landing. Even today, with sophisticated audiences long inoculated against the 'magic' of cinema, there is often a comic frisson at such moments of crossing from one world into the other, moments that seem to defy both spatial and temporal logic. There is something of the 'uncanny' in such transitions from the world of film into the 'live' world, as they draw attention to the virtual nature of the cinematic image and the performers who populate the screen, reminding us of the alchemical transformation which lies at the heart of cinema. With Méliès' background in magic theatre and his frequent use of routines of transformation, disappearance and re-appearance, he is unlikely to have passed up the opportunity to play magically with such a transitional moment.

Méliès himself played Satan – many of his films featured him playing Satan as a trickster figure, often in versions of the Faust legend. With analogies between devilry and magic well established in the popular imagination, Méliès seems to have extended the links to film itself – figuring film's capacity to capture images, destroy and recreate characters, and make them disappear or transform, as something diabolically magical. It is noteworthy that several present-day practitioners, including Elizabeth LeCompte, Marianne Weems and Robert Lepage, have also turned to the Faust legend and that they and Forkbeard Fantasy reference Méliès in their work.

Although these are the only recorded examples of Méliès creating film specifically for theatrical productions, his significance in the development of film techniques and the way he has been located in film criticism invite further consideration here, because of the light they shed on later uses of film and video in theatre and the debates surrounding them. Many fundamental techniques of film-making and editing derive ultimately from Méliès' early experiments, including:

- substitution splicing, whereby one image is seamlessly replaced by another;
- multiple exposure for dissolves between different images;
- matte shots, which allow different shots to exist side by side within the frame – as, for example, in *Le Portrait*, when Méliès filmed himself in conversation with a talking portrait of himself;
- model shots – filming miniature model sets as background to action which is then superimposed upon them.

As Elizabeth Ezra (2000) has demonstrated, Méliès also developed an approach to inserts that anticipates later developments. She illustrates his use of

- subjective inserts – images seen in dreams or hallucinations;
- explanatory inserts, as in close-ups of an object or person to underline their importance;
- displaced diegetic inserts – scenes from another time or place.

Although such techniques have been almost naturalised in dominant film practices, many were developed initially as part of the toolkit Méliès used for transferring the magic he practised in theatre into film. In the present context, we might observe that in the work of later theatre practitioners who use film or video, the relationship between recorded material and theatrical action might often be described in such ways. Film or video inserts allow spectators access to a character's subjective view of the action, or serve to underline a character's responses through the use of close-up, or depict action from elsewhere or another time. At the level of 'shots', we will also see film or video being used to provide multiple images of characters, to allow characters to talk to images of themselves, and so on.

Within cinema history Méliès was often portrayed as some sort of primitive, whose work was too theatrical, too wedded to tricks and spectacle to be of interest to theorists and historians of classic narrative cinema. More recently, however, the tendency to view earlier film from the perspective of classic narrative cinema, assuming a sort of teleological shift from the 'primitive' to a more 'proper' form of cinema, has been criticised and Méliès has been reassessed. Tom Gunning argues that he should be viewed in the light of a 'cinema of attractions' tradition, adopting the phrase from Eisenstein, who originally developed the idea of a 'theatre of attractions'. Gunning highlights the work's 'fascination in the thrill of display rather than the construction of a story', arguing that what narrative content there is functions 'as a kind of frame for the film's true subject: the process of appearance, disappearance, transformation and reappearance' (Elsaesser, 1990, 100). Suggesting that there is more of a balance between narration and spectacle in Méliès, Ezra argues that 'several of his films highlight the illusory nature of the realist aesthetic of mimesis'. Drawing on Jean Mitry's view that 'the real is nothing other than a form of the fantastic to which we have become accustomed', Ezra contends that consideration of Méliès highlights the misleading nature of the conventional opposition between fantasy and documentary, fiction and fact, spectacle and narration (Ezra, 2000, 4).

As we begin to trace the history of how recorded media have been used in theatre, the relevance of this debate over a theatre practitioner who became a pioneer of cinema and was perhaps the first to incorporate film into theatrical production will become clear. Much of the negative reaction to what might be seen as a 'theatre of attractions' approach in some of the work under consideration parallels certain cinema historians' reservations about a 'cinema of attractions'. Paradoxically, the cinema historians' suspicion of the 'theatricality' of Méliès' work finds a perverse echo in critical writing about multimedial and intermedial theatre that finds too much 'spectacle' and variation of focus in it, an attitude behind which one senses a preference for the clarity of classic narratives that also informs the dominant tradition of film history. Moreover, just as earlier critical treatment of Méliès was concerned with patrolling the borders of film and distinguishing it from theatre, so some writers on theatre desire to patrol its borders and repel suspected incursions from recorded media. In contrast, others argue that the play with appearance and disappearance in much contemporary multimedia and intermedial work and the mixing of genre influences challenges assumptions about, and the privileging of, a realist aesthetic in much discussion of theatre.

Early experiments

The tendency to portray Piscator as the inventor of the use of film in theatre owes much to his own 1929 book *The Political Theatre*, which documents powerfully the struggles he endured while developing a theatre that was as provocative politically as it was aesthetically. While Piscator did indeed employ film in more challenging ways, his often self-justifying account effectively ignores German precursors and contemporaries whose work he must have known. Before discussing Piscator, it will be worthwhile to take note of these and other examples elsewhere in Europe.

Much of the evidence for German precursors appears in a less well-known study whose first volume was published in the same year as Piscator's book. Franz Kranich's *Bühnetechnik der Gegenwart* (*Contemporary Theatre Technology*), an exhaustively detailed two-volume treatise, drew primarily on practices in German theatres, which at the time led the world in equipment and technological experiment. Noting that fifteen German theatres were already fitted with projection facilities, Kranich makes considerable reference to productions throughout Germany that employed film. In Volume II (1933) Kranich writes with apostolic zeal about film's theatrical potential, often espousing approaches seen as innovative when they were adopted by practitioners of the 1980s and 1990s. He argues that modern spectators, accustomed to the speed of cars and planes and the rapid changes of scene in films, no longer have patience for the long scene-changes associated with 19th-century theatre (1933, 127). Anticipating William Dudley's argument seventy years later, he suggests such changes of location could now be achieved using film, without awkward breaks in the dramatic illusion. He also argues that film could provide new ways of depicting onstage characters.

While Kranich draws mostly on work from the 1920s, he also mentions some earlier experiments. One has clear parallels with Méliès. At the Hamburg Operetta Theatre in 1911, the revue *Round the Alster* began with a film showing the arrival of Neptune at the docks in a submarine, followed by footage of the two main characters fleeing through the streets of Hamburg up to the theatre's entrance. As the film faded out, the two performers burst out of the orchestra pit onto the stage, followed by their pursuers (ibid., 132). The submarine's appearance parallels that of the car in *The Adventurous Automobile Trip* as a technology that was still excitingly new for spectators.[6] As with Méliès, film also shows characters travelling through familiar places, reflecting the element of thrill early filmgoers felt at just seeing somewhere familiar captured on screen. More particularly, the film here extends the offstage space of the stage: where the proscenium normally operates as a border to delimit the world of the play and the rest is left to the spectator to imagine, this device links the real world of the theatre's particular location with the supposedly fictional world of the stage.

Another early use for film was to cover scene changes. For example, in 1911 in a production at the Posen City Theatre, film depicted a performer climbing out of a window at the end of a scene and followed him off into further action while the set was being changed – again, film extends the fictional space beyond the space of the stage (ibid., 151).[7] Kranich suggests such use of film is particularly appropriate to revues, operetta, farces, and Christmas plays.

Kranich also describes early scenographic use of film in a 1913 production of Hoffmann's opera *Undine* in Stuttgart: film of waves was used in one scene and film of a waterfall in another (ibid., 132 and 313). He notes that this was already-existing film, rather than footage especially shot for the performance. Such usage was a logical development from 19th-century dioramas and the use of continuous slide projections described in André Antoine's account of a Saxe-Meiningen production in 1888: 'After an extraordinary torrential rain, obtained by means of projections, I was disturbed to see the water stop abruptly, instead of letting up slowly' (Nagler, 1952, 582). The scenographic use of film to depict waves, clouds, landscapes, flights, and railway trains was taken further in subsequent years at State Opera theatres in Dresden and Berlin, then elsewhere. In most instances these were probably 'actuality' filmstrips that could be readily purchased in the early days of film.[8]

Discussing productions from the 1920s for which film was especially shot, Kranich begins with what in fact was a 'fake' use of film – in Georg Kaiser's *Side by Side*, produced in Berlin in 1923. A central character was a sleazy would-be filmmaker. To set the atmosphere, the curtains opened onto projections of credit titles, along with a list of Kaiser's plays. For subsequent scenes location titles were projected, accompanied by flickering light produced by running a blank film through a projector, so that the titles appeared to be projected film. A 1928 production of Ludwig Fuldas' *Filmromantik* in Hanover echoed this, but used real film to show title credits as the curtains opened – a device subsequently used by Robert Lepage, for productions such as *Elsinore* (1994) and *La Casa Azul* (2003).

Kranich praises a Stuttgart production of Busoni's *Doctor Faustus* because 'for the first time a film was made the timing of which was tied exactly into the music' (1933, 132). Although it probably depicted some of Faust's visions, frustratingly, Kranich provides no details of the film used; but he does describe the attempt made to integrate the film and its projection into the overall design, so that it had the effect of a vision rather than a piece of film. The projection screen was covered with a gold wash and then a thin scrim placed in front of it; the filmstrip itself was tinted with brown and yellow; and the window of the projection box was given a yellow wash. (We should remember that film was generally in black and white, although a certain amount of colouring by hand might be done.) Additionally, clouds were projected onto the scrim, to blur the figures so that they would not seem too unrealistic.

After noting other operas that employed film, Kranich enthuses about the marvellous opportunities for the opera director, making detailed proposals for employing film in Wagner. He discusses its potential for spectacular scenes such as the storm in *The Flying Dutchman*, arguing that film could provide the answer for smaller theatres lacking the funds and technology demanded by 19th-century approaches to spectacle. He suggests film also provides an economical way for such theatres to present sequences requiring a large cast.[9] He also asserts that film provides a more artistic solution for scenes that place unusual demands on live singers – such as when the Rhinemaidens are seen swimming in *Rheingold*. He suggests that singers should deliver their songs standing in the wings, while film depicts their action.

Kranich adopts a fairly pragmatic approach to how film might enhance the spectacle in opera and in popular forms such as revue and farce. He shows little interest in the sort of ideological potential Piscator was exploring contemporaneously and his domination by a realistic aesthetic leads him to have reservations about its use in mainstream drama. Addressing technical issues to do with lighting, the size and nature of the screen, and the use of sound, he claims the mythic scope of opera can accommodate more effectively the merging of the filmic and stage worlds. Although he acknowledges the powerful montage effects sought by Piscator, Kranich is much concerned with disguising the rectangular nature of the screen and with ensuring that there is not too sharp a contrast in lighting when film appears – since this draws attention to the fact that film is being used. Blurring of the incorporation of film into productions is more achievable with the more painterly settings of opera, with their air of fantasy. For all that Kranich initially espouses the greater 'realism' film lends to scenery and spectacular moments, there is then, paradoxically, still an underlying concern that its introduction in more realistic dramatic productions may seem disruptive, and that the 'filmness' of film needs to be disguised.

Before examining Piscator's work, mention should be made of other key productions during this period in Paris, Berlin and Moscow. The first is surprisingly not mentioned by Kranich: Yvan Goll's surreal *Methusalem*, which premiered in Berlin in 1922.[10] This satire of bourgeois life, in the style of Alfred Jarry's Ubu plays, is a rare early example of a text that includes instructions for the use of fantastic film sequences. Although the film for its German production has not survived, some remarkable footage shot by Jean Painlevé for its 1927 Paris production has, and my discussion will focus on this production.[11] Mostly known for his startling natural history films, Painlevé was an associate of the Surrealists and included Antonin Artaud in his cast for the *Methusalem* film, which consists of five separate sequences.

Goll's play begins with a domestic scene establishing the shoe-manufacturer Methusalem and his wife as a Pa and Ma Ubu couple; they are grotesquely fat, with the cigar-smoking Methusalem wearing bandages over a gouty leg and his wife Amalia wearing a filthy apron over a silk dress, along with strings of diamonds. Following an absurd exchange of banalities that anticipates the beginning of Ionesco's *The Bald Prima Donna* 30 years later, Methusalem falls asleep and dreams. The window of the house becomes a screen for the first film-clip, a subjective insert. Here Painlevé's film diverges from Goll's directions. Goll suggests a film of Methusalem picking up a woman in the street and taking her to a restaurant. As they dine, the woman's identity changes constantly – to his cook, a prostitute, the wife of a business associate, and so on. When Methusalem addresses them, a text-bubble should appear with the words, 'Oh my darling, no matter who, Be to me faithful, be to me true, Always wear a Methusalem shoe' (Goll, 1980, 83).

Such a sequence combining Methusalem's erotic and capitalist fantasies would have been ideal for some substitution splicing shots in the style of Méliès (whom the Surrealists greatly admired). Instead, Painlevé's film focuses more on Methusalem's business dreams, in the process locating the production securely in Paris. Initially, Methusalem's corpulent belly is shown turning into a crudely constructed globe, around which one of his shoes flies. His name then appears in bright lights on a series of Parisian landmarks, including the Stock Exchange, the Eiffel Tower, and the Théâtre National Populaire. A Surrealist in-joke appears at this point, as a placard appears on the theatre door: 'RELÂCHE pour dernières repetitions de Hamlet'. While the meaning – Closed for dress rehearsals of *Hamlet* – links the scene forward to the next sequence, the capitalised RELÂCHE will have recalled the Surrealists' infamous 1924 multimedia performance that jokingly bore the name *RELÂCHE*.

The next dream sequence begins with Josephine Baker's understudy at the Moulin Rouge (as the title proudly announces) energetically dancing the Blackbottom on top of Yorick's grave. Thereafter, Painlevé adheres more closely to Goll's directions, as Methusalem barges in on a rehearsal, grabs Yorick's skull and replaces it with a Methusalem shoe and takes over as director. Following this, Methusalem plays a general briefing his officers. The three officers (including Artaud) are farcical figures with fake moustaches, while Methusalem waves about a floppy rubber sword.

As Methusalem wakes from his dream, he 'snorts, groans, wriggles about restlessly' (ibid., 84). Subsequent scenes include one in which stuffed animals stage a revolution against human rule, and scenes introducing Methusalem's thrusting young businessman son Felix (who has a copper megaphone mouth, a telephone receiver nose and a typewriter hat), his dreamy ninny of a daughter and her revolutionary student lover. When Felix discovers the student has impregnated his sister he challenges him to a farcical duel, which is interrupted by the next film sequence, of a funeral, again shown through the 'window'.

The coffin is carried on Painlevé's own Bugatti, while the cavernous-eyed Artaud plays the bishop leading the mourning procession with exaggerated piety. The mourners follow behind pushing scooters, until the procession collapses in disorder as the chief mourners begin brawling. Although the film appears on the window/screen, there is no attempt at a *trompe l'œil* approach – presenting it as though the activities were just being seen through the window. The change of location and shifts of point of view of the action make it clearly an extra-diegetic insert, just like the subsequent wedding scene.

As the film ends, Felix and the student begin insulting each other again, only to be interrupted by a further film sequence, this time of a wedding procession of bourgeois citizens prancing along in the style of the Monty Python School of Silly Walks. Again, a supposedly solemn event is undermined by a brawl. The play resumes with the duel once more, resulting in Felix killing the student and the latter's soul flying up to heaven in the shape of an overcoat – before the student himself jumps up and tips his hat and departs! Later, after the resurrected student shoots Methusalem, the play ends with a brief coda in which he and the daughter are shown destitute on a park bench, a banal couple with their baby, discussing frankfurters and dreams of bourgeois success.

At a narrative level, neither film insert is integrated in the same way as the subjective insert of the dreams in the first scene; they seem to appear at random, as part of Goll's general commitment to what he calls Alogic. Originally mounted with designs by Georg Grosz, *Methusalem*'s surreal Alogic and revue-style farrago of scenes and characters happily accommodated such incursions. Indeed, given the Surrealists' fascination with film (particularly the fantasy tradition which emerged out of Méliès' work) and their experiments in both film and theatre, it's surprising that Goll's experiment was relatively isolated. Mention has been made already of *RELÂCHE*, a notorious collaboration between Erik Satie, Francis Picabia, Man Ray, Marcel Duchamp and others, but it is not fully comparable.[12] The event had a revue format, which accommodated a variety of happenings, including a fireman pouring water in and out of a bucket all evening, a naked couple posing as Adam and Eve, obscene songs and an alternative ballet. During the interval a film called *Interval* was shown. It showed a bearded male dancer in a tutu dancing on a glass floor, from below which he was filmed; Duchamp and Ray playing chess on the roof of the theatre; and a parodic version of a funeral, in which a camel-drawn funeral carriage, covered in advertising posters and hung with various foods, processed through an amusement park. The style of the film parodies contemporary newsreels of state funerals. After the coffin fell off the hearse a grinning corpse sat up inside it and THE END came up on screen. Echoing earlier examples, the performers burst through the screen to resume the live performance.

A similar eruption through the screen also occurred a year earlier in Moscow, in Sergei Eisenstein's stage production of Ostrovsky's 1868 satire of the Russian bourgeoisie, A Wise Man.[13] The film shot for this was the first that Eisenstein directed – his enjoyment of the process contributed to his subsequent transition from theatre into cinema. Inspired by Meyerhold, Eisenstein stripped down Ostrovsky's comedy of manners text and gave it a circus-like performance. The arena stage was set up like a circus-ring, with a trapeze and high wires, vaulting-horses and so on. There were strong influences from Commedia dell'Arte and plentiful acrobatics and clowning. For example, when the character Glumov attempts to seduce a woman, he does so while walking a tightrope, symbolising the underlying emotions of the situation; at other times characters would end a sentence with a somersault. At one point Glumov's diary comes alive as a film. The film continues the circus approach, with substitution shots enabling a clown to transform magically into a donkey, and later into a field gun. It also contains a spectacular chase sequence, in which Glumov, as a masked bank-robber, climbs a high tower and leaps off into his accomplices' car. The performer then bursts through the screen and onto the stage.

Eisenstein's interest in circus, clowning, and music-hall reflected both an aesthetic and political interest in popular culture, which was complemented by the dynamism associated with early Soviet film – cinema was seen as the art-form of a dynamic new society. These interests fed into his arguments for a theatre of attractions built around a series of 'turns' or 'acts', as opposed to one based primarily on dramatic narrative for sustaining interest. He wrote:

> Instead of static 'reflection' of an event with all possibility for activity within the limits of the event's logical action, we advance to a new plane – *free montage of arbitrarily selected, independent attractions* – all from the stand of establishing certain final thematic effects – this is montage of attractions. (Seton, 1952, 62)

As we have seen, this term was later adapted by cinema theorists discussing early cinema, which they contrasted negatively with classic realism. Although Eisenstein developed the idea in a more dialectical fashion – note the idea of it 'establishing certain final thematic effects', the notion of 'arbitrarily selected independent attractions' continues to inform much present-day intermedial work.

Investigating Soviet theatre further, we might expect to find film used elsewhere, given the wealth of experiment undertaken by directors and writers such as Meyerhold, Tretyakov, Evreinov, Mayakovsky and so on. Meyerhold and others did assert that theatre needed to become more cinematic, and slide projections, cinematic lighting and montage often appeared in their productions. For example, Meyerhold's productions of Tretyakov's *Earth Rampant* (1923) and of *The D.E. Trust* (1924) included cinema-style captions for scenes along with projected quotations from figures such as Lenin and Trotsky. His 1926 production of Gogol's *The Government Inspector* included projected scene-titles, and lighting created the isolating effect of close-ups at certain moments, while scenes were played on a series of pre-set 'trucks' which appeared in the set's central doorway – in order to achieve the pace of film editing as it moved from scene to scene. Meyerhold claimed, 'Thanks to the methods of staging ... we have been able, in the language of cinema, to shoot the principal scenes in close-up' (Braun, 1979, 218). Spencer Golub describes how Evreinov saw a kinship between his theatrical work and the cinema and argued that 'the future of theatre was in talking pictures' (Golub, 1984, 144). In a 1925 play, *Radio Kiss*, Evreinov called for a 'film within a play' rather along the lines of Goll's *Methusalem*, but the work was never staged. In view of these and other examples, it seems surprising that actual film does not appear more often on the Soviet stage. This may have been affected by the constant shortage of film stock in the Soviet Union during the 1920s, or it may have reflected a political climate that became increasingly hostile to avant-garde experiment in the later 1920s, as Socialist Realism became installed as official doctrine in the arts. Whatever the case, the next practitioner considered, Erwin Piscator, was perhaps justified when he rejected claims that his work had been strongly influenced by Soviet practitioners such as Meyerhold.

Erwin Piscator

In the examples of early work discussed so far, film was used in three main ways: scenographically; to create narrative sequences, often involving actions which would otherwise be difficult to achieve as effectively on stage; and for purposes of spectacle, comedy or 'magic'. Building on such antecedents, Piscator was the first director to integrate film regularly into his productions and to explore its potential more extensively. In contrast with a concern with the fantastic in earlier work, political concerns led him initially to draw on film's emerging documentary tradition as a means of historicising the action in his productions, although he subsequently developed an appreciation for more wide-ranging rhetorical effects achievable through the interaction of film and onstage action.

Piscator's general approach emerged in the tumultuous cultural and political climate of Germany immediately after World War I. After military service he became involved in Communist politics and with the Berlin Dada group (including Yvan Goll and Georg Grosz).[14] The Dadaists' iconoclasm and liking for mixed media events remained with him even as he moved, via his involvement in the Proletarian Theatre and his experiments in AgitProp, into a more established role directing plays for the Volksbühne in Berlin.[15] There he developed a Total Theatre approach, in which the use of projections, film, revolves, elevator stages, treadmills and so on contributed to a technically complex spectacle, the constant motion of which reflected the turmoil of society outside the theatre.

A product of his Marxism, his aim in all this was:

> to super-impose on the subjective stage-action the *objective* controlling forces which were not present in the text. He wanted to include world politics, world economics, and the class struggle as integral elements ... to show the whys and wherefores, the subjective and objective aspects, action and the motives behind action. (Kipphardt, 1979, 10)

Piscator argued that the dominant literary drama, with its focus on the individual, could not capture the range of social, economic and ideological forces that shape human behaviour. Film could transcend the individual and demonstrate how the stage action typified a larger historical moment, sometimes highlighting contradictions between the characters' outlook and the movement of society around them.

Piscator's experiments also reflected a modernist embrace of contemporary technological advances. Although technical innovations 'were never an end in themselves', he argued that in an 'age whose technical achievements tower above its achievements in every other field the stage should become highly technical'. For him, theatre architecture and machinery had become hopelessly out of tune with the times, and 'the shabbiest film contained more topical interest, more of the exciting realities of our day than the stage' (Piscator, 1980, 188–9).

Piscator began using slide projections and film in ways that recall earlier German examples. In his 1924 production *Red Revue*, projections of photographs, statistics and satirical cartoons by Grosz, along with film of the repression of the 1919 Spartacist uprising, accompanied a medley of scenes depicting the class warfare of the time. Film appeared more extensively in the revue *In Spite of Everything!* (1925) and Paquet's *Tidal Wave* (1926). The former, produced for the German Communist Party conference and aiming to demonstrate that the Social Democrats had betrayed the proletariat by endorsing German involvement in the war, depicted the founding of the Communist Party in 1918, the subsequent repression of the Spartacist uprising, and the assassinations of the Communist leaders Rosa Luxemburg and Karl Liebknecht in 1919. A stripped down set with platforms, ramps and steps on a revolve stage, backed by a large projection screen, helped maintain the pace and underline the montagist relationship between the twenty-four scenes, most of which reconstructed historical occasions. Party and government archives were mined for the text and for film-clips, which mainly functioned as explanatory inserts or displaced diegetic inserts.

As the move to war was portrayed, Piscator showed film of a parade of European royalty. Film of Liebknecht distributing anti-war leaflets in 1913 was followed by a staging of a meeting of the Social Democrats at which Liebknecht protested against the clamour for war. When they voted to approve the raising of War Loans, archive film of slaughter at the Front immediately appeared, showing 'flame-thrower attacks, piles of mutilated bodies, and burning cities'. Piscator noted that 'war films had not yet come into fashion, so these pictures were bound to have a more striking effect on the masses of the proletariat than a hundred lectures' (ibid., 94). Film also depicted post-war demobilization and the Spartacist revolt.

As Piscator attempted to bring reality into drama and present reality dramatically, the resulting montage of film of real events, dramatic reconstruction, fictional drama and commentary largely anticipated modern methods of producing television drama documentaries. For all Piscator's theorisation of the political rationale for using documentary footage and his focus on the supposed objectivity of film, he was acutely aware of the powerful rhetorical effect of juxtaposing film and stage action. He argued that using film clips was

not only right for presenting political and social mechanisms, but also in a higher sense, right from the formal point of view ... . The momentary surprise when we changed from live scenes to film was very effective. But the dramatic tension that live scene and film clip derived from one another was even stronger. They interacted and built upon each other's power, and at intervals the action attained a *furioso* that I have seldom experienced in theatre. For example, when the Social Democrats' vote on War Loans (live) was followed by film showing the first dead, it not only made the political nature of the procedure clear, but also produced a shattering human effect, became art, in fact. … the most effective political propaganda lay along the same lines as the highest artistic form. (Ibid., 97)

Despite Piscator's rejection of traditional aesthetics, he attempts to justify the use of film artistically as well as politically. Although celebrated by some critics, he was attacked by some on the left for formalism, while simultaneously his mixing of media and his political focus was dismissed by more conservative critics as simply political propaganda with no artistic merit. Hence he tries to establish the principle of dynamic montage of elements as a significant artistic advance as well as a politically inspired example of Marxist dialectics.

Tidal Wave saw Piscator for the first time shooting film specifically for a production – showing actors from the play in further scenes. Set in St Petersburg, the play was a melodramatic romance inspired by the October Revolution of 1905. Piscator used film to ground the more far-fetched aspects of the play in something more politically relevant. At its simplest, it functioned scenographically, providing, for example, images of the harbour in St Petersburg as a backdrop for a ship-deck scene. The fictional and real worlds merged when archival footage of the October Revolution was shown behind the central character, Granka, as he addressed an onstage crowd of revolutionaries. Elsewhere, a scene of a capitalist selling off his shares was followed by a clip of panic-selling on the New York Stock Exchange, drawing an analogy between the fictional action and recent experience.

The narrative was also carried further by film: in one instance, after Granka quarrelled with his lover and exited, film showed him then wandering through the streets. Such use to cover scene changes worked in a way similar to dissolves in film. However, critic Herbert Ihering, normally one of Piscator's supporters, objected that when Granka 'ambles off sadly the decline into bourgeois sentimentality begins. Film in plays should stick to documentation and never try to touch the emotions' (Piscator, 1980, 105). Undeterred, Piscator continued to experiment with more expressive uses of film alongside documentary approaches.

The film in his 1927 production of Ehm Welk's *Storm over Gottland* aroused tremendous controversy. The play portrayed a 14th-century conflict between the Hanseatic League, a trading federation, and the Vitalians, a proto-communist community on the island of Gottland. With the Vitalian leader Asmus made up to resemble Lenin, Piscator introduced film to underscore the conflict's contemporary relevance. A prologue film exploring the socio-political context of the period concluded with a brilliantly effective use of substitution splicing to demonstrate the rebellion's continuing significance. The film showed Vitalian rebels moving towards the audience, initially in Mediaeval dress; as the film proceeded, their costume kept changing and they came to represent various proletarian movements throughout history, including the Paris Commune and, finally, the Russian Revolution. As the film ended, they burst on to the stage, effectively as Russian revolutionaries. What has been seen as a developing trope – characters emerging from film onto the stage, was adapted here to great political effect.

The parallels implied were emphasised in Eisensteinian fashion when one of the revolutionaries was to be executed: a film was projected of Lenin seemingly being beheaded, again and again. Each time he was beheaded, he returned, only to be beheaded again. This powerful image of revolutionary struggle always resurfacing despite continual defeat was described by the critic Alfred Kerr as 'one of the most deeply moving shots, one of the most unforgettable film clips' (Piscator, 1980, 146). Here the substitution splicing employed by Méliès for magic shots of decapitation was manipulated to very different emotive and political ends.

Film also functioned in more familiar dramatic ways: for example, film of an approaching ship appeared on a scrim, which then opened to reveal a stage ship; subsequently, a sea-battle was also shown on film. The production concluded with further film of revolutions through the centuries following the play's action, right up to clips of recent uprisings in Shanghai. Although the newspaper *Vorwärts* called it 'a totally convincing demonstration of the possibility of combining film and live theatre', a storm of outrage burst over the production and the Volksbühne arbitrarily cut most of the film from it, claiming the author had said it engulfed his play. During the next, truncated, performance, one of the actors, responding to audience demands for Piscator, came out and declared, 'We have been raped; it is under constraint and against our will that we are acting without the film' (ibid., 148). There followed a war of words in the newspapers, questions in parliament, a public debate packed by 2,000 people, and effectively a breakaway from the Volksbühne by a large section of its supporters.

Leaving the Volksbühne, Piscator continued to employ film exten-sively with the Piscator-Bühne companies which he ran between 1927 and 1931, after which he spent several years in France and the Soviet Union. Most notable were his productions of Toller's *Hoppla! We're Alive* (1927), Tolstoy and Shegolov's *Rasputin* (1927), and an adapta-tion of Hasek's *The Adventures of the Good Soldier Schwejk* (1928). In these Piscator combined increasingly complex sets and stage machin-ery, which allowed for multiple sites of action and film projection, along with increasingly varied types of film and interaction between film and stage, so much so that these productions effectively fused the-atre and film. Working with his own company allowed him to collabo-rate consistently with a team who shared his aesthetic and political goals; key amongst them were the designer Traugott Müller, the film-maker Carl Oertel, and Otto Richter, the stage-manager responsible for satisfying his ever more demanding technical requirements.

The set for *Hoppla! We're Alive* was a huge multi-storied scaffolding structure on a revolve, with a large transparent frontcloth onto which the opening film was projected. This prologue showed a giant close-up of a general's chest having medals pinned on to it, followed by graphic battlefront scenes from World War I, with images of Kurt Thomas (the play's Communist hero) spliced into the documentary footage of real soldiers.[16] It concluded with the general's chest again, but this time being stripped of his medals. The cloth was then raised to reveal Thomas and other condemned revolutionaries in prison cells, with the tall central section of the set showing film of a sentry patrolling, magni-fied for Expressionist effect. Then came newscast film of political events during Thomas' eight years of imprisonment since 1919 – the Ruhr uprisings, events in the Soviet Union, the rise of Mussolini, Hindenburg's election and so on. This was intercut with footage of boxing events, par-ties, and dancing. Piscator reflected on this kaleidoscopic presentation of 'the terror, stupidity and triviality' of the Roaring Twenties, 'No medium other than film is in a position to let eight interminable years roll by in the course of seven minutes' (ibid., 211).

As the production depicted Thomas' disintegration after his release and the corruption at the heart of German society of the time, film, pro-jected onto individual screens behind the scenic units as well as onto the central scrim, was used extensively to locate action, carry the narrative forward, and heighten the audience's perception of onstage action. So, for example, when Thomas went searching for work, film showed him trudging through the streets of Berlin: the Expressionist vision of speed-ing traffic, high buildings and so on evoked the alienating atmosphere of city life. In an election scene, the onstage voters casting their ballots were echoed on the large central screen by close-up shots of voting papers falling into a ballot box. Towards the end Piscator created an effect that anticipated the use of LED displays in more recent work. After Thomas was thrown back into prison, the prisoners began knocking on the walls of their cells, passing messages along; this was accompanied by a running display of the text on the central gauze.

The set for *Rasputin* was a spectacular hemispherical dome, which unfolded outwards to reveal interior platforms. Film was projected onto screens and onto the dome itself (with attendant technical problems). The production again opened with a historical prologue. Contrasting films depicted four centuries of Czarist rule: one showed images of the Czars, while another showed working-class and peasant life. Towards the end, Czar Nicholas II appeared on the upper platform, while on the screen behind him the shadowy figure of Rasputin loomed, growing ever larger. Sometimes three different films were shown simultaneously, creating a dialectic not just between film and live action, but also between films. Again, documentary film and staged historical footage 'illustrated the factual contradiction between

Figure 2   *Hoppla! We're Alive*

the personal illusions of the characters and the true nature of the events in which they were involved' (Innes, 1972, 101). This could be savagely ironic: for example, while the Czarina was being reassured that all would be well, film on one side displayed a list of lost battles, while on the other side Soviet archive film of the shooting of the Imperial family played.

The synthesis between play, technology and film was developed further in *The Adventures of the Good Soldier Schwejk*. Piscator had two conveyor belts running across the width of the stage, with various scenic elements and performers gliding into position on them. With the production portraying its anti-hero's picaresque adventures in a decrepit, war-torn Europe, film was used for landscape purposes, as well as showing documentary footage and grotesque cartoons by Grosz, who also created huge dummy figures to populate the stage. The dummies and cartoons evoked a sense of the ghastly absurdity of the authority figures Schwejk encountered.

Piscator's efforts to achieve his total theatre were pursued in the face of continual pressures of time and money. Although he received financial support from wealthy sympathisers, and *Rasputin* and *Schwejk* attracted large audiences, the high technical costs worked against him, eventually forcing him to dissolve his first company. Financial pressures also enforced shorter development and rehearsal periods than such complex productions really required, resulting in equipment being installed and film being introduced right up to the last minute: in the case of *Hoppla!* the final message-tapping film was still being edited while the performance got under way. When the conveyor belts in *Schwejk* were first used, 'they rattled and snorted and pounded so that the whole house quaked' (Piscator, 1980, 252). Worse was when the race to incorporate film material led to bungles, such as when Piscator was expecting the superimposition of two films at a climactic moment in *Schwejk* and only one appeared – the operator had forgotten to take the lens cover off.

Accused of not focusing sufficiently on the acting in his productions, Piscator admitted:

> At first my apparatus will seem strange, even hostile, to actors who are accustomed to the bourgeois stage. They feel lost amid the gigantic mechanical structures. ... They have problems in adjusting to the precision with which film forces them to come in on their cues. (Ibid., 213)

But he argued that his approach ultimately supported the actors 'by incorporating them into the production as a whole in a meaningful way'. He rejected the assertion that 'actors cannot perform in front of a projection screen because the flatness of the screen clashes with the three-dimensional nature of acting', claiming the screens were simply the equivalent of the 'old painted backdrops' of the previous century. This begs the question that theatrical reformers of the previous century had attacked the very same backdrops for their flatness, as they urged the claims of three-dimensional scenery.[17] Piscator himself ultimately accepted that 'a definitive acting style for the new stage apparatus has not yet been worked out' (ibid., 213).

Issues of scale sometimes caused problems. With the shadow of Rasputin behind the Czar or the giant sentry patrolling the prison in *Hoppla!*, a powerful effect could be gained through setting the live performer against larger-scale screen images, but at other times performers seemed dwarfed or were absorbed into the busyness of the screen images behind them, resulting in a dynamic dialectic between stage and screen being replaced by a sense that the stage was being overwhelmed by the film – a complaint made about some present-day work.

Despite the criticism and difficulties, Piscator's experiments advanced the use of film in theatre considerably and anticipated many of the ways current practitioners work with video. Furthermore, *The Political Theatre*, written during the hectic period when he was creating a string of major productions and fighting for his company's survival, provides many valuable insights into the issues surrounding his practice. As we have seen, Piscator's overriding justification was film's capacity to set the live action against the socio-political context that shaped it. He also suggests that the use of film contributes to establishing theatre as a contemporary form, with the increased pace created by dynamic cutting between live scenes and filmed sequences reflecting the greater pace of a technological society. He recognises how perception and consciousness were being affected by changes in technology and particularly visual technologies. Similar arguments around reflecting the simultaneity of experience in the modern world and the impact of media on everyday perception recur frequently amongst apologists for video sixty years later.

Analysing his own practice, Piscator usefully supplements Kranich's sketch of film's possibilities and further anticipates later practitioners (Piscator, 1980, 236–40). He describes three broad categories of use:

(1) Didactic (the dominant kind in his work): film supplements the onstage drama by presenting objective facts and information that broaden the subject in terms of time and space.

(2) Dramatic: film carries the action forward and is a substitute for the live scene, 'but where live scenes waste time with explanations, dialogue, action, film can illuminate the situation with a few quick shots'.

(3) Choric: 'Film commentary accompanies the action in the manner of a chorus. It addresses itself directly to the audience ... . It levels criticisms, makes accusations.' Recalling how the chorus functions in Greek tragedy, as a device for establishing the narrative, public and moral context of the action, while drawing mythic parallels with the events of the play and clarifying their implications for wider society, we can see that the 'choric' use covers more than just 'criticism and accusations': it is at the heart of Piscator's desire to situate individual dramatic events in a broader public political context, in the face of what he saw as the more naturalistic theatre's limitations in revealing such aspects. The prologue sequence to *Storm over Gottland* and the film interlude covering Kurt's eight years in prison in *Hoppla!* might, then, be equally seen as choric uses of film. It is arguable that Piscator's handling of film was at its strongest dramatically and politically when used in various choric ways.

As well as these categories, Piscator might well have mentioned the scenographic use of film and the use of subjective inserts, both of which he employed occasionally. In combination with Kranich's work, Piscator provides the beginnings of a typology that can be informative for discussing subsequent work.

The 1930s

Although beset by financial difficulties, Piscator continued working until the National Socialist takeover in 1931 led to his departure abroad. One might have expected the notoriety of his work and the publication of *The Political Theatre* to lead to an upsurge in similar experimentation in the 1930s. Yet this did not occur. We hear of a few other German productions, but none achieved anything as complex as Piscator's work or fulfilled the potential Kranich predicted. This may have been influenced by the fact that such practices were so closely identified with Piscator's political theatre, which had been increasingly condemned by the reactionary press. Also, many other radical theatre and film artists, including prominent Bauhaus members, fled Germany in the early 30s.[18] In the Soviet Union, Eisenstein's example found few imitators and the Stalinist clampdown on anything radical in the 1930s deterred further experimentation that might be condemned as formalist. Piscator himself left for the US as the purges of 1936 began, while practitioners such as Tretyakov and Meyerhold paid for their 'deviation' with their lives.

More generally, we might speculate about the impact of the appearance of 'talking pictures' in 1928. All the examples discussed so far made use of silent black and white films. With silent films replaced by the talkies, and with black and white beginning to be displaced by colour from the mid-1930s on, the potential for film use may have seemed greater, but the challenges presumably also seemed greater – apart, of course, from the increased expense involved. A reaction seemed to be setting in against scenic use, as demonstrated by Fuerst and Hume's comments (see Note 17). An audience used to hearing screen actors talk would now expect this also to occur if film were being used in the theatre. What problems would this pose for the actors? And if colour film were to be used, what difficulties would this pose in terms of matching up film with the onstage picture?

Looking to Great Britain and the US, there seems to have been little take-up of the idea of using film, even though Piscator and Meyerhold inspired the use of slide projection by groups involved in the British Workers' Theatre Movement and in the American Federal Theatre Project's Living Newspapers. A few Living Newspapers made very limited use of film; so, for example, the Seattle production *Power*, depicting battles for control of the power industry, in order to liven up a scene which 'ended flatly' and to 'point up the show locally', included a two-minute collage of film from the Seattle City Light Company displaying 'snow, ice, glaciers, streams, rivers, waterfalls and finally double exposure energy coursing through turbines'.[19] Piscator himself, despite his reputation, had difficulty getting directing work and spent the 1940s teaching at the New School in New York. Perhaps just as informative is the fact that when the influential American designer Robert Edmond Jones published his wide-ranging study of *The Dramatic Imagination* in 1941, he made radical suggestions about the possibility of using film in theatre without indicating an awareness of anyone else having already done so.

Known for his own Expressionist approach to staging, especially in productions of Eugene O'Neill's plays, Jones advocated a more poetic theatre, as opposed to the realism that dominated American theatre. Discussing Hollywood's impact on theatre, he celebrated cinema for taking over realism and doing it much better: this would allow theatre to revert to its 'true role' of accessing the Unconscious, a 'vast dynamic world of impulse and dream' (Jones, 1941, 16). Paradoxically, he saw film as 'the perfect medium for expressing the Unconscious in terms of theatre' suggesting that, 'In the simultaneous use of the living actor and the talking picture in the theatre there lies a wholly new theatrical art' (ibid., 17).

Excited by film's capacity 'to move forward or backward in space or time, unhampered by the rationalisations of the conscious mind', and unwittingly reversing Piscator's scheme, he imagined:

> Some new playwright will presently set a motion-picture screen on the stage above and behind his actors and will reveal simultaneously the two worlds of the Conscious and the Unconscious ... the outer world and the inner world, the objective world of actuality and the subjective world of motive. On the stage we shall see the actual characters of the drama, on the screen we shall see their hidden secrets. (Ibid., 19)

That Jones could write as he did, despite being a well-travelled, progressive theatre practitioner, suggests that, despite the influx of European practitioners into the US in the mid-1930s, the broad range of experiment discussed so far had little impact beyond Europe. And it was in a perhaps unlikely corner of Europe that Jones' vision came nearer to being fulfilled, in the work of Czech scenographer Josef Svoboda.

2 Polyscenicness: Josef Svoboda and Laterna Magika

A notable exception to the dearth of experimentation in the 1930s was the work of the Czech director Emil František Burian, who provides a link between Piscator and the next major innovator in the field, Josef Svoboda. Working in Prague with an experimental political theatre company, Burian was inspired by Piscator and by Meyerhold. With designer Miroslav Kouřil, he devised a system for combined film and slide projection called the Theatregraph, first used for his 1936 production of Wedekind's *Spring Awakening*.[1] The performance took place behind a large transparent scrim (onto which film was projected) and in front of a further opaque screen, with the effect that the live performers seemed to be performing *in* the world of the film, rather than up against a filmic backdrop. Film heightened the production's Expressionist aspects – enlarging a bed of flowers in which Wendla lay down, showing water swirling about, zooming in until the audience saw a close-up of characters' eyes filling the whole screen, and so on. The performers' engulfment in the filmic world became an image of their own engulfment by their society. Similar use to suggest the subjectivity of characters occurred in Burian's 1937 production of the opera *Eugene Onegin*, where, for example, film showed Onegin's sleigh-ride to a ball, while a voice-over spoke his thoughts and memories. Subsequently, and anticipating several of Svoboda's productions, the ball merged both live and filmed dancers. Like Piscator before him, as Socialist Realism came to dominate Soviet aesthetics, Burian was attacked for formalism by the very Communists whom he supported. His career was then interrupted by the German invasion and he spent much of World War II in concentration camps.

Burian's legacy was taken up after the war by Josef Svoboda, whose many years of experiment, adapting and developing the traditions of both Piscator and Méliès, form a significant bridge between such early pioneers and current work. Svoboda began using film in his work from 1950 onwards.[2] Although Svoboda was a scenographer, working on productions which others directed, he played a strong role in conceptualising the production approach, and from 1973 he was Director of Laterna Magika, the company with which he particularly explored the possibilities of combining film and live performance.[3] During a long career, he worked on over 700 productions in Czechoslovakia and abroad. Obviously, only a few productions will be touched on here, with discussion of some early examples of his use of film in the scenography for more conventional dramatic works being followed by closer examination of some Laterna Magika productions that illustrate different stages in his evolving approach to the wholesale integration of film and live performance.[4]

Strongly influenced by Edward Gordon Craig and Adolphe Appia, and aware of Bauhaus thinking about synthesising the arts, Svoboda desired to create theatrical spaces which were readily transformable and had a dynamic rhythm to them rather than a concern for naturalistic detail. He argued,

> the goal of the designer can no longer be the description or copy of actuality, but the creation of its multi-dimensional model. The basis of a theatrical presentation is no longer the dramatic text, but the scenario, the evidence of the fusion between direction and scenography. (Burian, 1971, 31)

Like Piscator, he continually explored different technological innovations that would help him to create the sort of poetic fluidity he sought. For him, 'Modern technical progress belongs in the modern theatre just as an elevator or Laundromat belongs in a modern building' (ibid., 23). He saw film editing as a model for theatrical presentation:

> We're at a disadvantage in relation to film; we can't use rapid cutting techniques or enlarged details; we always have to work with the scene as a whole. We manage to create focus and tension by a contrapuntal accord between actor and props, movement, sound. (Ibid., 29)

To escape the 'static theatre in which scenery rigidly gazes down on actions played out within its space' (Svoboda, 1993, 17), he developed the notion of 'polyscenicness':

an expression of a free and many-sided time-space operation, in which one and the same action is observed from several optical and ideational angles ... it means breaking up the linear continuity of theatre action, and its transformation into separate events or moments. (Ibid., 21)

As with Piscator and Meyerhold, scenography was aimed at creating a 'machine for actors' to work with. He frequently deployed multiple screens of varying shapes and sizes on different planes, so that he could project different types of material. Film provided a heightened sense of the context of the drama, introduced supplementary material in the manner of Piscator's choric use, juxtaposed extra-diegetic inserts with the staged action and enlarged details of the stage action or figures. Particularly with Laterna Magika, he employed film more for dramatic narrative than Piscator, and utilised film to reveal the subjective experience of characters, either through explanatory inserts such as flashbacks, dreams and close-ups, or through using the camera for two-shot sequences or POV (point of view) shots. He also developed a greater interactivity between the onstage actors and figures in the film world, taking further the fantastic tradition of Méliès and the Surrealists.

Svoboda's first attempt to weave together stage action and filmed action was in a 1950 adaptation of F. F. Šamberk's 19th-century play *The Eleventh Commandment*, directed by Alfred Radok, who had previously worked with E. F. Burian, and was subsequently to become one of Svoboda's principal collaborators and co-founder of Laterna Magika. Svoboda described it as 'a slapstick farce', in which the film drew 'from magazines of the period, which featured, in addition to sensational reports of automobile and flying events, the Emperor Franz Joseph himself' (ibid., 110). Film also showed the characters in external locations and there was at least one example of interplay between filmed and live performers. A chase sequence involving a policeman and gangsters was shown initially on film. Then, in a way that develops earlier examples of characters entering the stage from film, the detective appeared on stage and engaged in a shoot-out with an onscreen gangster, eventually shooting him.

A further example of a dynamic interplay between live action and film to create a polyscenic version of an event is found in the 1959 production of Josef Topol's *Their Day* (directed by Otomar Krejča). Svoboda describes one incident in which a car knocked down a pedestrian:

His last steps on stage ... were accompanied by two simultaneously running filmed shots. The first used a slowly tracking camera to follow the side of the road;

the second followed the speeding automobile in the opposite direction. Then the penetrating sound effect of squealing brakes and tyres. The pedestrian fell, the stage went to blackout, the projected image froze, and the sound of the engine receded in the distance. Then the image of a peaceful road bordered by grassy trenches appeared on all the screens. (Ibid., 55)

Production photographs suggest an almost Cubist approach to projection, with the set dominated by nine large mobile screens hung at various angles. Employing six film projectors as well as slide projectors, film and still images of street lamps, shop windows and advertising billboards were projected, to create 'a mosaic of city life that evolves with the action of the play' (Burian, 1971, 93). These heightened the sense of divisions amongst the characters of the piece, which explored the 'milieu of altered cultural values in the post-Stalinist era', along with the conflict between an older generation's 'bourgeois grasping for security' and their children who 'grope uncertainly for ideals in the midst of disillusionment' (Burian, 2000, 96). In a play that explored conflicting outlooks, the polyscenic use of film enabled multiple viewpoints to appear at any one time.

Figure 3   *Their Day*

In 1958, Svoboda collaborated with Radok on the Czech exhibition for the Brussels World's Fair. With greater funding than usual, he developed the technology for a more complex interplay between live and filmed action. This was the first example of what Radok dubbed Laterna Magika, recalling the 19th-century magic lantern precursors of early cinema. The name was subsequently adopted by the company that carried on developing the concept. The first production was more like a revue than a full-scale dramatic production. In keeping with the World's Fair context, projected film included footage of Czech scenery and industry, along with cultural activities. The performance also involved live musicians and performers interacting with their filmed selves and filmed images of other performers. In an echo of Méliès' use of the matte shot in *Le Portrait*, a female emcee held a conversation with two filmed images of herself; and a live dancer performed a duet with a filmed partner. Projection varied from full-scale Cinemascope projection that filled the back-cloth to smaller projections onto other surfaces.

Laterna Magika initially seemed more concerned with a Méliès-like trickery than with the integration of film within more serious theatrical production. Along with Svoboda's development of his so-called *polyecran* – a forerunner of video-walls, that synchronised many different films on a large number of screens, it caused a considerable stir and went on to be developed in a more commercial way as a tourist attraction. After working with the company in 1962 on a production of Offenbach's *The Tales of Hoffmann* which included fantastic Expressionist sequences, Svoboda withdrew to focus on other work, but he sometimes introduced there techniques he discovered while developing the Laterna Magika principle.

Two productions which illustrate his development in the 1960s are Radok's production of Maxim Gorky's *The Last Ones* in 1966, and Luigi Nono's opera *Intolerance* in Boston in 1965. The former was very much in the Piscatorian tradition, with simultaneous action across three or four staging areas extending it beyond Gorky's naturalistic treatment and filmed material employed as a counterpoint to onstage action. A central plotline involved a policeman, Jakorevov, courting Vera, the daughter of a senior police officer, Kolomnitzev. Although Kolomnitzev promotes himself as a figure of honour, justice and patriotism, projections and film presented a rather different picture of Czarist society, effectively serving as an ironic choric commentary on the actions and characters. For example, at one point, while onstage the young woman's maids gently stroke her naked back with birch twigs, the screen displays film of a young prisoner's back being whipped. In another sequence, while Jakorevov tells Vera a heroic account of pursuing and shooting a fleeing prisoner, a documentary-style film shows a very contrasting picture of what actually took place. Later, when Jakorevov attempts to rape Vera and she returns to her house and throws off her clothes and washes herself, the same film returns.

Figure 4   *The Last Ones*

In a similarly Piscatorian vein, Svoboda's work on Luigi Nono's *Intolerance* is the earliest example I have encountered of extensive use of television in theatre. Nono, a leading avant-garde composer, was active in the Italian Communist Party and knew Piscator well. Drawing on the political situation of the period, in particular the brutalities of the Algerian war of independence, struggles around racism and anti-fascist demonstrations in Italy, the opera dealt with the sufferings of a political refugee. For Sarah Caldwell's production, with the Opera Group of Boston, the assistance of the local television station enabled Svoboda to use projected live relay. Now, when audiences are accustomed to the ease with which digital technology allows simultaneous recording and editing of live material during performance, it is easy to forget how cumbersome (and risky) such an experiment was in 1965. Svoboda had cameras on stage, inside and outside the auditorium, and in two television studios several miles away. An Outside Broadcast Unit outside the theatre edited together material from the various sources, with the results projected onto three large onstage screens. One studio recorded various documents – photographs, texts, slogans and so on. In the other members of the chorus were filmed – while they themselves followed the conductor's baton on video. In the theatre itself, cameras were trained on both performers and audience: resulting images were mixed live with the other sources and relayed onstage, as they might be at a rock-concert today.

In one scene, instead of showing the chorus live on stage as a group of strikers, a more dynamic effect was created by having images of strikers projected onto dozens of placards carried about the stage. Then cameras captured images of (real-life) racist demonstrators against the opera, who were marching outside the theatre with placards denouncing Jews and Communists and demanding that mixed schools be closed and black people be sent back to Africa. As Svoboda describes it, 'The subject of intolerance dealt with in the opera, and the intolerance in the live context in which we presented it, were suddenly confronted' (Svoboda, 1993, 79). Here a trope which had first appeared in 1911 – using the camera to show the real world outside the theatre – was adapted to create a powerful political effect rather than just a comic frisson or moment of recognition.

Appropriately in a production dealing with race issues, Svoboda also played sometimes with showing images in negative. For example, the image of a white singer suddenly switched into negative, so that she was shown as black. A similar effect was applied to video of the spectators: as they were videoed live, their image appeared in negative on the screens, showing an apparently black audience. When this led to some people protesting, their indignation was in turn recorded and shown onscreen.

We might note Svoboda's use of television technology here did not make use of monitors and their associations in the way that other practitioners working with video subsequently did. The images were projected on a larger scale, equivalent to the way in which he used film. However, the technology allowed him to bring the sense of immediacy that comes with 'live' reporting on television. Rather like Piscator's use of the prologue film to *Storm over Gottland*, which forcibly drew out the links between a 15th-century story and contem porary political struggle, Svoboda used television's association with actuality reporting to make an opera set in Algeria directly relevant to its American audience.

Having become Chief Scenographer at the National Theatre in Prague in 1970, in 1973 Svoboda also became Artistic Director of Laterna Magika. Svoboda felt that Laterna Magika had not progressed far in developing a coherent approach to the interplay between the live and the filmed and had largely remained at the level of an entertaining curiosity, appealing to tourists and children through its visual gags. For it to progress, he 'would have to create a real theatre out of Laterna Magika' and 'expand and deepen its current expressive resources' (1993, 116). Identifying the need to rethink its dramaturgy, he cites *The Wonderful Circus* (1977) as a major milestone on the way to rectifying the situation. This was the first time Laterna Magika produced an original continuous story. Directed by Evald Schorm, with collaboration from filmmakers Jiři Srenek and Jan Švankmajer, even this production relies largely on its comic visual appeal, despite Svoboda's conviction that its more coherent narrative and thematic concerns signalled an advance.[5] In contrast with the more Piscatorian handling of film in his work on opera and drama, Svoboda played more with the potential 'magic' of the relationship between live and filmed, even when it had more serious thematic concerns.

As with most Laterna Magika shows, the performance uses dancers and primarily juxtaposes dance and pantomimic movement with film. (This wordless approach ensured the productions' appeal to a tourist market in Prague and to the international touring network: *The Wonderful Circus*, for example, had successful runs on Broadway, in Paris and many other cities.) The production takes the form of a comic fable with allegorical overtones. An opening film reveals two clowns washed ashore on a mountain lake; under the eye of a malevolent Ringmaster they encounter their first vision of womanhood – filmed floating over the water like Botticelli's Birth of Venus. The production follows their quest for love, symbolised by the Venus figure, who appears in various guises throughout; always, just as they reach her, they are thwarted by the intervention of the Ringmaster who snatches her away. By the end their wigs have gone grey, their outfits are tatty, and Venus remains beyond their reach. En route, film enables them to go on a rollercoaster drive through spectacular scenery, perform in circuses, take a ride in a hot air balloon, and get into various scrapes, such as setting a circus tent alight or being beaten up by a motor-cycle gang. Yet still they chase the ever-elusive Venus.

Film runs throughout *The Wonderful Circus* and most Laterna Magika shows. When not used scenographically, it is used to carry the narrative forward and for close-ups; there is also much play with characters slipping in and out of the film. Projection is onto a stage-width semi-circular backcloth, composed of three sections. The semi-circular shape echoes a circus tent, and indeed red and white stripes are projected onto it for the circus scenes. While occasionally three different activities are projected onto the canvas, often projected scenes cover its whole width, a cinemascope effect achieved by filming scenes with three cameras simultaneously and then projecting them together.

Continuing the tradition of Méliès, film is at its most effective in lending a fairy-tale air to proceedings, as in the opening scene and in landscape scenes such as their careering car-ride. In this the live clowns throw their bodies about astride a stepladder in front of the backcloth, while the camera tracks rapidly through changing scenery. As the onstage clowns switch between facing the film and facing the audience, the camera's POV switches to and fro between that of the clowns themselves as they seem to rush headlong towards oncoming scenery and that of an observer being charged at by them. Towards the end the clowns spot Venus and run into the film after her. With the scenery shifting continually from country roads to forests to wintry mountains, not only does the film transport them around the world, but swift seasonal shifts collapse time, suggesting that many years pass between the beginning and end of the sequence.

In such scenes, the overwhelming presence of the film has a dynamic function, which is reinforced by the cinemascope-style projection. Similarly, when the clowns are thrust into performing in a circus and the camera pans around a circus audience, turning their applause and laughter into something grotesque and threatening, the effect is very powerful. After the clowns move into the film, huge close-ups of their faces flank the central canvas on either side, as a grotesque Punch and Judy style 'puppet show' is played out partly onscreen and partly by live dancers onstage. As the figures become more violent, the camera creates a whirligig effect with distorting close-ups of the puppet heads, the clowns' faces, and the menacing Ringmaster. The dynamic interplay between the different images and the live performers moves beyond simple trickery here to create a nightmarish effect. (The design of the puppets and the dizzying editing are familiar trademarks of Švankmajer's other film work.)

At other times, however, the film threatens to overwhelm the performers. Sometimes this is simply an effect of scale, sometimes the film assumes such narrative prominence that the live performers seem merely to be making up the numbers in a story that might as well be shown as a film. A law of diminishing returns operates with some of the attempts at *trompe l'œil* interaction between live performer and filmed action and figures. For example, the Ringmaster, live, is shown doing a lion-taming act, with a troupe of filmed lions leaping to and fro above his head. While this works initially as an amusing sight-gag, as the sequence goes on longer, the effect wanes, and the gap between film and the live figure cracking a whip in the void reasserts itself: it

Figure 5   *The Wonderful Circus*

eventually seems merely a mechanical trick. This impression becomes even more pronounced when, soon after, he reprises the act, but this time with Venus moving to and fro between stage and screen (where she is depicted in the lions' cage).

Viewing the production today, the show's sexual politics and developments in circus, choreography and film since the 1970s conspire to reinforce the impression that *The Wonderful Circus* has become something of a museum piece; yet in 1977 the production was innovative and it laid the foundations for Svoboda and Schorm's subsequent development of productions in which such continuous, or near-continuous, use of film became the norm.[6]

The 1986 production of *Odysseus* (dir. Schorm and Jaroslav Kučera) makes more successful use of devices found in *The Wonderful Circus*. The primary scenic element is again a large backcloth, which hangs at an angle from the flies and sweeps down onto the floor over a supporting scaffolding structure. Film is projected onto this, the floor and a platform suspended from the fly-tower that also serves as a raft for Odysseus and his companions. The film is more stylised and dynamic. Sometimes it sets the scene quite literally, with plenty of seascapes and sea-washed shores throughout. At other times it functions more emblematically, as when Odysseus leaves Penelope for the Trojan War: streams of molten lava pour down the screen and over the floor, followed by rapid intercutting of cannon-barrels, a Zeppelin in flames, World War I bi-planes speeding across the sky, and burning buildings, all creating an engulfing trans-historical image of the maelstrom of war, in which the isolated figure of Penelope is swallowed up.

Film also establishes some of the situations in which Odysseus finds himself. When he journeys down to Hades, the live performer stands centre facing the backcloth, while film shows dozens of bodies hurtling outwards at him from a central point. The threat of the giant Cyclops is depicted through close-ups of a huge hand and eye as seen from Odysseus' point of view. The home of the wind-god Aeolus is suggested by dozens of sheets of paper and kites blown about on film, with a shot of Penelope's face moving about amongst them, always eluding Odysseus – Svoboda here combines scenographic and narrative functions with a subjective insert.

The fact that *Odysseus* is another quest story, tracking the central character through various places and adventures, lends itself to film. With film covering the huge cloth and the floor, the performers are literally enveloped. Yet the scale of film and the interaction with the live performance is more effective. The shape and flow of the cloth

Figure 6   *Odysseus*

mitigate the sense of watching performers moving about in front of a movie screen, while the scale suggests the overwhelming forces Odysseus faces: the fury of war, the anger of the sea-god Poseidon, the monstrous Polyphemus, the whirlpools of Scylla and Charybdis, and so on. Odysseus and his men remain on stage and do not enter the film like the clowns in *The Wonderful Circus*; rather they battle against the awesome forces represented in it. Furthermore, the continual return to sea-imagery, whether calm or stormy, sets a rhythm to the journey as well as underscoring the metaphor of the sea of life that pervades the myth. These factors, along with the mythic nature of setting and story, as opposed to the rather coy humour and cloying sentiment of *The Wonderful Circus*, perhaps contribute to the production still working well twenty years after its premiere.

Although Svoboda employed video projection in *Casanova* (1995), the use was filmic rather than televisual. A richly layered production, it warrants further exploration since the video operates in more complexly expressionistic and self-reflexive ways than in previous Laterna Magika work. With video functioning as more than just a tool to make the narrative more dynamic and fluent, the production self-consciously plays with the style of video used and with the chronology of the action in a challenging, if not completely successful, attempt to explore the continuing appeal of films of the 'rake's progress' sort.

Although it explored another classic story that could be expected to appeal to its international audience, there was a more immediate link to its Czech context, since Giacomo Casanova spent the last thirteen years of his life as a librarian in the Duchcov Castle in Bohemia. The historical Casanova has been superseded by his legendary reputation as a heartless seducer; like Don Juan, he is seen emblematically as a narcissist who attempted to fill an existential void through his continuous amorous conquests. Popular myth usually ignores his activities as a scientist, musician and translator of the *Iliad*, who mixed with the likes of Mozart and Voltaire on his travels. Although the programme note's reference to him being 'an extremely educated and cultured man' might lead spectators to expect these aspects to appear in the production, the focus remains largely on a picaresque tale of his amorous exploits, which is then resolved through a final sequence that casts his behaviour in a psychological light as that of an extreme narcissist.

Video projection (from four mobile projectors) is employed extensively, sometimes conveying the narrative on its own, especially in the opening prologue scene and a final coda. The simple set essentially demarcates a playing space with projection surfaces: there is a large central projection screen, above which hovers a further large mobile screen with a reflective surface; on each side there is a further crenellated screen, onto which video is also projected. A front scrim is also used for projection at the beginning.

The performance opens with projections of historical medallion portraits of Casanova that give way to an image of an old man on his deathbed covered with a cloak. In an atmospheric prologue that recalls *Citizen Kane*, snow begins falling on him and the film flashes back to a fairy-tale like scene in the snow, in which Casanova as a young boy encounters a mysterious young woman – who wears the same cloak as the dying Casanova. As the child turns into a handsome young man through substitution splicing, she covers him in the cloak, gives him a glowing pendant, a rather trite image of igniting his love for women, and departs. At this, the front scrim drops and reveals the dancer who plays Casanova.

While video alternates between more general depiction of Venetian Carnival revellers and close-ups of Casanova and a young dancer whom he watches, the story of Casanova's first amour is played out on stage. Briefly, Casanova falls in love with a dancer named Angelika, but in the confusion of Carnival, is seduced by another. When Angelika discovers them, she unmasks the interloper and flees. Casanova pursues her, but Angelika escapes on a gondola – having run off and reappeared on video. The whole scene is given an Expressionist atmosphere through having dancers reflected on the upper mirror surface and through projected close-up reaction shots.

The opening scenes set the pattern for much of the subsequent action. Video establishes setting and context, and is then used to amplify onstage action (with full period costume and sets as opposed to the balletic costuming of onstage dancers and minimal scenic indicators). It is also used for close-ups of people watching onstage action: this allows the same action to be shown from different points of view (Svoboda's *polyscenic* principle) and contributes to a pervasive atmosphere of intrigue and voyeurism. The reflective upper screen also sometimes provides a multiplication effect, occasionally compounded by special effects doubling of the videotaped images.

The next few scenes depicting Casanova's descent into lechery culminate in the full company of dancers engaging in a stylised bout of sexual gymnastics onstage, echoed by video images of writhing naked bodies and Casanova cracking a whip. When the Inquisition raids the orgy and arrests Casanova, onstage priests and soldiers are doubled on video by a posse of incense-waving priests. Thrown into a cell, Casanova is haunted by memories of Angelika: spot-lit on the darkened stage, his body is reflected onto a large revolving shot of her in nun's habit, merging a doubling of the live performer with subjective images from his consciousness. Video then depicts his escape through the prison roof.

Before leaping from the roof, however, he swaps his wig (by now grey) for a top-hat: the video switches to a 19th-century Parisian cabaret featuring a Can-Can act. In one deft move, to be echoed later, video shifts the action on a century from the time of the historical Casanova, as it attempts to turn his portrayal into that of a timeless archetype. Video use becomes even more self-reflexive in the following scene, in which Casanova seduces a General's wife and fights a duel. As the onstage lovers dance, the video includes footage of a man cranking the handle of an early film projector, along with images of old HMV records; the accompanying music increasingly resembles film melodrama music as it climaxes with the General shooting at a door, causing the film projectionist to look up, startled. As the General dances onstage and challenges Casanova to a duel, video shows an adjutant lowering a backdrop showing a ruined building – which then becomes the setting for a videotaped depiction of the duel. After using

Figure 7 *Casanova*

video in the first half to establish or continue onstage action or expressionistically heighten its impact, the production here develops a more ironic vein. The spectator is caught between a dramatic response to the unfolding story and more metatheatrical reflection on its depiction as a set-piece of melodramatic cinema.

Following scenes depict Casanova's reunion with Angelika and his subsequent abandonment of her for a peasant woman; while the former scene sets a lyrical dance duet against a videotaped depiction of the story, the latter narrative is conveyed through video alone. Its final image of Casanova riding a horse across a river transmutes into a scene in a 20th-century theatre, where a musical called *Casanova* is being presented – the name shines out in neon lighting, in the graphic style of posters for the film *Cabaret*. A top-hatted nightclub chanteuse in the mould of Sally Bowles sings a ragtime number while making up to Casanova, now wearing bowtie and tailcoat but still astride a horse! This provides the backdrop for a live chorus-line routine by three men in classic black tailcoats in the style of Fred Astaire, and six women, whose skimpy white tailcoat outfits, with white toppers and canes, recall Marlene Dietrich. Again, costume and video locate the action knowingly within a filmic tradition.

As the routine ends, video shows Casanova entering the chanteuse's dressing room. Removing her wig, the chanteuse is revealed as Casanova himself. Clever use of doubles and two-shots allows the chanteuse Casanova to approach Casanova and kiss him, only to be repelled. Casanova throws a suitcase at his alter-ego, destroying a mirror along with his double. As the camera pulls away, it gradually reveals a film set, containing props that have been used throughout the piece: a bed, snowballs, the horse, a crucifix. Casanova strips naked in front of the crucifix as the production moves towards its Expressionist finale, all accompanied by strident strings and percussion. After a brief cutaway to a performer's eye view of a grand 19th-century theatre auditorium, the video alternates between moodily lit images of garishly attired streetwalkers and footage of the naked Casanova running. The dancer Casanova staggers backwards onto the stage and video begins showing successive images of the ageing Casanova, leading up to the first deathbed image. While Casanova stumbles about onstage, a group of streetwalkers blindfold him and circle about, caressing him (all doubled by fleeting videotaped images of myriad females). Finally abandoned, he rips the blindfold off and watches video of his dying self, intercut with film of his Fairy Godmother and of him kissing a woman. As he runs into the screen, the film shows the

Fairy Godmother covering his dead body with her cloak. The performance ends with the medallion of Casanova from the prologue now containing the face of the performer, who blows a flirtatious kiss towards the audience.

This kiss illustrates a problematic ambiguity about the way the performance as a whole flirts with a more critical reading of the Casanova story. Noting how the intertextual play of the videotaped material locates the subject and style of the piece self-consciously within cinematic tradition and plays knowingly with the continuing seductive appeal of such stories, it is tempting to see the production as attempting a complicit critique of the voyeurism inherent in the spectator–screen relationship. Furthermore, the programme note might suggest the company is adopting a feminist response to the tale:

> He faces a shocking revelation: all his loves and passions were nothing but a cover for a morbid love of himself. ... He was unable to give, only to take in handfuls. But how many men of his kind have passed through this world? And how many Angelikas?

Yet the production nearly always depicts women as temptresses or flirts, or as powerless victims like Angelika, who still pines for Casanova after her seclusion in the convent. And the framing of the story around Casanova's self-discovery and death places the progress of the piece within a humanist tragedy paradigm. Video (particularly the close-ups, dynamic editing and multiplication effects) combines dazzlingly with lighting, music, and make-up to create an atmosphere of Expressionist grotesquery in the portrayal of Casanova's orgiastic life. But, as often with stage and film treatments of the rake's progress sort, the production rather enjoys its 'naughtiness', foregrounding the sensuous appeal of the women dancing attendance on Casanova and the ravishing visual display of the video. While the production utilises the dynamic interplay of live and videoed more adventurously and critically than previous works, ultimately, it ends up engaging less radically with the story than its sophisticated self-consciousness might suggest.

Graffiti (2001) was the last production that Svoboda worked on with Laterna Magika before his death in 2002. It is notable for a technical innovation that he developed for it and for a greater abstraction in both video and dance, with CGI playing a major role in the video material. The production comprises four distinct sections, each choreographed by members of a new generation of Czech choreographers, to music by Peter Gabriel, Michael Nyman and Philip Glass. A young filmmaker, Petr Kout, provided video material. The production suggests that the company recognised the need to find a new way forward if it was not to become simply a museum of old performances.

For *Graffiti* Svoboda designed a system for projection which enabled the projected material to appear on a non-existent 'screen' cutting across the full width of the stage – to create images literally in thin air. Suspended from the flies, at an angle of 45 degrees and reaching to the stage-floor, is a large screen made of a polycarbonate material that is both transparent and reflective (it is also slatted, like Venetian blinds). In the flies above the screen is a large mirror surface. Video projection bounces off the screen onto the mirror surface and back down onto a virtual perpendicular plane behind the angled screen. This produces the effect of the projections appearing in mid-air, so to speak (there is no actual 'screen' for them to appear on). Performers behind the angled polycarbonate screen are, therefore, able to operate along the same plane as the projected video. They can interact with the 'phantom' figures created by the video or appear actually to be in the (often abstract) settings established by the video, without appearing to be up against a two-dimensional material surface. Those familiar with Victorian theatre and the history of illusionism will recognise that Svoboda was here developing a more complex version of the screens and mirrors apparatus used for the so-called Pepper's Ghost illusion, named after its inventor J. H. Pepper. In the late 19th century theatre this technique was initially used to produce ghostly apparitions with whom the onstage performer could appear to interact.[7] While the technology here draws on 19th-century spectacular theatre for inspiration, the production's overall look is very contemporary, with some video material being in the style of music videos.

The programme notes describe graffiti as 'a subversive expression within the context of contemporary urban culture' and 'a metaphor of the contemporary world. The central motif in the story is a hope residing in our urge to perceive the existence of traces that are left behind the others' "life" stories as a mark for future "re-generations".' The first section responds most literally to the notion of graffiti and to ideas around urban alienation which produce it, while the subsequent three sections play more with the notion of personal traces. The performance opens with video showing accumulating footage of trains and stations and graffiti artists tagging them, using close-ups of sprayers and tags, colourisation, and dynamic editing to create an imagistic backdrop. An ensemble of six dancers performs an abstract, angular dance, working off geometric shapes, suggesting an interpretative response to the video imagery. The virtual screen is then filled by CGI in the style of drip paintings, creating an abstract impression of roots or tendrils that seem to entwine a male dancer who performs a solo amidst them. The video then shifts to more urban imagery, creating the sense of a racing city, while the ensemble returns for more abstract geometric routines. The section closes with a return to further images of trains and graffiti.

The following three sections revolve more around a series of dances depicting relationships, between couples or between individuals and the group, with video projection providing more or less abstract settings or being used to echo or expand upon the relationships depicted through live dance. In section two, for example, a man and a woman dance a lyrical duet, while the video moves between a large-scale, highly colourised version of their love-making and shimmering, impressionistic images of a cityscape by the water at night. When the woman leaves, the man performs a dance of loss and yearning, while the screen is taken over by fleeting close-ups of her, as though depicting his memories of their love-making. When she returns, their dance is again echoed on video, before water washes over their image. While section three is provided with narrative framing by a video showing the ensemble completing a performance and heading off into the Prague night, the focus is primarily on another romantic duet. A swirling pillar of light is projected centre-stage, forming a virtual barrier between a male and a female dancer. Each is joined in turn by video doubles of the other, creating the effect of each in isolation dreaming of dancing with the other. Eventually the woman passes through the pillar towards the man.

The mixing of video to establish setting and to depict more subjective dreams or fantasies continues in the concluding sequence, which again deals with a man in isolation dreaming up a lover. During an opening ensemble sequence the video tracks through a cityscape once more, then up a building to a window. It then depicts a perspective sketch outlining three walls of a room. Onstage a male dancer begins dancing on and around a chair and table. After a brief ensemble interlude, he is left isolated. As the virtual screen fills with a series of geometric planes, a female dancer appears in duplicate, with one image being much larger than life. There is a transition between video and live, as the life-size image dances to the side and is replaced by the live woman, who then dances with the man. On departing, she is shown ascending a high abstract mountainside on video, while the man shelters beneath the table.

Figure 8 *Graffiti*

As this account suggests, the performance relies much more on abstract video imagery than the company's previous work. A romantic, ghostly atmosphere is created, and even the city settings are filmed in such a way as to render them more like Impressionist paintings than straightforward cityscapes. Where the performers themselves appear on video, their images are often fleeting and evanescent, an effect made more pronounced by their projection onto a virtual rather than material surface: the mode of projection fits with the phantasmatic nature of their existence in the minds of the onstage characters who dream them up. In contrast with some earlier work, there is a sense for most of the performance that the focus is on the live dancing out of the various relationships that are explored. Apart from the more pointed subjective use, when it conjures up the dreams or memories of the onstage figures, the video complements the dance atmospherically, rather than taking over from it. The dancing itself, with the choreographers having danced with such companies as Nederlands Dance Theatre and Munich Ballet Theatre, is more contemporary than some of the dance in earlier productions.

The production might suggest then that, just when the death of its founder might have put its future in doubt, the company is in the process of renewing itself, while still drawing on his legacy. There is some truth in this, but it is perhaps not so simple. Ironically, considering the technical innovation involved, the effects achieved recall early 20th-century views of film being most suitable for fantasy scenes or ghostly apparitions. Furthermore, for all that the references to graffiti and the computer animation insert an element of the contemporary, as do the dance vocabulary and its more explicit sensuality, the romantic lyricism with which the relationships are explored, pervaded by atmospheres of loss and yearning, also harks back to an earlier era. For all that the production looks forward then, it also returns, under the guise of its innovative scenography, to the world of late 19th or early 20th-century romantic fantasy, revues and magic.

3 Big Screen to Small Screen

In 1965, the year that Svoboda collaborated with a Boston television station for his radical production of *Intolerance*, the arts were about to be revolutionised by Sony's introduction of the PortaPak – the first portable video-recording system. Up until then video was generally shot on bulky cameras attached to massive recording decks which used two-inch videotape. Location shooting demanded use of an O B Unit stacked with gear and personnel. The few available domestic video-recording systems were cumbersome and expensive, like the Ampex system introduced in 1963 and selling for $30,000, which included camera, monitor and a video recorder weighing about 50 kilograms, disguised in a large wooden cabinet resembling an old-fashioned phonogram. Even when Sony introduced its PortaPak, the camera (still B&W) was much bigger than current cameras and was connected to a large video-recording machine, carried with a shoulder-strap: a reasonably hefty person could manage both, but usually someone would trail around behind the camera person lugging the recorder along. Editing still involved a clumsy process of lining tapes up on different recorders and recording from one to the other. Nevertheless, the PortaPak kick-started a very diverse video art movement, which expanded rapidly over the following decade and influenced the way video came to be used in theatre.

Legend has it that the Korean artist Nam June Paik bought a PortaPak the first day it went on sale in the US, went out and videotaped the Pope, who was visiting New York, and then showed the results that night in the Café Au Go-Go, thus begetting the video art movement. Martha Rosler has rightly satirised what she sees as the 'sanctification' of Paik and the moment in question (Hall and Fifer, 1990, 44) and critiqued the way in which his supposedly radical work was readily absorbed by the art institutions. Nevertheless, a flyer issued alongside his first videotape showings was prophetic: 'As collage technic replaced oil-paint, the cathode ray tube will replace the canvas. ... Someday artists will work with capacitors, resistors & semi-conductors as they work today with brushes, violins & junk' (Paik, 1974).

Behind Paik's view that video would become a key tool for artists and the way in which it was deployed in performance work from the late 1960s on lie broader artistic developments during the preceding decade, especially the resurgence of interest in creating collagist, intermedial art – in which film often played a part. Before discussing some early uses of video in performance that paved the way for its appearance in theatre, it will be worth sketching something of these developments.

In Chapter 1 (Note 18) I briefly noted John Cage's collaboration with other artists on a large-scale multimedia project at Black Mountain College in 1952, an event that was to have a legendary status amongst subsequent experimental artists. The involvement of Cage, who was strongly influenced by Surrealism and Dada, at the Bauhaus-inspired BMC suggests something of the confluence of influences that impacted on developments from the mid-1950s on. A revival of interest in Dada and Surrealism coincided with renewed enthusiasm for a synthesis of art and technology and for the sort of multimedial performance espoused by Bauhaus figures such as Gropius and Moholy-Nagy, both of whom had explored how they might disturb conventional ways of showing film. This contributed to a flurry of activity on both sides of the Atlantic that challenged the autonomy of art-forms, distinctions between low and high cultural forms, and dominant conventions for the presentation and distribution of various art-forms (all of which were part of the early stirrings of postmodernism in the arts). The late 1950s saw the rise of Happenings and the emergence of the Fluxus Group as two key influences on the shape of 1960s intermedial activity. Figures such as Cage, Allan Kaprow, Dick Higgins, George Brecht, Nam June Paik, Carolee Schneemann, Yvonne Rainer, Wolf Vostell, and many others, experimented, theorised and argued with each other about how to break down barriers between art and daily life and between different art-forms.[1]

Happenings and Fluxus events celebrated hybridity and collagism, with actions, sound, text, visual images and film often layered against each other, and with barriers between performers and audiences broken down in diverse ways, whether through surrounding them on all sides with activity, having them move between different spaces, or giving them actions to perform. Higgins coined the term 'intermedia' to describe such types of activity in 1965. The arts moved out of galleries, theatres and cinemas into cafes, lofts and train stations. As new relationships were explored between art-forms, artists and spectators, formal experiment and processes were often privileged over semantic concerns and the production of finished commodities. Multiplicity and simultaneity were catchwords, as events were built around alogical juxtapositions and structures that rejected coherent narratives and self-reflexively played off representational conventions, especially those of media such as film and television.

Whether as part of Happenings or other intermedial events, film, and subsequently video, played a significant part. Amongst Kaprow's collaborators on Happenings at the Reuben Gallery in 1960 was Robert Whitman, who became one of the leading exponents of mixing film with live performance. For *The American Moon* (1960) the spectators were located at the end of six narrow tunnels that converged on a central performance space, with sheets of plastic occasionally lowered down to provide screens for film projection. In *Prune Flat* (1965) a film of two young women was played while the same women and another performed in front of it. The piece played with the perceptual challenges posed by synchronicities and discrepancies between the live and filmed action. In other installational pieces, Whitman played with projections onto objects. So, for example, he projected an image of a woman washing herself onto a shower and a woman applying variously coloured skin creams appeared rear-projected onto the surface of a dressing table mirror: 'she became blue, red, green, while now a river, now a city street, now trees were seen behind her' (Kirby, 1966, 52). (The shower device was echoed by DV8 in 1999 in *The Happiest Day of My Life* and Forkbeard Fantasy played similar games with rear-projection onto a mirror in *Frankenstein*.)

Around the same time Roberts Blossom was also experimenting with what he called 'filmstage'. Rather in the manner of Svoboda's first Laterna Magika show in 1959, in performances such as *Duet for One* (1963) and *Scene Unresolved* (1964) he had dancers performing in front of films of themselves or other dancers. The live or filmed dancers anticipated or followed their 'partners' in the other medium, while film also showed close-ups of the dancers' faces or legs. In discussing his work Blossom echoed much of Robert Edmond Jones' language, celebrating the camera's ability to 'examine an object from all sides, close up and/or far away' and suggesting that his work combined 'the unconscious (recorded) with the conscious (present)' (Blossom, 1966, 70).

In Ann Arbor, Michigan, from 1958 on, Milton Cohen ran his Space Theater in a loft; suspending adjustable mirrors, prisms and triangular screens around the space, he projected films onto them from different angles, while the spectators viewed them lying on cushions or moving about the space. The film used included abstract patterns and images, along with more representational footage; sometimes performers also moved about carrying out seemingly unrelated actions. Cohen was also involved in Ann Arbor with the Once Group, which organised events and festivals during the 1960s that brought together artists and performers who were part of the broader environment of Happenings and Fluxus – people such as Cage, David Tudor, Robert Ashley and the Judson Dance Group. Their best-known group performance was *Unmarked Interchange* (1965), for which a drive-in style screen was erected on the roof of a car-park. As scenes of Fred Astaire and Ginger Rogers in *Top Hat* were projected onto the screen, various panels in the screen opened to reveal live performers carrying out everyday actions: a couple at a table eating a meal, a man lifting weights, a pianist, a woman hanging out washing. As a man read passages from a French pornographic novel *The Story of O*, a woman sometimes walked across a catwalk in front of the screen and threw custard pies in his face. Much of the effect of the performance came from the incongruity of the live actions set against the glamour of the Hollywood musical.

As with much work in the period, the handling of women in some of these combinations of film and performance trod a fine line between celebration of sexuality and sexism, voyeurism and critiques of voyeurism. No stranger to debates about such issues was Carolee Schneemann, who aroused much controversy with her radical critiques of sexist hierarchies in the art-world, most notably in her performance *Interior Scroll* (1975), and celebrations of the erotic in mythic-ritual events such as *Meat Joy* (1964). A prolific, politically committed multidisciplinary artist, who was involved with early Fluxus activities, she produced sculptures, assemblages, films and video as well as performance events that involved all of these. Her approach was underpinned by the hypermediatic view that artworks should cast into stress the spectator's total sensibility, and that 'our best developments grow from works which initially strike us as "too much"; those which are intriguing, demanding, that lead us to experiences which we feel we cannot encompass' (Schneemann, in Sandford, 1995, 246). Notable multimedia events included *Snows* (1967) and *Illinois Central* (1968). In *Snows* the performance space and auditorium was hung with strips of white plastic and paper and white branches, creating an icy atmosphere. A collage of films played through the piece, including: a newsreel from 1947 showing, amongst other things, a volcanic eruption, a snowstorm, a car crash and the Pope; two films of winter sports in Zürich in World War II; film of a blizzard outside the theatre, along with further footage of winter activities shot by Schneemann; and a short film *Viet-Flakes*, in which Schneemann animated several photographs of a Vietnamese soldier shooting a supposed Viet Cong. Some of the film was projected onto the walls and ceiling, as well as onto the bodies of the performers, who carried out movements that included sweeping up snow, a series of grabbing and falling moves, pursuing each other and wrapping themselves in the hanging silver foil, before a snow machine was used to cover them with 'snow'.[2] At times film, lighting and James Tenney's sound collage were triggered by switches activated by the audience.

An important Fluxus activist in Europe and sometimes overlooked as a figure behind the emergence of video art was the German Wolf Vostell, who coined the word 'dé-coll/age' to describe his various installations and Happenings, which 'concentrated on the conjunction of destruction, violence and sexuality, especially as represented in the media' (Stiles, in Schimmel, 1998, 275). As early as 1958 he exhibited *Transmigration*, a slashed canvas alongside a flickering television screen: an ironic foretaste of the way video art would eventually displace painting in contemporary art. For *Nein – 9 Decollagen*, a Happening in Wuppertal in 1963, the audience was bussed to a cinema, where, accompanied by wailing sirens and with people lying about on the floor, they witnessed a dé-coll/age film of television material called *Sun in Your Head*; later a television was ritually shot. A similar destructive approach was adopted in the same year's *TV Burial*, presented in New York alongside other Happenings involving Kaprow, Higgins, and Rainer. While a television played various programmes (the first sequence featured Salvador Dali), cream cakes were thrown at the screen and then a slashed old oil painting was placed in front of it, before it was finally wreathed with barbed wire and buried.

While Vostell continued to confront television as an institution in his installations, his work came to be overshadowed by the less transgressive activities of Paik, a sound artist who became involved with Vostell and other German Fluxus artists in the late 50s. Having created sound environments and events that owed much to Cage's influence, in 1963 in Wuppertal he organised a large-scale event *Exposition of Music – Electronic Television*, which included various installations with prepared pianos, sound-tapes, a dead ox's head, and in one room, a dozen televisions randomly scattered about. Various means were used to distort or interfere with the programmes shown, with vertical lines and negative images being overlaid, for example. Paik also went to New York, and in 1964, with cellist Charlotte Moorman, he created the *TV Cello* installation, in which televisions were stacked up on each other to form the shape of a cello. Moorman moved her bow across the front of the structure, while the televisions played footage of her and other cellists playing. Subsequently, Paik went on to create numerous installations incorporating television monitors, ranging from smaller-scale sculptural objects such as robots and juke boxes made up of monitors to various versions of his Video-Buddha installations, showing a Buddha statue watching a collection of monitors. His work was often characterised by a certain dry, ironic humour, as he 'mutilated, defiled, and fetishized the TV set, reduplicated it, symbolically defecated on it by filling it with dirt, confronted it with time boundedness and thoughtlessness by putting it in proximity with eternal Mind in the form of the Buddha, in proximity with natural time by growing plants in it, and in proximity with architecture and interior design by making it an element of furniture' (Rosler, in Hall and Fifer, 1990, 45).

An increasing number of artists began to use video, sometimes on its own, sometimes in conjunction with performative action. During this initial flourish of activity, and in keeping with the time, 'for many video represented a tool with which to "revolt" against the establishment of commercial television. For others, it was an art medium with which to wage "war" on the establishment of the commercial art world' (Sturken, in Hall and Fifer, 1990, 106). As an upsurge in New Left and identity politics from the mid-60s onward coincided with increasing affordability and accessibility of video equipment, a strongly political community video movement also emerged in many countries, with the democratic potential of new media developments encapsulated in Hans Magnus Enzenberger's influential 1970 essay, 'Constituents of a Theory of the Media'. There he argued, 'For the first time in history, the media are making possible mass participation in a social and socialized productive process, the practical means of which are in the hands of the masses themselves' (Hanhardt, 1986, 98). Tackling what he saw as obsolete Leftist views of a monolithic capitalist media manipulating the masses, Enzenberger, in an argument that anticipated the Utopianism that now surrounds some proselytising about the internet, proposed:

The most elementary processes in media production, from the choice of the medium itself to shooting, cutting, synchronization, dubbing, right up to distribution, are all operations carried out on the raw material. There is no such thing as unmanipulated writing, filming, or broadcasting. The question is therefore not whether the media are manipulated, but who manipulates them. (Ibid., 103–4)

Crossing both the work of individual artists and community video, the construction and representation of identity became a favourite area of work, as issues to do with race, gender and sexuality were frequently explored through video, as in for example, Joan Jonas' *Vertical Roll* (1972), which Kathy O'Dell describes as 'paradigmatic of the early 1970s' (Hall and Fifer, 1990, 146).[3] In this examination of female identity and its construction/destruction, the video shows fractured shots of Jonas' masked head and body shot in close-up. The vertical hold control is used to make the images fall down the screen continually, disintegrating any attempt to hold onto or contemplate her image. The action is accompanied by an insistent banging noise – of a spoon on the screen. In early performances Jonas herself stood alongside, naked, examining herself with a small hand-held mirror.

Here is not the place to enter into detail about the achievements and limitations of the challenges made by video artists and community animateurs to dominant notions of television's properties and capacities through the 1970s. Some have argued that community video's aspirations belied the power relations that still resided in both the role of the animateurs who worked in communities and the controllers of distribution of work and that it often, despite its aims, ended up reproducing or only modifying dominant systems of representation associated with television. And critics such as Rosler have questioned the way in which Paik and other video artists soon became 'museumized' and their '(pseudo-)transgressions of the institutions of both television and the museum' were quickly accommodated by the artistic establishment, just as Dadaism and Surrealism had been before (Hall and Fifer, 1990, 45).[4]

Notwithstanding such qualifications, the rapidly evolving video work of the 1970s did in many ways anticipate later developments in theatre. Video installations played different images on different monitors against each other; monitors were taken out of the domestic space which is their normal domain and placed in public spaces such as parks or malls; closed circuit television was employed to replay images of spectators to themselves; video images were fragmented, slowed down or distorted, and the grammar, temporal conventions and subject matter of television pastiched or challenged; echoing earlier work with film, there was much play with the co-presence of performers and their video images, sometimes pre-recorded, sometimes relayed live; and as Paik predicted, increasingly sophisticated developments in editing and projection created a whole new palette for artists to play with in ways that referred back perhaps more to painting than to television itself, although, as David Antin noted, 'To a great extent, the significance of all types of video art derives from its stance with respect to some aspect of television ... whether or not the artist sees the work in relation to television' (Hanhardt, 1986, 162).

This rapid sketch suggests why one needs to treat with a degree of caution Wooster Group director Elizabeth LeCompte's comment, in a 1987 interview, that when she started putting televisions on the stage, in the 1981 production of *Route 1 & 9*, 'television just wasn't being used in the theatre', whereas she felt it was just as natural as 'Chekhov having a door open onto some artificial light'.[5] While The Wooster Group has led the way in contemporary use of video in theatre and LeCompte's comment broadly reflected the situation in dominant drama-based theatre, it not only takes no account of earlier work with film but also fails to acknowledge the wealth of intermedial performance and video art work in the 1960s and 1970s which established the context for her own collagist experiments discussed in the next chapter.

4 Postmodern Collage: The Wooster Group

Since using video in its 1981 production of *Route 1 & 9*, The Wooster Group has included video in all its theatre productions, consistently experimenting with the content and style of material used and the interplay between video materials, their means of display, and the live performers. In the process it has influenced many other companies in the US and abroad.[1] Unlike subsequent practitioners who have taken advantage of the opportunities afforded by developing technologies such as video projection and video walls, The Wooster Group is unusual in continuing to deliver video material on television monitors.

The company emerged, under the directorship of Elizabeth LeCompte, from a group of performers who were working in New York in the 1970s with Richard Schechner's Performance Group – a leading experimental company of the time which drew inspiration from the work of Brecht, Artaud and Grotowski, amongst others.[2] Its highly intertextual work is characterised by playful collaging of found materials and daily life activities with both 'high' and popular cultural forms and texts and by ironic, self-conscious performances. Their productions have incorporated a striking diversity of texts and performance approaches. Dramatic texts have ranged from neoclassical French drama (Racine's *Phèdre*), drama of a more naturalistic kind (*The Crucible, Three Sisters*), to a modernist experimental text (Stein's *Doctor Faustus Lights the Lights*); productions have also included texts from novels, biographies and films, along with autobiographical material and material found in rehearsal. Even more extensive have been the performance styles explored in both live and videotaped performance, as they 'face off' with the found texts (Kate Valk, in Rosten, 1998, 18). They have experimented with blackface, cartoons, musicals, soap opera, porn movies, chat shows, Polynesian dance, Japanese

Noh and Kyogen. LeCompte speaks of 'composing' the productions visually and musically and her background in the visual arts is often noticeable in her adoption of visual motifs from painting, as seen in recollections of Dali and Holbein discussed below. The Group's handling of video and its playing with different televisual styles must, then, be seen in the context of this broader collagist approach and ongoing play with different 'masks' for addressing and defamiliarising the chosen texts.[3]

Some critics portray such collagism and eclecticism as simply symptomatic of a depthless, ahistorical postmodernism and a fetishisation of the signifier at the expense of the signified, and comments by LeCompte and members of the company have discouraged the idea that a deliberate deconstructive project lies behind the work. LeCompte delights in testing to the extreme ideas about collage which derive from Dadaism, and accounts of devising sessions and rehearsals make clear that the company adopts a genuinely *experimental* approach to the collocation of different types of text, narrative or styles. Typifying Lyotard's postmodern artist who 'works without rules in order to formulate the rules of *what will have been done*' (Lyotard, 1984, 81), they *test out* what it might be like to have black-face performers doing crude comic routines while video plays a classic Thornton Wilder text performed like a soap opera, or what might be the effect of including a Polynesian dance in the middle of a Chekhov play, with LeCompte insisting on allowing different elements 'to be in the space together, without this demand for meaning. "Meaning" in quotes' (Kaye, 1996, 256).

Nevertheless, the Group's approach does, in effect if not intention, encourage a deconstructive response towards the various texts and performance styles, and towards representation in general. The very act of laying one system of representation against another (or in The Wooster Group's case, often several others) tends to call the differing systems into question, or at the very least, to denaturalise them. In handling video, the knowing play with particular televisual conventions leads to fruitful collisions with different conventions of dramatic writing and performance and brings to light the absences and erasures in each and the dynamics of authority which they instigate. While the dominant place of television within contemporary culture is reflected in the Group's persistent use of the television monitor rather than video projection, the way in which LeCompte continually reframes its location and contents challenges the place of television just as much as her use of video expands and challenges theatrical texts and conventions.

LeCompte cites two significant ways television practice influenced her broader approach to composition. She describes her love for old television shows such as *The George Burns and Gracie Allen Show* and *I Love Lucy*, in which the performers regularly moved to and fro between performing as characters and performing as themselves, breaking the televisual fourth wall to comment on what had just been done, before returning to the action – often with comic effect (LeCompte, 1990). As in contemporary shows such as *Curb Your Enthusiasm*, aspects of the performers' own lives were folded into the story-lines, blurring boundaries between the fictional and the autobiographical. Similarly, Wooster Group performers, especially in earlier productions, move fluidly between the characters they present and a stage version of themselves, as they speak to each other or the audience and aspects of their lives in the company appear in the productions. A version of this appeared in earlier Performance Group productions, where the influence of Brecht could be seen, and it was familiar in popular entertainments such as vaudeville and variety shows, but it is noteworthy that LeCompte identifies her own approach as influenced more by popular television.

In common with other contemporary theatremakers, LeCompte also likens the way productions flit to and fro between various narratives and modes of performance to channel-hopping on television, moving backwards and forwards between fiction, documentary, news, comedy, and so on. She sees no reason why, if we are comfortable doing this when watching television, we should not feel comfortable when theatre produces the same effect. Again, there are precursors in earlier forms of popular theatre, and such an approach is often seen as characteristic of much postmodern cultural production.

Route 1 & 9 (The Last Act)

In earlier productions, such as *Rumstick Road*, The Wooster Group collaged music, slide-projections and other sound-recordings alongside related and apparently non-related stage action. In 1981, however, for *Route 1 & 9 (The Last Act)*, LeCompte introduced video for the first time. Three distinct sections of video appeared; though controversial at the time, seen in retrospect today, their use seems quite straightforward in comparison with later experiments.

The first use was, for all its simplicity, quite disconcerting. The production began not with live performance, but with a twenty-minute video of performer Ron Vawter mimicking a 1965 educational film featuring Clifton Fadiman lecturing about Thornton Wilder's depiction of small-town America, *Our Town*. In early performances spectators watched this in a separate room in the Performance Garage before going down into the performance space for the rest of the production. In subsequent performances elsewhere, the video usually appeared on four monitors suspended above the performers and one on ground level, in the same space as the rest of the performance.

Vawter delivered the lecture in a very deliberate manner, deploying rhetorical gestures and illustrative materials in ways that mark the moment of their use. He studied Fadiman's film in great detail, and his prompt-script shows how closely he plotted every gesture – opening out his palms, placing his hands in each other, touching fingers and thumbs together in what he calls a 'church' gesture, and so on. He produces an almost Brechtian demonstration of Fadiman's lecture style. His stiff movements across the lecture theatre – to and fro between a toy theatre and a stepladder, were also filmed in such a way as to mimic the self-conscious variation of setting often found in educational television lectures. Capitalised sub-titles underscored certain points, as when the lecturer speaks of THE USE OF A CONDENSED LINE OR WORD. The video retained moments that would normally be edited out in a broadcast television programme: as well as awkward editing jumps, Vawter sometimes coughs, corrects himself, or repeats a line. All this served to expose how such television normally tries to operate seamlessly in order to generate an authoritative meaning. In refusing such seamless presentation, the video undermined the authority of the interpretation put forward in the lecture.

The lecture presents a traditional humanist analysis, focusing on the graveyard scene of Act Three. Fadiman endorses Wilder's idea that the inhabitants of Grover's Corners undergo universal, trans-historical experiences and feelings. He places *Our Town* within a Western tradition of art as consolation in the face of death. At the end of the play 'we see that Emily's life, and all our lives, are part of something vast and eternal'. It helps us 'to create order out of the confusion of everyday living'. He refers to a series of sculpted heads, from Greeks and Egyptians up to Degas and Picasso, images of which appear on the monitors. These are citizens of *Our Town*, 'just as we all are'. As Savran observes, the lecturer's use of the first person plural continually inscribes the spectators as sharing this humanist tradition. LeCompte herself acknowledges that she 'liked the Fadiman film, but was bothered about liking it. It touched nostalgic chords of comfort for me that made me angry' (Savran, 1986, 17). The style of the video here, however, problematises Fadiman's approach, provoking spectators to question the extent to which they are imbued with the beliefs assumed by the lecturer.

What follows the lecture is the antithesis of such art: it seems chaotic, grotesque, unsettling, and presents a view of America very different from the middle-class, white America that dominates *Our Town*. Where Wilder refers in passing to 'the other side of the railway tracks' as a place where Poles and various others live (but note, no mention of a black population), *Route 1 & 9* enacts an extreme version of an 'other side' – one that was not depicted in the dominant American drama of the 1930s, but largely relegated to marginalised theatrical forms such as vaudeville.

The live action begins with Vawter and Willem Dafoe, wearing blackface make-up and dark sunglasses with tape across them, constructing a skeletal house in the style of Laurel and Hardy, accompanied by a sound-tape of two men discussing house-building in New Jersey.[4] Their clumsy attempts to erect the frame and install a large window become a perverse echo of the Stage Manager setting up the houses of the Webb and Gibbs families early in *Our Town*, but here the builders are black labourers (or more properly, white performers blacked up) – a sort of *lumpenproletariat* not depicted in *Our Town*. As building work proceeds, Kate Valk and Peyton Smith, also in blackface, plan a birthday party. Adopting a black 'jive' voice, Valk phones friends to invite them and calls real local food outlets, trying to order food – with the shopkeepers' responses being amplified for the audience. Again, this parallels scenes of food and party preparation in *Our Town*: but in contrast with the homey, apple-pie female domesticity of the play, Valk orders chicken and mash from fast-food joints.

Throughout all this a television monitor inside the house-frame flickers with electrostatic 'snow' – an image of television's constant presence in modern homes. The upper four monitors show Wooster Group performers, shot in close-up, quietly speaking dialogue from *Our Town*. As the text competes with the interspersed dialogues of the live performers and intermittent sound effects of drills, gunfire, and alarms, it is only possible to decipher an occasional exchange when the volume is increased or other activities subside. The atmosphere is that of soap opera. LeCompte thought that:

> when you took the Stage Manager out of *Our Town*, it became a soap opera. ... We did improvs around soap opera style, using TVs. And we watched soap opera.

I would time the segments in between the ads. And from that, we got a kind of rhythm. The actor's pacing is soap opera, but the visual style is more 'portraiture', the actors speaking directly to the camera. (Savran, 1986, 34)

Wilder's Stage Manager was, of course, originally intended as a Brechtian device to defamiliarise the action of *Our Town*, and Wilder himself disliked the way the play was taken up as sentimentally as it was, with the Stage Manager often played as rather too folksy. The Stage Manger's removal and the remediation of the play here highlight the potential the text contains for such a sentimentalising take-up.

As the building concludes, the performers enact a wild, drunken party. The performers alternate high-energy dance numbers and raucous re-enactments of blackface comedy routines originally performed by Pigmeat Markham, including pouring 'castor oil' into a punch bowl (actually onto the floor) and a sequence in which Pigmeat defecates in his pants.[5] As the party reaches a crescendo, the four monitors are winched forward, until they loom over the heads of the performers at the front of the performing space – forcing spectators to crane their heads back in order to watch the subsequent sequence. As a loud alarm rings incessantly, the lights dim and the performers give way to twenty minutes of video.

Again using head-shots, the video includes much of Act Three of *Our Town*, in which the recently dead Emily joins the ghosts of those who pre-deceased her, in the cemetery above Grover's Corners. She wrestles with her in-between state, still feeling part of life 'down there'. Ironically, given her own coffined existence and her presentation here in a television 'box', she describes the living as 'sort of shut up in little boxes'. Allowed to revisit her life for one last time, she returns to Grover's Corners on her twelfth birthday. The bitter-sweet experience culminates in an elegiac farewell to Grover's Corners and her parents before she asks, 'Do any human beings ever realize life while they live it? every, every minute?' (Wilder, 1962, 89).

As Mrs Gibbs and Emily observe a tearful George falling to the ground in the graveyard, the video shows Dafoe's face contorted with pain – a sculptural image that echoes ironically the sculpted heads shown at the end of the opening lecture. The intimate sound, overtly manipulative music, soft focus and close-up technique of soap opera produce a wistful atmosphere. Swelling chords contribute to a sense of double-coding: spectators may be torn between the emotional impact of the presentation and a sense of irony created by the televisual framing and the excessive underlining of the scene's pathos. This is followed by crashing music accompanying Simon Stimson's bitter outburst, 'That's what it was to be alive. To move about in a cloud of ignorance.' The conflicted viewing of this is also underscored by the onstage activity, which reverses the background/foreground relationship between party and play earlier in the production. After remaining still initially, the blackface performers begin tiptoeing about, shifting furniture and whispering inaudibly, lit only by the glow of the monitors. Occasionally dancing slowly, they function as the partygoers of the previous sequence (and of Emily's twelfth birthday) and as stagehands preparing the scene for the next part of the show (the lower monitor is moved centre-stage and another monitor placed above it). While the silent cavorting initially heightens the melancholic atmosphere created on video, it gradually provides a counterpoint: a telephone rings, loud music suddenly erupts, and then a boisterous calypso starts playing. As in *Our Town*, life begins to resume amongst those left 'down below'. As the monitors freeze on the tortured image of Dafoe, the music is turned up full blast and the performers, with their make-up half wiped off, launch into a final frenetic dance:

> They approach the audience, blood streaming down their faces, their mouths gaping open to reveal vampire fangs. The restrained emotionality of *Our Town* and the constraints placed on the performers to remain quiet during the video now explode into a frenzy of bloodlust and rage. (Savran, 1986, 36)

If this brief dance is extremely confrontational, what follows is even more so. Following a further loud alarm, the performers abruptly stop and sit down, and the monitors flicker into life again. They show LeCompte and Vawter driving a van into New Jersey. Initially, this seems to invert early European examples of film showing performers coming through neighbouring streets to the theatre. Here they are shown leaving the theatre, heading into the real world through which Route 1 and 9 runs. But they soon pick up two hitchhikers. While the journey continues on the upper colour monitors, the smaller, lower black and white monitor begins to show the hitchhikers engaging in copulation and oral sex with each other.[6] The sequence focuses like a porn movie on the bodies of the performers: they are effectively headless sex objects. Just as the blackface routines suggested a grotesque contrast with the repressed world of *Our Town*, so the head-shots of the *Our Town* videos and the educational pieties of the lecturer (and his sculpted heads) seem to be answered by the obscene *bodily* display of this video. (It might also be seen as a riposte to the sentimental treatment of George and Emily's romance.) Throughout its playing there is no sound, no other distraction for the audience. When the videotape stops playing, the performance ends abruptly.

The controversies over the pornographic video and the use of blackface have been extensively discussed, and Savran and Vanden Heuvel provide stimulating readings of how the various elements play against each other. LeCompte herself claimed that when she started working, she 'didn't have any idea that these routines from Pigmeat Markham would have anything to do with *Our Town*. ... I was working on Pigmeat Markham material because I was interested in it formally' (Kaye, 1996, 254). She 'just overlapped and scissored', refusing 'to judge what material was relevant and what was not' (Savran, 1986, 41). Nevertheless, Vanden Heuvel argues that the antics of the blackface performers and the pornographic video expose the falsifying 'order' of Wilder's supposedly universal portrait of middle-America and alert the spectator to what the play represses:

> Framed outside Wilder's text and town, these disorderly phenomena (sexual threat, racial difference, violent physicality, death rather than eternal verities) find representation in *Route 1 & 9* as local perturbations which will – as they cannot in the closed system of *Our Town* – cause widespread transformation of the overall system. (Vanden Heuvel, 1995, 68)

Of course, the contrast drawn is made problematic by the use of white performers to play the blackface routines; the critique of Wilder is framed by The Wooster Group's own recognition that it, as a group, does not have any black performers.

While such arguments are persuasive, Savran warns against too readily attempting a conclusive dialectical reading of the production, and in *What Is This Dancing?* (2004) I suggest that the quest for meaning production may too easily smooth over the production's gaps and contradictions, to produce a coherent, politically progressive interpretation, at the expense of sufficient acknowledgement of the libidinal impact of the performances and of the extent to which its radical structuring challenged attempts by early spectators to read the production as a whole. Even spectators who were familiar with the avant-garde scene in New York initially found the work highly offensive and less neatly dialectical than subsequent analysis suggests. Here we might note how LeCompte's deployment of video, for all that it appears quite simple in comparison with later usage, was, at the time, striking in its divergence from previous practice with film, in particular the Piscatorian model favoured by political theatre. LeCompte effectively inverted the sort of use Piscator and, to some extent, Svoboda made of film. Where they used film to expand the world presented by the play-text that was being enacted live, LeCompte placed *Our Town* on video, and set up a stage world that, at first sight, seems to bear no relation to its world or to the preceding lecture. To the extent that one implicitly 'comments' on the other, the stage world seems to function as a contrast to the videoed world, rather than vice-versa. Where earlier practitioners exploited film's potential to shift scene and show large scale action, LeCompte confined herself mostly to the 'talking heads' more normally associated with television. The continuous length of the videos exceeded previous practice (excepting Laterna Magika): the first runs for almost twenty minutes, and the *Our Town* material lasts over thirty. Although there was some simultaneous action during the *Our Town* tapes, running the first and third films on their own exceeded anything Piscator or others had attempted with film and owed more to the collagist practices of video installations. In common with contemporary video art, it also played more knowingly with the formal properties of the medium than earlier practitioners.

LSD (... Just the High Points ...)

Developed during 1983–84 and shown over the next six years, *LSD* (... *Just the High Points* ...) combined a collagist treatment of the drug culture of the 1960s (particularly the activities of LSD guru Timothy Leary) with a scrambled treatment of Arthur Miller's play *The Crucible*.[7] Video did not play a great part, although it is worth noting briefly how LeCompte introduced certain practices which were explored more fully in subsequent shows.

In the first of its four Acts, the performers, seated behind a long table, provided a quick snapshot of the 1950s and 1960s by reading excerpts from works by Kerouac, Ginsberg, Burroughs and others, interspersed with memories of Leary's baby-sitter. Act Two originally involved a condensed, rapid-fire reading of excerpts from *The Crucible*, but after Miller had the company prosecuted, Michael Kirby provided a text that closely paralleled *The Crucible*. In Act Three the performers re-enacted a rehearsal during which they worked on *The Crucible* after taking LSD, a sequence that was variously comic, tedious, and quite dark and frightening. This merged with re-enacting a riotous drug-fuelled party at Leary's farm, Millbrook. Meanwhile, a parallel narrative on video involved a man in Miami arranging a gig in a hotel. Act Four drew on the fact that in the 1980s Leary and Watergate burglar Gordon Liddy toured a staged debate in which they discussed issues to do with the individual and society. The performers enacted an incident when a man who had been shot by someone on LSD confronted Leary. Alongside this, a fake Spanish dance troupe, Donna Sierra and the Del Fuegos, performed a hilarious dance.

The video material was shown on two monitors, one placed on the table beside the performers, the other in front of it. The first usage was not originally planned, but was a product of circumstance; it nevertheless initiated a subsequent line of development and raised questions about the place of an actor's literal presence in theatrical performance. When Kirby was unavailable for a few performances, some of his contributions were videotaped and played when appropriate. The collagist structure made the substitution easier than it might have been in a more naturalistic performance, especially as the presentational style, with the performers often reading from books or scripts, or delivering the text at breakneck speed, generally challenged traditional notions of actorly presence. As LeCompte rejects the spurious authenticity associated with a Method approach to acting, she saw Kirby's appearance on video as just another mask, and subsequent productions began to include such video substitutions, reaching its logical conclusion in *Fish Story*, when video footage included appearances by Ron Vawter, who died while the show was being made.

When Kirby subsequently returned, some of the video was retained, producing a doubling effect, as 'live' Kirby sat alongside his video image. This led to a wittily structured comic effect in the drug party scene. Kirby enacted a version of the notorious incident in which William Burroughs shot his wife – when attempting an Annie Oakley style trick-shot. Here a fused image of the real Kirby and his televised arm 'shot' at the live Nancy Reilly. Such a moment functions as a comic turn or 'attraction' (and recalls Svoboda's shoot-out scene in 1950), but its hallucinatory quality also seemed apt, coming during a party in which everyone was high on drugs. The cyborgian fusion of live and videotaped performer also further marked the making of the performance, showing it as a product of mediation and refusing to naturalise its depiction of events; in later work such cyborg-like images become almost a Wooster Group trademark. Subsequent use of video in Acts Three and Four was relatively minor in significance, although it did contribute to the emotional texture of the acid-trip scene.

Frank Dell's The Temptation of Saint Antony

More complex integration of video was found in *Frank Dell's The Temptation of Saint Antony* (1987), aptly described by Elinor Fuchs as 'part mystery play and meditation on morality, part an in-the-theater burlesque filled with tricks, gags and numbers' (1988, 104). This drew on a bewildering array of source materials, including: Ingmar Bergman's 1958 film, *The Magician*, in which a magic troupe under investigation by the police is forced to demonstrate their tricks; Gustave Flaubert's 1874 closet drama *The Temptation of St Antony*, which depicts the 3rd-century hermit being tempted by the Devil with manifestations of the Seven Deadly Sins; dances devised with director Peter Sellars; a biography of the comedian Lenny Bruce, who adopted the name 'Frank Dell' in one of his routines; Geraldine Cummins' 1932 book, *The Road to Immortality* – in his last weeks Bruce had his assistant read extracts from this to him; nude chat shows of the sort shown on late-night cable television; a hallucinatory film made by Ken Kobland; and incidents and interruptions which occurred during the rehearsal process.[8] As Savran has noted, 'No other Wooster Group piece ... is as complex and deeply intertextual; no other will as consistently frustrate any attempt to fix the freeplay of references or to contain the plurality of signifiers' (1990, 43). Such complex layering of activities prevents any attempt here to do anything more than provide a rudimentary sense of action and text, so that its use of video may be more fully explored.

The action is nominally set in a hotel room in Washington, substituting, as the Programme suggests, for Flaubert's 'sunset in the desert' location. In practice, the set consists of the long platform from *LSD*, behind which a long wall with two doors and a window is lowered and raised at certain points. Centre-stage is a metal-framed bed. To the sides are two television monitors, with a third suspended above. While the published text gives no clues as to setting, performance approaches or the use of video, the layout, in two parallel columns, does reflect something of the underlying structure of the production's seven episodes. One column consists mostly of a long, rambling text delivered by Vawter as Frank; the other consists of dialogue of other cast members, who sometimes interact with Frank, but often follow an almost separate track of activity.

Frank merges three main identities: he hosts a nude television chat show (with the activities shown on the upper monitor); as the leader of a performing troupe, he veers between recounting a Lenny Bruce style autobiographical monologue and attempting to rehearse two women in a dance version of the St Antony story;[9] as both figures he slips in and out of playing St Antony, making observations about life, death and God, while also being visited by various visions from Flaubert's text – Ammonaria, Hilarion, and the Chimera. Vawter's monologue is punctuated by exchanges with the production's technicians and an assistant called Sue (who reads him extracts from Cummins and Flaubert and goes shopping for him), and by videotaped phone-calls from Dafoe. Wearing a bathrobe and sunglasses, with a hand-held microphone, Vawter performs mostly down in front of the platform on which the rest of the cast generally performs. Here Onna and Phyllis (Valk and Smith) move between partying, recalling past disastrous performances, and rehearsing a melodramatic tale of drugs and death. In Episode Six, in a scene derived from Bergman, they stage some magic acts, for which Vawter is enlisted. In the final episode Phyllis announces she is abandoning theatre, while Onna organizes a hasty departure, responding to a request for a performance from the King of Sweden, again a trace of Bergman's narrative.

From the opening lines, in which Vawter tests the sound levels and asks 'JJ' (James Johnson) to 'throw that tape on' and 'Dieter' for a little music (blurring Jeff Webster's role as both sound operator and a character), the production becomes 'a piece about the making of the piece', as LeCompte described it (Cole, 1992, 96). The quest to get things right, the banalities surrounding rehearsal, the highs and lows of performance and relationships with audiences are constantly referenced. The use of lighting, sound, music, and video to manipulate atmospheres and affect audiences is often marked in the very moment of their use. Taking its cue from *The Magician*, the production plays with, but also exposes, the 'magic' of theatre. Interwoven with the metatheatrical playing about are frequent encounters with mortality, a desire for ecstasy and transcendence, and a recurrent collapse into a soulless eroticism.

Typical of the mixing of sacred and profane, the profound and the banal, and also illustrative of the tightly integrated use of video, is a sequence in Episode One: The Monologue.[10] Vawter riffs about a quasi-mystical experience on drugs, interspersing a vision of stars with a flippant account of an encounter with a woman. The vision is soon undercut by his comment, 'the harmony of the planets gave me a real pain in the old proverbial butt' (The Wooster Group, 1996, 269). As the video shows him with a naked woman, Vawter lip-synchs a brief dialogue with the woman, doing her voice as well as his own. (He

reverses the sort of lip-synch associated with music-video performances: the live Vawter speaks into his microphone, synchronising with
the videotaped figures, whose voices are silenced.) They are then
joined by Dafoe, naked and wearing a markedly fake moustache.
Dafoe is introduced as Cubby from Wales. As they engage in a faltering discussion of the attraction and repulsion of stars and the appearance of the Milky Way, Vawter lip-synchs Cubby's dialogue also. He
then looks at his script and prompts himself to get going on 'that bit
about the prayers, tears, physical suffering'. After speculating about
'the absolute and the big questions', he calls a bearded woman to come
to him (Ammonaria from the St Antony story) and continues:

> Everywhere, everywhere here is ... there's no bounds ... the infinite ... the
> infinite ... you can never reach the top ... you can never come to the bottom.
> Because there is no bottom. There's no bottom? Let's see if there's no bottom. You
> wanna ... toss that thing around? (Ibid., 271; ellipses are in the text)

Over this last section the video, which has shown a naked bearded
woman joining him, closes in on her crotch. After musing about
'something beyond death, something beyond God', Vawter adopts a
female voice to say, 'Maybe appearance is the only reality.' To this he
replies, in leering fashion, 'Well, appearance is the only reality ... and
what an appearance.' So the scene proceeds, mixing metaphysical
speculation with asides, chat-up lines and sight-gags, while the video's
naked figures gyrate with a jaded lassitude and Vawter's lip-synching
becomes an increasingly virtuosic display of the performer's skills.
Pathos and bathos combine towards the end as, in the face of
Ammonaria's acknowledgement that you can't 'ever see the cradle
without seeing the grave' (ibid., 274), Vawter calls for a little dance to
cheer them up: the video displays them in a naked line-up jigging
about, with the camera trained on their pubic areas.

In the following three episodes, while Onna and Phyllis dance and
rehearse and Vawter alternates between the various tracks of his
monologue and his dialogues with the others, the videos are used
principally to show his encounters with the figures from the St
Antony narrative, such as the bearded lady, the Sphinx and the
Chimera. He interviews them, they lounge about or dance, always
naked and with the camera often freeze-framing shots of the chest to
pubic area. The effect is more comic than erotic, as in, for example,
Dafoe's appearance as a sand-dancing Chimera crying out 'You can't
catch me, I'm the gingerbread man.' While the style mimics its cable

television model, its framing also recalls the iconography of Salvador Dali's *The Temptation of St Antony* (1946). Dali shows a naked St Antony raising a crucifix up against an elongated white horse that advances on him from above, followed by four elephants carrying images of sensuality. One of these is a naked female torso (from the neck to the pubic area) framed in the doorway of a Renaissance cathedral. This was strikingly echoed in the way Vawter at ground level stood looking up at the video monitor's freeze-frames of similarly naked torsos. The mixture of sacred and profane in Dali's painting thus reappears, but with the television monitor as the contemporary equivalent of the cathedral.

At a narrative level, video apparently has a simple theatrical function, to show the visions that distract St Antony from 'concentrating on holy things'. It recalls Robert Edmond Jones' vision of film showing characters' thoughts, dreams, and fantasies. But the style of presentation has further implications and effects. There is a suggestive parallel with the 19th-century touring versions of the story. Just as they exploited the surface moralism of the overall tale as an excuse for playing out scenes of lust and excess, so the conversations on the chat shows are only a pretext for their real interest – the titillating exposure of the naked participants. Furthermore, where Flaubert's text embraces a rich range of temptations, spiritual, carnal and fantastical, the reduction of these to the soft-porn of late-night television suggests a poverty of both spiritual and erotic imagination in a world saturated with quasi-pornographic imagery. We are presented with a rather pathetic version of 'temptation-lite', more ridiculous than erotic. For all the supposed seductiveness of the naked flesh on display, the close-up televisual framing eventually reduces the bodies to mere objects, stripped of humanity and eroticism.

The underlying melancholia is evoked forcefully in Ken Kobland's *Flaubert Dreams of Travel*, sections of which play later in the production. The film shows Vawter, sometimes wearing a moustache and goatee beard (modelled on Georges Méliès), sometimes with a turban, moving in desultory fashion about a desolate motel room. Other cast-members appear in various states of disguise and undress. Hand-held camera shots, colourisation, distorted angles and close-ups lend a surreal air. At times Vawter stares at a naked body splayed out on the floor, tracking its contours with a cane: the layout recalls how Lenny Bruce's naked body was found after his morphine overdose. The body has the ghastly tonalities of the British painter Stanley Spencer's studies of naked bodies, bodies reduced to cadavers. The film's atmosphere suggests a post-orgiastic torpor, a sense of decadence turned sour.

The further major use of video is for three phone-calls between Dafoe's Cubby and Vawter. Cubby reports that he has gone to Hollywood to act in a movie about Christ – echoing Dafoe's real-life absence, performing in Scorsese's controversial *The Last Temptation of Christ*. Coming between the various temptations, and conveying Cubby's excitement at being out in Hollywood, the calls operate at two levels: they suggest another potential aspiration or temptation for Frank / St Antony and they reflect how Dafoe's developing film career was affecting the company's work.

The final call, however, assumes more complex resonances. Having endured his dark night of the soul, Vawter / Frank summons up the energy to begin playing St Antony once more. While, above him, Onna calls on Frank to hurry, because they have to get out of the room/theatre, he repeatedly addresses the absent Ammonaria, asking, 'What are you afraid of? A big black hole?' Hearing no answer, he asserts, 'there is happiness, happiness to be found. Birds, birds in the air. OK, you can join them ... [my ellipsis] and uh ... fly into the winds' (The Wooster Group, 1996, 313). He soon qualifies this, 'Don't, don't feel that you have to fly always. You can walk. Walk on.' As Vawter prepares to leave, Cubby phones, and simultaneously Onna receives a phone call summoning the group to the King of Sweden's palace. Cubby holds up to the camera a picture – of Dafoe as Christ. The St Antony story coalesces here once more with that of the performing troupe. In Flaubert's text St Antony finally sees a redemptive vision of Christ's face in the sun as it rises. In Bergman's film the travelling troupe is saved by a last-minute summons from the King, and as they head off the sun shines down on them, an image echoed here by a bright light coming up on Valk and Anna Kohler dressed for travel. But this being The Wooster Group, the ending is not as simple as this neat coalescence might suggest. Vawter ignores Onna's calls and seems not to hear Cubby, who desperately tries to attract his attention, whistling and repeatedly calling him. Without looking at the image of Christ, Vawter switches the monitor off, puts on an overcoat and walks off, leaving Sue calling out to an empty theatre, 'Frank?' As if the portrayal of Flaubert's Christ by a videotaped photograph of a movie star playing Christ, a multiply deferred signifier, had not been ironic enough, Vawter's ignoring of the image, and of Onna, serves to underline even further the sceptical handling of the *deus ex machina* endings of both source texts.

Brace Up!

After such complexities, the next production, *Brace Up!* (1990), seems like a relatively direct response to Chekhov's *Three Sisters*, with more of the core text being delivered than in previous shows. This was a fresh, colloquial American translation by Paul Schmidt, a noted scholar of Russian theatre, who also performed as Chebutykin. A framing device was provided by the group's researches in Pacific Island dances and Japanese theatre and film. Paralleling *Saint Antony*'s use of Bergman's travelling troupe, the group studied a documentary about a Japanese Geinin troupe and developed the idea that Chekhov's play was being presented by such an itinerant group in New York. This influenced costume and set design and certain aspects of the gestural and movement style.[11] Excerpts from Japanese films also occasionally accompanied the stage action. A major development was the use of live relay to capture and frame live action on monitors.

Live relay played a significant part in the way, from the start, the production declared its intention to clear away the dead wood of a tradition of handling Chekhov in a reverential, naturalistic fashion. The play begins with a typical Chekhovian exposition scene, with the eldest sister Olga effectively delivering a monologue (punctuated briefly by 'feeds' from others), in which Chekhov introduces the members of the Prozorov household, their past, their removal from Moscow, and so on. Such expositions often seem heavy-handed to contemporary audiences. LeCompte wittily sidesteps any awkwardness by openly acknowledging the expository function. While the audience enters the auditorium, performers move about the platform set, adjusting props and chatting to each other quietly, before taking up positions about the set and on a long bench behind it. Performers' faces appear on two monitors located on parallel floor-tracks – on which they move to and fro throughout the performance. Kate Valk, microphone in hand, gets the show underway, reading Chekhov's stage directions to set the scene. In chat show style, she interviews Peyton Smith's Olga, asking her about the family, the weather and such like. Smith, who is seated to the rear, is videoed as she responds, and her image relayed live to the monitors. Such remediation makes the sequence more palatable for a contemporary audience and draws attention to its expository function.

This defamiliarisation process carries on as the scene proceeds. When Chekhov indicates a clock striking twelve, Valk's request for a sound effect is answered by loud bonging; when Chekhov indicates that Masha whistles under her breath, Valk says the actress playing

Masha hasn't arrived yet – so she whistles briefly. She subsequently introduces the performers, including Beatrice Roth and Joan Jonas: Roth, in her 70s, plays the 21-year-old Irina, and Jonas, in her 50s, plays the middle sister Masha. Valk also introduces two 'video performers', informing us that, 'Since the actor playing Soliony cannot be here tonight, every time he has to speak, we'll turn the TV loud'; creating an amplified static noise, this does have a certain appropriateness for the argumentative Soliony.[12] She announces that since the woman playing the servant Anfisa is too old to travel, she will appear on video. Anfisa's words were spoken by Josephine Buscemi, the 95 year-old great-grandmother of actor Steve Buscemi, whose wife videotaped her at home, while Buscemi fed her the cues. The overall effect of these first ten minutes is to establish that The Wooster Group is presenting its encounter with a text in the 1990s, rather than attempting to create a naturalistic portrait of the Prozorov household in the 1890s. This is underscored by the way cabling for microphones and monitors, extra floor lights, and people wielding cameras, all lent the setting the atmosphere of a television studio, with Valk sometimes resembling a Floor Manager coordinating the production.

Subsequent use of live feed recalls some of Svoboda's rhetorical effects: it is employed for close-ups and to multiply points of focus in a scene, as well as producing style-shifts through jumping from one medium to the other. For example, when Anna Kohler's socially inept and fashion-challenged Natalya first appears, she remains in the background, while her image is shown on video; when Olga remarks cattily on her green belt, the screens fill with a close-up of the offending belt. When Chekhov has Natalya rush from the dinner (here replaced by a comic stick-dance), tears are shown welling up in Kohler's eyes. When Dafoe's Andrei declares his love, it is played out on video, with Kohler sitting with her back to the audience, while Dafoe sits at the bench behind the set. Turning the scene into a soap opera proposal scene filmed in two-shot heightens its sentimentality, just as the sound of it on video underscores its intimacy. Simultaneously it ironises it in a gently comic way.

Further distancing is achieved through having Schmidt, doubling as both translator and Chebutykin, sit for much of the production in an upstage corner watching a monitor – with a camera, in turn, trained on him. Valk occasionally asks for comments. For example, introducing Act Two, Valk, rather like fast-forwarding a video, suggests that they skip the early expository part and asks Schmidt to summarise it – which he does, on video. Later, when Vershinin, Tusenbach and Masha are philosophising about life, Valk suggests fast-forwarding once again, but Schmidt interrupts, 'No, Kate, let Masha say the lines; it is a beautiful speech.' Jonas chimes in:

I remember, Paul, she says, 'I think a person has to believe in something, or has to look for something to believe in, otherwise his life is empty, empty ... Just to live, and not to know why the cranes fly, why children are born, why there are stars in the sky ... Either you know the reason why you are alive, or nothing makes any difference.' That it?

As Arratia observes, this 'dramatizes the multiplicity of choices involved in selecting and editing the text' (1992, 130). It also foregrounds these lines and contributes to an ongoing, witty marking of Schmidt's role in the production. His continuing appearance on one of the monitors observing the action produces the effect of seeing the author/translator watching over the production.

LeCompte describes the video usage as evolving in a way that may seem haphazard:

I had originally thought that the three sisters would not be on video, and almost everyone else would. Then that broke down. I like Peyton on video; she has a wonderful, soap opera performance quality. But basically it was who was near the video cameras, and who wanted to be onstage, and who was going in and out a lot. (Mee, 1992, 146)

She also describes the scenes as being structured like autonomous 'islands' between which Valk provided bridging commentary, allowing some to be omitted if necessary:

We may have people coming and going because of the money situation. So I developed from the beginning the idea that anyone could come and go without disturbing the piece ... Willem went in the middle of St. Antony, and I substituted him on video, but it wasn't an easy process. (Arratia, 1992, 128)

LeCompte's presentational approach and readiness to mix videotaped and live performances facilitates such pragmatic responses to the company's circumstances. Nevertheless, as *Brace Up!* evolved, certain patterns and effects emerged. LeCompte saw the space as divided into different zones of performance:

The back area becomes the area of 'most private performance.' Performers in the middle section put their dark glasses on and 'think pure dance.' ... the front section is the place for a 'declamatory style, speaking to the whole room.' (Ibid., 129)

The 'most private performances' were mostly those relayed on video, while Vershinin and others often delivered their philosophical musings into a microphone in the front zone, underlining their grandstanding, and contrasting with the soap opera intimacy of encounters in the back area.

As well as live relay and pre-recorded performances, public domain film appears periodically, sometimes illustrating events in a way that is both literalising and amusingly at odds with the supposed setting of the Chekhov text. For example, when the fire rages through the town, Chekhov's stage directions state, 'A window, red with the glow of fire, can be seen through the open door. The sound of a passing fire engine is heard.' For this LeCompte substituted video of a fire sequence from *The Harvey Girls*, a 1946 musical featuring Judy Garland.[13] Also, underlining the fact that most of the male characters are army officers who are eventually mobilised and despatched to a garrison in Poland, scenes from samurai movies occasionally appear, along with Kenneth Branagh's film of Shakespeare's *Henry V*. In the October 1990 version the latter played against the departure scenes of Act Four. While the incongruity of seeing Branagh rallying troops for battle was comic, it also provided a provocative parallel to the mobilisation: these men whom Chekhov portrays as idling about purposelessly in a sleepy provincial town are suddenly shipping off to a potentially dangerous posting.

The overall design, the use of video, microphones and other sound technology, the destruction of the fourth wall, the fluctuating performance styles and the almost Brechtian episodic presentation (emphasised by Valk and Schmidt's functions) all combined to overturn most of the conventions usually associated with Chekhovian production. Nevertheless, *Brace Up!* managed to shine a sharp light on Chekhov's text and evoke something of the ironic comedy found in the most satisfying Chekhov productions, 'opening up the full subtlety, pathos and irony of Chekhov's drama, analysing its elements, demonstrating how these can still work through and alongside the barrage of fragmented images that makes up modern cultural experience' (J. McMillan, *Guardian*, 4 November, 1992).

House/Lights

From the point of view of video usage, the 1993 productions *Fish Story* (a further reworking of *Three Sisters*) and Eugene O'Neill's *The*

Emperor Jones largely marked a consolidation in the company's approach. Play between live relay and pre-recorded material and the use of hybridised live and mediated figures were taken further, in ways that *House/Lights* (1998) would more fully exploit; there was also some exploration of special effects editing and video was employed for setting purposes in *Emperor Jones*, although in an ironic manner very different from earlier practitioners' scenographic use of film. LeCompte abolished the naturalistic clutter that O'Neill's detailed stage directions call for, in favour of an almost empty playing space – except for a television monitor, which in the first half showed a plantation house, and in the second half a jungle. A fake palm tree stood alongside. The effect was to mark wittily the production's refusal to fulfil expectations of the sort of full-blown naturalistic set associated with Broadway productions of O'Neill.

In *House/Lights* LeCompte returned to a more complex interplay between live and mediated, mixing publicly released film with pre-recorded and live relay material, and playing with CG effects and cyborgian interfaces between live and mediated performers. The centrality of video, both pre-recorded and live, was emphasised by placing two monitors centre stage: while one was raised and upstage, the other sat waist-high downstage and performers continually delivered lines or performed actions behind it, often creating a hybrid live/video image. Paradoxically for a production in which Faust's disillusionment with technology was thematically significant, *House/Lights* was one of the company's most technologically complex shows.

Central to the production was the recreation of a film on stage. As discussed in the Introduction, early cinema frequently adapted theatre texts for the screen; subsequently, as cinema became the dominant medium, popular films were adapted for the stage. One of Mark Lawson's complaints, apart from the presence of video in the theatre, was that London's West End increasingly relied on such adaptations; in 2006, for example, productions such as *The Thirty Nine Steps*, *The Producers*, and *Billy Elliot* all originated in successful films. Given LeCompte's work with various film or television sources in earlier productions, it was a logical progression to adapt a film to the stage, but this was very different from the examples cited. For one thing, she showed excerpts of the film simultaneously with the action, showing the actors mimicking the film's action; and the film itself was Joseph Mawra's little-known sexploitation thriller *Olga's House of Shame* (1964), which was set off against a rarely performed avant-garde opera libretto, Gertrude Stein's *Doctor Faustus Lights the Lights* (1938).

Having encountered the film while developing another project, LeCompte decided to transpose its action to the stage:

> We had the performers watching the *Olga* film on TV and mimicking exactly what they saw gesturally and translating the logic of the camera – close-up, medium shot, long shot – into the theatrical space. It was making for a very quirky physical vocabulary. (Rosten, 1998, 17)

Only subsequently did she decide to play Stein's text against it. These materials were supplemented by several other sources, including films by Mel Brooks and the Marx Brothers, Hollywood musicals, an episode of *I Love Lucy*, and music by Hans Peter Kuhn.

Olga's House of Shame follows the fortunes of Elaine, a jewel-smuggler for a sadistic crime boss, Olga. Having betrayed Olga and attempted to escape through a forest, Elaine is captured and tortured by Olga's sinister brother Nick, until she agrees to become Elaine's lieutenant. Olga engages in some lesbian 'party games' and then enlists Elaine's help in treating another girl to some 'horse discipline'. By the end Olga, like God creating man, has 'created Elaine in her own image and likeness. Now there were two of them. Two vicious minds working as one' (The Wooster Group, 2000, 56). Shot in black and white, the film has a low-budget look, with settings alternating between the forest and a minimally furnished backwoods cabin. Much of the narrative is conveyed through a male voice-over delivered in the style of a documentary crime-series. Action is more suggestive than explicit – there's little flesh on display, and violence is more implied than shown.

Stein's adaptation of the Faustus tale is full of her characteristic repetition and rhythmic riddling language. Faustus sells his soul in order to discover the electric light. Disappointed with a world always filled with light, he rebels against Mephisto and claims he had no soul to sell. Margaret, whom Faustus seduces in Goethe's version, is transformed into a character called Margarete Ida and Helena Annabel (hereafter MIHA), whose very name marks her thoroughly confused identity. She first appears lost in a wood; bitten by a viper (with all its sexual and biblical connotations), she seeks a cure from Faustus. Saved from death (simultaneously acquiring Faust's knowledge), she sits wearing a halo, a cross between a Madonna and a movie star, surrounded by candles and a chorus that sings and dances attendance. Falling for a 'man from over the seas', she spurns Faustus when he seeks to take her to Hell with him. Faustus, who has been accompanied much of the time by a boy and a dog that repeatedly says 'Thank you', shoots them both on Mephisto's orders and descends to Hell.

Stein's frequently comic gloss on the tale supplements the usual themes of knowledge, power and identity that circulate around Faustus with a further theme to do with the effects of fame. Stein wrote the libretto after a trip to the US in 1934 had turned her into a celebrity, culminating in having her name in lights on Broadway. Unsettled by her public notoriety, she began writing *Ida*, a story in which she attempted 'a study of the effects of publicity on a personality' (Neuman, 1988, 171). Its plot, of a girl with a dog who is lost in a wood and bitten by a viper, anticipates the opera libretto, which she commenced after putting *Ida* aside, unfinished. Although Faustus' disillusionment with electric light, which erases the difference between night and day, may be read as a metaphor for disillusionment with modern technology and the broader Enlightenment project associated with it, Stein also employs electric light as a metaphor for fame and celebrity, embodied in two 'ballets of lights' mounted for Faustus and MIHA: rather than clarifying their identities, light is seen as confusing them.

Recalling *Route 1 & 9*, the production essentially layered the two core sources against each other, although the interweaving was more complex. While *Olga's House of Shame* appeared on monitors, an edited version of Stein's text was intercut with text from the film. Most of this was delivered by Valk through a downstage microphone. Much of the stage action mimicked the film's action. Doubling the playing of roles pointed up provocative parallels between the narratives and central characters of the two very different sources. As well as delivering most of the text, Valk also played Faustus and Elaine – both seekers of power and rebels who try to escape their 'bosses'. She also played MIHA, whose wanderings were relayed on video in a way that echoed Elaine's flight through the woods. Suzzy Roche, wearing trashy plastic devil horns, doubled as Mephisto and the sadistic Olga, reflecting the narrator's comment that 'To incur Olga's wrath is to invite the Devil from Hell.'

Seamless transitions between scenes heightened the sense of parallels. For example, towards the end of Act One, Scene One, Olga strikes a devil's bargain with the captured Elaine, just as Faustus attempts to renege on his bargain with Mephisto, with attendant ironies in the conflation of the two narratives:

Olga: Well after what you've gone through here do you think you're willing to talk business with me?

(Faust):	Oh you devil go to hell, that is all you know to tell, and who is interested in hell just a devil is interested in hell
Elaine:	I think so.
(Faust):	Whether I stamp or whether I cry whether I live or whether I die, I can know that all a devil can say is just about going to hell the same way,
Olga:	Well ... I think now's the time I'm in a position to offer you ... some nice work with some nice dividends.
(Faust):	Get out of here devil, it does not interest me whether (you can buy or I can sell);
Elaine:	Oh, I'm always interested in nice ... dividends.

(The Wooster Group, 2000, 23)

Here the interwoven sequences produce divergent responses. Subsequently, in Act Three, Elaine, having rejoined Olga, is described as enjoying her new power of life and death and being 'like a god here' – just like Faust, who also holds the power of life and death over MIHA, the boy and the dog. Olga persuades Elaine to join her in disciplining Nadja; while the video shows Olga using a whip and reins to walk Nadja about like a 'filly', Roche and Tanya Selvaratnam play out the scene live. Simultaneously, Valk, as Faustus, shoots the boy and dog, before taking over the reins to train Nadja, just as Elaine does on video.

The interweaving of seemingly disparate texts and actions and the abstracted mimicry of the film action was all made more coherent by Jim Findlay's set which exemplified superbly the company's Meyerholdian approach to sets as 'theatre machines'. Attached to a metal railing at the front were a microphone, a video monitor, stools, and a pair of small tables (one of them supporting a laptop computer at which Selvaratnam sat orchestrating a series of noises that punctuated the text's delivery). Behind it were two seesaws, each with a sliding table attached. Further back were two tall frames carrying monitors which could slide up and down. Four large light bulbs swung periodically above the heads of the performers.

Valk's delivery, which she described as 'channelling', derived from listening through a wireless receiver to the composer Kuhn reading the text and then repeating it, a device that helped avoid any temptation to produce a psychological interpretation. This was further estranged by computer manipulation of her voice, frequently producing a strangulated high-pitched sound. The mimed action assumed a cartoon-like appearance, as performers heightened and abstracted the melodramatic action of the film, often to hilarious effect. For example, while the monitors show Elaine being pursued through the woods, Valk and the others run to and fro across the stage, up and down the seesaw

Figure 9   *House/Lights* Pictured (l-r): Sheena See, Helen Eve Pickett, Kate Valk, Roy Faudree, Tanya Selvaratnam, Suzzy Roche. Photo: © Paula Court

ramps in a precisely choreographed cartoon chase. At times live action and video intersect. Soon after Elaine's capture, for example, when Nick asks if she enjoyed her swim, the video shows a shot of the lower part of a seated man wielding a pair of pliers menacingly. Onstage, Roy Faudree moves behind the monitor, his upper body completing the picture; further back, Valk stands with her bound hands raised in the air, an image then echoed on the video monitor. Conventional distinctions between live and videotaped performers become confounded and a sort of cyborgian representation occurs. Along with the contribution of technology to the creation of Valk's various characters, a Frankensteinian dynamic pervades the production.

In the sequence following Elaine's torture, while Valk delivers MIHA's lament over being lost in the woods, the video superimposes Valk's head on a tracking shot through the woods, giving the effect of her head floating through them. When the film voice-over interrupts to describe 'a very special party', the video shows a woman doing a belly dance. Valk begins to belly dance, with her image superimposed over the *Olga* material. Two men then tip her upside down and Roche enters and sticks her head between her legs – all relayed live on the upstage monitor. While Olga's narration describes the girls as 'ready to go the limit', Roche moves over to fondle Selvaratnam, with a close-up being superimposed on the film. Meanwhile, as Stein's text describes MIHA being lost in the wood, an overtly fake tree is brought on. Live relay of Valk shot through the tree is then intercut with the Olga/Elaine material. The whole sequence, only a few minutes long, becomes a dazzling display of video editing crossed with live performance and live relay, conflating in an ironic fashion the erotics of MIHA's wander in the woods (and her viper bite) and the scenes in Olga's house of shame.

In addition to facilitating the merging of identities and narratives, video frequently expands the resonances of particular moments, usually through shadowing the Stein text with scenes from popular film or television. When MIHA visits Faustus, for example, the upstage monitors show a sequence from Mel Brooks' *Young Frankenstein* in which the monster is brought to life. Foreshadowing Faustus' saving of MIHA's life, this also evokes the alchemical tradition that links the Faustus and Frankenstein myths and the way their treatment in literature and film embodies a continuing suspicion of the role of science and scientists.[14] Soon after, when Stein calls for MIHA to be depicted with a halo of lights, the videos display Valk's head superimposed on a floating circular chorus from a Busby Berkeley water ballet. Later, when MIHA, confused at the sight of Mephisto behind the man from over the seas, whispers, 'They two I two they two that makes six it should be seven they two I two they two five is heaven,' Valk's head is accordingly multiplied on video, followed soon after by the halo of swimmers again.

The production's overall approach is embodied in the literalising response to Stein's number play here, as Valk's multiplied head is echoed by the multiplied female bodies of this aquatic halo. Where Stein's adaptation of the myth multiplies and splits the personalities of MIHA, Faustus and Mephisto, LeCompte uses technology and her supplementary sources to multiply everyone even further. The crossing of Stein's figures with figures from film, the play with hybrid images of performers, the doubling of onstage action with live relay, and Valk's channelling of the text, all operate as figures of the divided selves of Stein's play and undermine any possibility of employing conventional notions of a unified self as a way of approaching it. Foregrounding the literary and filmic construction of the characters and obviating any potential spectatorial desire for a naturalistic portrayal, they provide a dazzling theatrical response to Stein's anti-psychological mode of

Figure 10 *House/Lights* Pictured (l-r): Suzzy Roche, Kate Valk (upside down), Ari Fliakos. Photo: © Mary Gearhart

writing. Equally, the abstracted, condensed mimicry of Mawra's film estranges its narrative and performing conventions, echoing the way Stein's treatment of the Faust myth functions to defamiliarise conventional Faustian productions.

This approach also, of course, contributes considerably to the theatrical energy of the production. The technical ingenuity and the sheer bravura with which the performers play out the intersections between the various materials produce a theatre of attractions writ large: watching it, one could sense the audience around thrilling to the roller-coaster ride of the performance. The pyrotechnics of the performances and production match Stein's linguistic pyrotechnics, with the rhythmic choreography of the production answering the rhythmic play of Stein's text. The resulting focus on the signifier rather than the signified echoes the spirit of Stein, a writer more concerned with the processes of representation than the object of representation, and for whom the shape and rhythm of a sentence was always paramount.

To You, the Birdie! (Phèdre)

Jean Racine wrote his adaptation of Euripides' drama about Phaedra's love for her stepson Hippolytus in 1677, just before quitting the theatre and becoming Louis XIV's royal historiographer. It signalled his reversion to Jansenism, an extremely puritanical version of Catholicism – a turn that coincided with a growing sobriety at Louis' court. Arguing that dramatists should be 'as keen to edify their spectators as to amuse them, thereby complying with the real purpose of tragedy', Racine defended his portrayal of Phaedra's illicit passion:

> The slightest transgressions are severely punished. The very thought of crime is regarded with as much horror as crime itself. ... The passions are portrayed merely in order to show the aberrations to which they give rise. (Racine, 1963, 147)

When LeCompte received Paul Schmidt's translation in 1993, she felt the play was too Catholic, 'tedious, boring and stupid'. Six years later, after Schmidt's death, she was persuaded to direct it by Valk, 'who wanted to play the queen, and because it was her I trusted that there was something there' (Gardner, 2002). The resulting production contained few of the collagist elements usually found in Wooster Group productions. There were no parallel texts layered against Racine's text, which was delivered fairly faithfully (bar a few cuts and minor additions); there were no extracts from public domain media or extra-dramatic footage of Wooster Group members. Indeed, framing devices were relatively sparse. The production's title derives from the French term for a shuttlecock, *oiseau* or 'bird', reflecting the fact that the royal court effectively became a badminton court. All the characters played badminton at some point – with the goddess Venus as referee. Phaedra's near-death state as a result of her guilty passion was graphically represented by having her tended by servants administering drips and enemas. Inverting the situation in *House/Lights*, most of Valk's lines (and Dafoe's as Theseus) were spoken by another performer, Scott Shepherd (who also played Theramenes). The overall effect was seen by some critics as a terrible undermining of what is generally seen as one of the great tragedies in the Western canon, with Charles Isherwood asserting, 'The triumph of Racine's "Phèdre" was its ability to evoke compassion for a monstrous woman; The Wooster Group reverses the equation, and makes us feel practically nothing for her. ... Game, set, match to the postmodernists!' (*Variety*, 25 February, 2002).

The set resembled a modified version of the *Brace Up!* set – a metal frame enclosing the playing space and a low bench behind it. Replacing the television monitors found in most Wooster Group productions, upstage and downstage centre were two 'video totems' – metal structures which allowed a large plasma screen on each to rise and fall. Additionally, a large Plexiglass screen moved laterally to and fro. Perhaps a nod in the direction of the Hall of Mirrors at Versailles, the effect was to continually reconfigure the playing space, to create more or less intimate areas, appropriate enough for a court full of intrigues and people looking over their shoulders.

Video appears from the start. The performance opens with Hippolytus and Theramenes, semi-naked apart from short kilts, sitting behind the downstage screen, which obscures their lower bodies. Where Euripides and Racine portray Hippolytus' hyper-masculinity and misogyny through his devotion to hunting, LeCompte shows him as a sports jock: the discussion of Theseus' long absence and Phaedra's apparent hostility towards Hippolytus becomes a locker-room chat. The video plays comically with their masculinity. With a sound-track of intermittent laughter, cheering and bird-calls, the (pre-recorded) video appears to show the obscured action of the lower half of the men's bodies (in a hybrid image of the sort seen previously in *House/Lights*). They cross and re-cross legs, scratch buttocks and fiddle with genitals. Comically capturing a common male bodily behaviour, the activity also evokes the latent homo-eroticism of the locker-room.[15]

Figure 11 *To You, the Birdie!* (*Phèdre*) Pictured (l-r): Scott Shepherd, Ari Fliakos. Photo: © Mary Gearhart

The scene also initiates the frequent use of video to isolate and draw attention to parts of the performers' bodies and to play with notions of revealing the hidden. Framing the images on plasma screens and playing with their colouring often also lends a painterly feel to their use. Valk's first appearance illustrates this. Wheeled in by a maid, she barely staggers to her feet before her servant Enone knocks her over with a shuttlecock. Helped to a seat behind the (lowered) downstage screen, her legs are substituted by videotaped legs. While the maid washes her feet (again mixing live and video image), Phaedra complains that her shoes are not suitable for playing badminton. Others are brought and placed on her feet – also shown on video. Her grand address to the Sun is punctuated by her calling again for her seat: the wheelchair, which has a toilet attached to it, is brought over, with another change of shoes. The video doubling of the maid's servile ministrations underlines a view of Phaedra as a pampered, neurasthenic aristocrat, an impression borne out by the fact that Phaedra does not even speak her own words – Shepherd delivers them into a microphone behind the platform. The disjunctive voicing of her lines and the video dislocations of her body also operate as figures of her being torn apart, being *disintegrated*, by her passion for Hippolytus. This is reinforced soon afterwards. Valk stands behind the screen, her head hidden, while the video shows an enlarged image of her face trapped behind a barred window. Even as she moves away, the image of her face, mouth agape, remains briefly. A hitherto broadly satiric device for isolating and doubling parts of the characters' bodies becomes at this point an Expressionist, painterly device for amplifying a subjective feeling that is beyond words.

The grotesque imagery around Phaedra's enemas is similarly ambiguous. Just before revealing her passion for Hippolytus, her maids help Phaedra to squat and defecate. When she subsequently encounters Hippolytus semi-naked by a swimming pool, she declares her love, grabbing at him and rolling to the floor, in a scene that tips Racinian decorum on its head. Her desperation becomes increasingly grotesque, as maids wrestle her into a chair and administer an enema, while she grabs at Hippolytus' naked buttock. As she pursues the retreating Hippolytus the enema tube trailing behind is reproduced on the video screen. Towards the end of the play, wracked by guilt, she undergoes another enema. Having poisoned herself, she confesses to Theseus and collapses. Her death is portrayed in another hybrid moment, with her upper body revealed, while her lower body, enema tube trailing behind, is again shown on the downstage video screen.

Figure 12 *To You, the Birdie!* (*Phèdre*) Pictured (l-r): Frances McDormand, Kate Valk, Ari Fliakos. Photo: © Paula Court

Almost inevitably, in performance, such business appears initially as a satiric device. However, as the performance continues, it becomes a disturbing literal playing out of the effects of Phaedra's passion, particularly as Schmidt's translation handles it. Immediately after her first enema, Phaedra describes her passion for Hippolytus in terms of disease: 'I sweat and shivered both at once ... I had Venus like a virus in my blood.' Here Schmidt changes Racine's original metaphor of Venus making Phaedra her prey into one of infecting her with a virus. Any present-day audience is likely to sense the shadow of HIV behind the language here; the sort of integral audience that forms a large part of The Wooster Group's audience and is aware of the history of its members, could hardly avoid thinking of the deaths of Ron Vawter and Schmidt himself from AIDS-related illnesses.[16] The enemas, then, become a powerfully loaded medical image of the effects of passion. Moreover, they also seem to reflect literally the notion of tragic *catharsis*. Aristotle's famous term derives from Greek medical practice, in which illness was treated with emetics and enemas as a way of purging the body of infection. When Phaedra undergoes her final enema, accompanied by screaming that seems to mix agony and ecstasy, it has the appearance of a final literal attempt at *catharsis* before committing suicide.

The videos also play a major part in reconfiguring Venus' involvement in the play. Immediately after the opening dialogue, the raised upstage plasma screen reveals an image of Venus: Suzzy Roche, with red hair frizzed up, filmed against a blue sky with wispy clouds floating by. Again, there is disjunction at work, since Venus' lines are spoken from behind the stage by a live performer, Fiona Leaming.[17] She announces that she is the referee, tells how she made Phaedra fall for Hippolytus and declares that 'this is the last day he will look upon the light'. Here the text draws on Aphrodite's vindictive prologue in Euripides' *Hippolytus*. Although Racine's characters blame Venus for their plight, neoclassical decorum inhibited him from having the goddess appear. In *The Hidden God*, Lucien Goldmann defines Racinian tragedy 'as a spectacle under the permanent observation of a deity', observing that, 'though he is *always present*, this God remains a *hidden god*, a god who is always absent' and 'never shows the hero which path he should follow in order to realize an authentic existence' (1964, 7). Reverting to Euripides, The Wooster Group makes present the 'hidden god(dess)' of Racine, but in a bifurcated way: while the live Venus calls faults and awards points in a game which Phaedra is too feeble to play, the virtually present Video Venus impassively observes all.

Again, initially comic imagery becomes increasingly sinister. So, the first badminton match, under Video Venus' watchful eye and refereed by the live Venus, is fast and furious and accompanied by a series of buzzes, tweets, and whistles – a cartoonish arcade game soundtrack. Such games function throughout as an image of the players' capacities for waging the personal and political struggles at court. The boys' energetic playing displays a sort of narcissistic vitality, whereas the enfeebled Phaedra can barely lift her racquet and hits the weakest of shots. Later, Theseus fires shot after shot against Hippolytus, figuratively destroying him before his prayer to Neptune actually brings about his death.

Video Venus' recurring appearances become increasingly ominous. When Phaedra discusses her first encounter with Hippolytus, Video Venus pops up on cue. As Phaedra describes having Hippolytus banished, Venus' head drops comically off screen, only to reappear almost immediately when Phaedra reports the consequences of being reunited with him during Theseus' absence – 'it's Venus clawing at my heart, drinking my lifeblood'. She later witnesses Phaedra's desperate appeal to Hippolytus. After sending Enone to offer Hippolytus the Athenian crown, Phaedra pleads with Video Venus: 'Avenge yourself on him, not me! Make him love me!' When Enone reports Theseus' imminent return, Video Venus watches her persuade Phaedra to accuse Hippolytus of attempted rape. After Theseus banishes Hippolytus, Phaedra momentarily repents, but her intended confession is forestalled by Theseus' revelation that Hippolytus had admitted his love for Aricia. Sure enough, Video Venus surfaces to watch Phaedra's convulsion of grief at this news. Finally, Phaedra's death takes place under the eye of the absent yet present goddess whose virus has brought such destruction.

The scenes with Theseus before Phaedra's death further illustrate how video provides ironic visual commentary. Theseus' entrance is heralded by comically thunderous crashing noises, accompanied by video images of a classic male torso set against a green background. Dafoe appears, a strutting, puffed-up cockerel wearing only a short white tunic, made more ridiculous by the weedy nasal voice Shepherd adopts to deliver his lines. When Phaedra exits, Theseus lies down to be massaged by two maids. After his first encounter with Hippolytus, the maids carry him down and line him up with the lowered downstage video screen – so that his head is hidden and replaced by an enlarged video image. The resulting image recalls Hans Holbein's 1521 painting of *The Body of the Dead Christ in the Tomb*, while the maids' action of washing his arms and feet resembles a corpse being laid out for burial. While the hybrid image continues devices from earlier in the production, the referencing of the Holbein burial adds a tremendous visual power to the image, setting in play many resonances. Although Theseus lives at the end of Racine's play, the image foreshadows both the laying out of Hippolytus' corpse and a sort of death-in-life for Theseus that will come from Enone's allegations. The image also, of course, recalls Dafoe's film portrayal of Christ.

After calling on Neptune to drown Hippolytus, Theseus jumps up and begins striking macho poses – while both screens display shots of male torsos again. After Phaedra decides not to confess, thus sealing Hippolytus' fate, the background to the torsos becomes red. As she grieves over Hippolytus' love for Aricia, not only is she watched over by Video Venus, but also the downstage screen switches to an image of a closed purple theatrical curtain, a metatheatrical reference to both the impending end of the play and the mounting melodrama of the situation.

As with other Wooster Group productions, closer examination reveals a very precise structure behind what may initially seem to be a

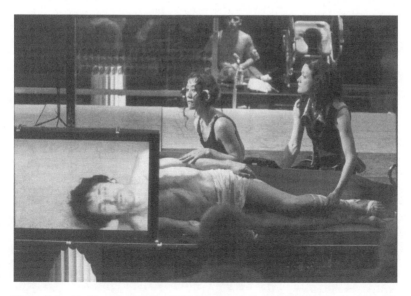

Figure 13 *To You, the Birdie!* (*Phèdre*) Pictured (l-r): Willem Dafoe, Koosil-ja Hwang, Ari Fliakos, Dominique Bousquet. Photo: © Mary Gearhart

bizarre surface. While the different performance frames operate at a broader emblematic level, they are closely modulated to the evolving moment by moment action. Again, much of the play with sound and video technology functions emblematically, suggesting a world in which characters are alienated from themselves, in which their language and bodies are in a continuous state of dislocation and disintegration, as they are wasted by Venus' virus. But their deployment at particular moments is precisely organised around the drama of the moment, amplifying or ironising individual actions, or marking a moment of crisis. After years of experimenting with very different uses of video, here The Wooster Group seems to move towards employing it in ways that recall Piscator's choric use of film: to a large extent, the video material highlights or brings out a sort of sub-text to the action. While the overall result is not a production that leaves in place the tragic world of Racine's play, neither is it simply a postmodern mockery of Racine's tragedy, as some critics suggested. To be sure, the production takes a cynical view of the royal court (and by implication the 17th-century court for which Racine wrote); there is no final sense of redemption or of suffering as ennobling, but, against expectation, as the production evolves, there is a growing darkness to the grotesque vision embodied in Phaedra's portrayal and the increasingly sinister presence of Video Venus.

Surveying LeCompte's use of video in the works discussed, what is remarkable is the variety of ways in which it has been incorporated in relatively few projects. There is a constant development from the more segregated use for three very different sequences in *Route 1 & 9*, through the more integrated dramatic use in *Saint Antony* and the use of live relay for a mix of dramatic, rhetorical and choric purposes in *Brace Up!*, to the interweaving of film and avant-garde text in *House/Lights*, followed by the painterly rhetorical and choric use in *To You, the Birdie!*. Along the way, a wide range of films and television programmes have been incorporated or mimicked, with the video material created by the company always playing knowingly with the televisual or cinematic genres being mimicked. Often very different styles have been collided against each other, inviting the spectator to read the different performing media and styles against or through each other. The underlying dialogue between the materials often acquires multiple resonances, tempting, if sometimes also ultimately defying, dialectical or synthesising readings of the relationships. After *LSD* the appearance of hybrid or cyborg images of performers becomes a growing feature; while at one level it appears as an 'attraction', it also becomes more emblematic of the hybrid nature of Wooster Group performances, calling attention to diverse mediations which occur in their work, whether literally through transfer of text or action to electronic media or simply through the adoption of the various stylistic 'masks' they employ.

LeCompte is very matter of fact when discussing her use of video, suggesting she sees it as just something that is part of the contemporary cultural context in which she works, which, therefore, should be available as a tool for her work. While sometimes her accounts of the seeming randomness with which she begins to collage materials may seem disingenuous, given the resonances particular collocations of material evoke, they are testimony to the creative experimental processes that the company uses. That the process does employ a lot of trial and error playing with different materials should not, however, disguise the fact that, as the productions evolve, a very precise selection process also comes into play which depends on LeCompte's astute sense of what materials work well in dialogue with each other. Thus what sometimes seem to be at first sight arbitrary juxtapositions often emerge as very precisely organised imagistic, textual or sensory structures.

5 Third-hand Photocopies: Forced Entertainment

Established in 1984 in Sheffield, Forced Entertainment produces a theatre of collage and quotation which plays around with set, texts, narratives, video material, acting and non-acting in ways that bear some resemblance to The Wooster Group's approach, but which also has its own distinctive qualities. During the late 1980s they worked with video in ways that exerted a strong influence on a number of other young British companies that began to appear in the 1990s – by which time they themselves were moving away from incorporating video in their work.

The company was initially influenced by Impact Theatre, a leading British experimental group of the early 1980s that created strange, hauntingly lit worlds that drew on movie culture, dance and physical theatre to evoke atmospheres of loss and confusion, featuring people caught up in worlds over which they had little control. They based themselves in Sheffield deliberately: the work is very much concerned with a sort of 'mapping' of life as it is lived in the combination of decay and hi-tech modernity that has appeared in post-industrial cities over the past 30 years. Director Tim Etchells reflects this postmodern viewing of, and interaction with, the city:

> The work has been informed by a shift in the way cities are talked about and per-
> ceived; the shift from a planner's eye view of cities as places of collective order
> and rationality, causality and order ... to a view of the city, and the individual within
> it, as the meeting point of a vast system of signs and messages.[1]

In *A Decade of Forced Entertainment*, a show marking the first decade of the company's existence, the company describes wandering the city observing strangers and collecting random objects and texts – rather like Baudelaire's *flaneur*, a strolling voyeur who draws inspiration from city life. They describe themselves as 'interested in the margins of life never the centre' and trying 'not to talk about the people who made decisions but about those people who were affected by decisions made in other areas and other places' (Etchells, 1996, 77).

This rejection of the metropolis in favour of the 'margins' was accompanied by a desire to respond to what Etchells describes as the wider media-scape:

> We've talked a lot about growing up in a house with the TV always on in the corner of the room. ... Our immediate landscape is what we can see out the window. But we have so many other landscapes. So where does our visual image bank locate itself? The space that we really live in is a kind of electronically mediated one. And it feels like one's landscape – the source of one's images, the things that haunt you – are likely to be second, third, fourth-hand. (Kaye 1996, 236)

Early on, Etchells described the company as creating a theatre of trash which is 'fast, aggressive, immediate, sweet, ironic, visceral, chaotic, fragile, double-knowing, bitter, naive, foolish, stupid, spacious and sentimental' (Etchells, 1989). This sprawling list is typical of Etchells' writing style in the productions: they often feature lists of events, feelings, figures, or imaginary titles for books or news items, or litanies of questions or confessions – delivered with a sort of allusive rapidity which allows spectators little time to dwell on individual details. There is a sense of appearing to attempt the fullest possible inclusiveness, while suggesting that language and theatre can never *fully* describe or embrace the range of possible events, feelings, characters and so on that we experience in life: the very plenitude of the lists marks their incompleteness. The list also reflects another aspect of the work: within the sort of trashy, aggressive world depicted there are half-glimpsed moments of tenderness and beauty.

Through long devising periods the company works with found characters, events, texts and objects, along with imagery from popular culture, particularly music, film and television. It has drawn on a very diverse range of performance styles and texts, including *film noir*, news programmes, children's Nativity plays, Maoist confession sessions, and a Japanese Noh play. Unlike The Wooster Group, however, final productions contain very little direct presentation of a source text or texts. Instead, the texts, which Etchells writes during the devising period, bear traces or echoes of the source materials: Etchells describes them as like poor third-generation photocopies. Similarly, the performance style adopted at any point gestures towards an original, but usually conspicuously fails to fully lay hold of it. As with the lists that mark their own incompleteness, various strategies are adopted to mark the failure, or refusal, of the performers to inhabit fully the characters or worlds created. Etchells relates this approach to a radical scepticism about the possibility of authentic language or behaviour:

> Everything we say is already borrowed from somewhere, even when we are not aware of it explicitly. Within the work that's usually pretty obvious – that the characters are speaking in tongues. ... It's as much perhaps that those borrowings or quotations or second or third-hand things that these people have got are to them probably the only language they know. As such, it's the language they use to try to define and to construct and come to rest about themselves and their world. (Kaye, 1996, 246–7)

Etchells' own phrasing here echoes Richard Rorty's discussion of language in works such as *Contingency, Irony, and Solidarity* (1989).[2]

This all informs the approach adopted towards performing, in the video work as much as in the onstage action. In his manifesto on Zero Theatre, Polish director Tadeusz Kantor spoke of 'dismembering logical plot structures, building up scenes, not by textual reference, but by reference to associations triggered by them, juggling with CHANCE or junk, ridiculously trivial matters, which are embarrassingly shameful, devoid of any meaning and consequence' (Kantor, 1993, 63). Kantor advocated performances characterised by 'slowing of pace, loss of rhythm, repetition, elimination through noise, stupidity, clichés, automatic action, terror; by disinformation, withholding of information, dissection of plot, decomposition of acting; by acting poorly, acting "on the sly", acting "non-acting"' (ibid.).

Kantor's list might equally describe the Forced Entertainment approach to performance. There is continual playing around with the extent to which action or speech is 'real' or 'fictional', as performers move between adopted roles and some version of themselves. Performers freely shift between referring to themselves in the first and third persons and between presenting events as though they are happening in a fictional present and describing them as having happened in the past. What might conventionally be seen as 'bad' acting is mixed with quite convincing 'realistic' acting and with seeming 'non-acting', as noted in *A Decade of Forced Entertainment*:

> They told you so many times they weren't acting, that when they did act they hoped you'd think it real. And on a good night that's what happened. They pretended to be dead. They pretended to be Elvis. They pretended to be drunk. They pretended to be angels. They pretended to be drunks. ... And often they pretended to be themselves. (Etchells, 1996, 81)

All this, of course, challenges assumptions about 'authenticity' that are frequently found in discussion of performance and problematises notions of the 'real' or its representability, an issue which also informs their use of media in the work. It is based on a sense that all performance is an act of mediation and on scepticism about the notion of any performance being immediate: whether performers are on video, performing with microphones, apparently acting as characters or as themselves. The self-reflexive use of video in several productions operates, then, as part of a general interrogation of representational practices that pervades their work.

Although discussion here focuses on three productions from their first decade that employ video, much of their work before and since drew inspiration from particular film and television genres. For example, their first show, *Jessica in the Room of Lights* (1984), dealt with a cinema usherette whose life becomes mixed up with the movies she sees; and in *(Let the Water Run its Course) to the Sea that Made the Promise* (1986) the characters obsessively re-enact dying scenes from the movies – with tomato ketchup bottles spurting 'blood'. The company first worked with videotaped material in *200% and Bloody Thirsty* (1987); they explored further ways of using video in the next three productions, *Some Confusions in the Law about Love* (1989), *Marina and Lee* (1991), and *Emanuelle Enchanted* (1992), before they 'somehow got tired of answering the question: "Where shall we put the monitors?" ' (Etchells, 1994, 94). Even so, the next show, *Club of No Regrets* (1993) was built around rapid-fire enactments of clichéd sequences from gangster movies, played in a way that 'posits the camera somewhere out in the audience' (Lowdon, in Kaye, 1996, 238). Although the company returned to using video in *Disco Relax* (1999) and *Instructions for Forgetting* (2001), discussion here will focus on the earlier productions.

Although film genres are referenced in Forced Entertainment work, it is always video and live relay that are used, not film, and these are presented on old-fashioned domestic monitors – there's no video-projection or plasma screens.[3] This reflects a sense of the ubiquity of the television set and of television as a dominant cultural medium. Furthermore, it chimes with both the channel-hopping aesthetic which characterises the collagism of their earlier work, and the 'poor' quality of the televisual images they create (compared with the finished look of commercial television) complements the trashy sets, costumes and props, just as the light that emanates from television monitors plays a significant part in the overall 'half-light' look of their productions.

200% and Bloody Thirsty

> The best-performed piece we saw all decade was the Hilton School Nativity Play on hand-held Video 8. We liked the transparent simplicity of the structure, the content and the acting. We liked the weak expositional dialogue, the complete lack of subtext, the token props. (Etchells, 1990)

> Was it really true that the only way to see Britain properly was to see it through the eyes of a drunk? (Etchells, 1996, 77)

Forced Entertainment productions frequently contain drunken figures, often involved in a wild party, which usually gives rise to a post-drunk stupor. *200% and Bloody Thirsty* opens on just such a scene: a woman and two men (Cathy Naden, Richard Lowdon, Robin Arthur), dressed only in underwear, lie sprawled out on a set littered with the contents of a dozen wardrobes and bordered by dead trees. With the words '200% and Bloody Thirsty' picked out in red neon against a blue sky backdrop, the lights gradually fade up on the slowly stirring figures, accompanied by a few sparse piano notes. As the performers begin to gather clothes, two video monitors suspended high above the set upstage spring to life. They reveal portrait shots of a pair of glum-faced angels, their heads circled by tinfoil haloes against a cloudy blue sky, poor iconographic relations of the angels who perch in the upper corners of Renaissance paintings or stained glass windows in churches. As they proceed to observe and comment with wry sympathy on the happenings below, they also recall how angels have functioned in movies from Frank Capra's *It's a Wonderful Life* (1946) through to Wim Wenders' *Wings of Desire* (1987).

They deliver the opening dialogue to each other across the messy world below them – a disconcerting image as one monitor 'speaks' to the other, male to female angel. Delivery is flat and deliberate, with long pauses:

Male:	I'm trying to get my life in order.
Female:	Well let's start right away.
Male:	Will you answer me a question?
Female:	One question if you like.
Male:	Are there tears in the world? Is there pain?
Female:	Does the snow fall from the sky?
Male:	You're brave. You know. Much braver than I am.
Female:	So answer me a question.
Male:	One question if you like.
Female:	Are there tears in the world? Is there pain?

The mixture of colloquialism and cod-poeticism, the repetition with variation of speaker, the subdued delivery and lighting, all contribute to an atmosphere of delicate ambivalence, with the pathos of the questions balanced by a faintly comic air. This develops further as, with quiet birdsong coming on cue, the angels recall a human past and enthuse (as much as these melancholic angels can) about life in heaven:

Male:	Our favourite sound was always the birds singing in the streets of the city at dawn.
Female:	Now that we're angels in heaven we both have plenty of time.
Male:	Here we sit with fine clouds in green parks and gorgeous open spaces.
Female:	Here all our streets are grand and wide and there are fountains and waterfalls in everybody's garden.

After they repeat the earlier routine in abridged form the video snaps off. Dramatically, the sequence prepares the audience for the evocation of a crisis in spiritual faith that emerges as a significant aspect of the show to come. The visual and aural structure of the section (during which the live performers slowly move about, getting dressed) recalls the *Our Town* cemetery sequence in *Route 1 & 9*. There is a similar double-coding at work, as the production toys with the sweet pathos of the exchange, while at the same time inviting an ironic viewing of the performers' angelic identity and their banal vision of heaven. While presenting it all as slightly absurd, the sequence foreshadows the way their subsequent appearances play with the persistence of a nostalgic desire for such a vision, to which the use of angelic visitations in movies contributes and responds. The staging, as these televised figures seemingly observe the live

Figure 14 *200% and Bloody Thirsty*

performers, also, of course, inverts the usual relationship between live and recorded figures.

After this introductory chorus (for that is how the video angels function throughout the show), the live performers embark on a wild, drunken party, tearing about the space, laughing, embracing, weeping, splashing beer about, compressing the activities and emotions of an all-night Christmas party into ten minutes of frenetic action. (The Christmas setting recalls Capra's film, in which an angel visits Earth to

Figure 15   *200% and Bloody Thirsty*

save James Stewart's character from committing suicide.) As the energy and Elvis Presley's *I'll be Home for Christmas* fade, Arthur lies down on the bed. The others climb the scaffolding behind it, adopt the pose of children performing angels in a Nativity play, arms stretched high above their heads, and try to revive the 'dead' man, declaiming with the awkward naiveté of child performers:

> *A:* Wake it up stupid dead person for we are angels and do everything!
> *B:* Wake it up and listen hard for we are real and fantastic angels!

They pour soap-flake 'snow' over him and describe him as having been at a 'fuck and wild man Xmas party', where he 'did act of a drunk and nativity play'. As their attempt to revive him fails, the video angels reappear. They note the scene below, then begin doubting their own angelic status:

> *Female*: Are you sure that we're angels?
> *Male*: Yes, I'm pretty sure we are.
> *Female*: Now we're interested in even the lowliest sparrow.
> *Male*: You know I find it pretty hard to take.

Mixing cliché with absurd invention, they describe their activities in heaven, 'playing harp music and singing in a choir', 'moving clouds around the world', and when they're bored, organising 'a power cut to make a whole town blind'. The live would-be angels then try their magic again, this time successfully.

The three performers then embark on a frantic version of the Christmas story. In five minutes they rush from the Annunciation, through the trip to Bethlehem (or Bedlam as they aptly call it), the search for shelter and the birth of Christ, to the Adoration of the Magi. The dialogue is rushed gibberish, of which only an occasional phrase is decipherable; the action resembles a fast-forward version of a children's Nativity. It is a ritual gone haywire, emptied of meaning. At the end the performers look at a loss as to what to do next, before Naden lies down on the bed. Then it all starts over again: a failing attempt to raise her from the dead, a choric intervention from the video angels, another resurrection, another nativity, this time with the performers stumbling about with paper bags over their heads, and with roles swapped. Lowdon takes his turn as the dead man, with the angelic resurrection taking even longer, and the video angels becoming more fanciful in their imaginings of what to do in heaven.

During a further, increasingly jaded-looking nativity performance Arthur 'dies' before the narrative is completed; Naden and Lowdon look nonplussed before carrying on as best they can, condemned to finish the ritual. Attempting to raise the 'dead' man, they become increasingly desperate, screaming at him and jumping up and down, all to no avail. Eventually, they strip him and themselves back down to their underwear, don tatty cardboard wings and play out the nativity for a final time. This time the video monitors stay on and the video angels watch, the light of the monitors casting a soft glow over proceedings. It is a quiet, gentle playing, with the delivery hoarse and barely audible, backed this time by music on piano and synthesised strings. Sound and light conspire with the performances to create a haunting, poignant atmosphere. As the performers complete the nativity, they take three orange dummies, which they have previously flung about as fellow partygoers and figures in the nativity, and carefully place them on the bed. In the fading light they sprinkle snowflakes on them, while the video angels recite a litany of good-nights:

> Goodnite to kids made out of wire and shadows. Sweet dreams.
> Goodnite to the lights across the water. Sweet shine.
> Goodnite to murderers, murderesses and car thieves. ...
> A sad goodnite to half things. Like half-light. Half-naked. Half-covered in snow. ...
> The best goodnite to drunks still sleeping, half covered in snow.

Much is lost in the attempt to recount a show such as this, dependent as it is on the sensory impact of the performers' exhausting routines and the seductive manipulation of light and sound. The affective experience perhaps outweighs what *post hoc* discursive sense we try to make of it. Etchells has spoken often of the importance of the notion of witnessing in Forced Entertainment's work, of spectators bearing responsibility for what they witness. And much of the impact of the company's work comes from being in the space with the performers, witnessing them exhausting themselves, exposing their vulnerability, doing stupid things, doing 'bad acting', looking at a loss. Performances become draining for spectators as well: we too may become frustrated with the playing and replaying, exhausted by the noise and expended energy, and be drawn into the sense of entropy towards the end. Attempts to explore the shows discursively inevitably incur a sense of the gap between the experience and the way we order it to write it, recalling the Lacanian gap between our experience of the world and the way in which the Symbolic Order structures our way of perceiving the world – territory with which much Forced Entertainment is implicitly concerned.

At an initial level the show recycles Christmas imagery in a way that suggests its hollowness in a world where, for most people, it has lost any real connection with its originating story. It becomes a time of 'forced entertainment', an excuse for drunken parties that are more desperate than life-enhancing, a time of ritual re-enactments of nativities that are copies of copies, divorced from any original or any sense of meaningful content, a time for watching sentimental old movies in which miracles bring grace to a world that no longer actually believes in the miracle doers. A look that the performers occasionally turn towards the audience, which seems to suggest the question, 'Do we really have to keep doing this?', works reflexively to suggest that even they are caught up in this obligation to repeat *ad nauseam* the rituals they present: theatre's representational practices seem to be directly challenged, as the performers seem on the brink of rebelling. Nevertheless, within all the 'mess' there are interactions, half-glimpsed in the half-light of which Forced Entertainment is so fond, which touch us; and although, 'like crap magicians', they show us the tricks as they do them, there is still a naïve charm to the snowflakes, the angelic gestures, the cardboard wings and so on, which evokes the charm of just such children's Nativity performances as Etchells recalled in 1990.

All this is underscored by the recurrent refrains of the video angels, whose ethereal nature is literal – they are just beams of light from a box, absent presences, who seem aware of their own corniness, their implausibility; yet, somehow, they succeed as images of a sought-for transcendence, a longing for a world where miracles and beauty do occur, even when we least expect, even for a 'drunk man lying out in the snow'. The video presentation of the angels thus makes a significant contribution to how an audience experiences and attempts to make sense of the piece. Although the video monitors may be seen as physically marginalised and their texts may be primarily choric in relation to the onstage action, the affective impact of both their performances and their televisual delivery moves them beyond simply being choric, intertextual devices.

Some Confusions in the Law about Love

We made a show not about Elvis Presley but about an Elvis Presley impersonator in Birmingham, England. We didn't want anything authentic, we wanted a third-rate copy – we loved that more dearly than anything original. (Etchells, 1996, 77)

In Plato's *The Symposium* a group of Athenian intellectuals is portrayed having an after-dinner discussion about the nature of love: physical love, spiritual love, the love of wisdom. Hardly the stuff of a Forced Entertainment production, one might think. But then again, 'symposium' literally means 'drinking session', and most of Plato's participants are suffering hangovers from the night before, the comic poet Aristophanes is depicted having the hiccups, and Alcibiades, declaring his love for Socrates, announces that he is thoroughly drunk. When more revellers arrive, they settle down to drink, talk and sleep the night away.

Belonging to a tradition six centuries old, Japanese Noh theatre moves at a slow, stately pace, and is regarded by many contemporary Japanese as a fossilised relic of the courtly world in which its tales are set. Behind its sparse setting and texts lies a Buddhist aspiration for beauty founded on subtlety and depth. Again, it might not immediately seem to be Forced Entertainment territory – until we recall that the central player, the *shite*, often plays the ghost of someone who comes back to haunt the place of his death, the deaths are often those of star-crossed lovers, and the plays are suffused with an autumnal melancholy, as leaves fall and winds blow by faded moonlight.

And then there's dead Elvis – or the myriad Elvises of tabloid culture: the 'still alive' on some far-off island Elvis, the ghost Elvis who appears to fans, the Karaoke Elvises who haunt the local pub, and the Elvis impersonators who populate Elvis look-alike contests. Add to this the sort of seedy live-sex shows found in Soho basements, and you have the unlikely ingredients of *Some Confusions in the Law about Love*, a production in which love, sex, drink and death are just some of the ways the five performers portray their characters seeking a form of transcendence or escape from themselves.

The production is set on a metal-framed platform, creating the effect of a skeletal room, equipped with a bed, chair and two trapdoors. Two television monitors draped in muslin hang from the upstage corners: blue neon strip lighting above combines with their static glow to cast a soft light over the action when the monitors are not showing video. A backcloth is scattered with electric stars, a remnant of some tatty nightclub show.

The production features more identifiable, continuous 'characters' than earlier work. Recalling *Frank Dell's The Temptation of Saint Antony*, it depicts a lousy Elvis impersonator (Robin Arthur) and two tawdry showgirls (Cathy Naden and Terry O'Connor), during a long, drunken night in a hotel room. Occasionally, without much conviction, they pretend to do some of their act, but they mostly talk about love, sex, drugs, and death, and fantasise about going to heaven or to Graceland – anywhere to get away from the 'shit-hole' Birmingham where it always rains. They are sometimes visited by Seijuro and Onatsu, stray skeletons from a Noh play, and at other points 'so-called Presley' speaks to a couple who appear on the monitors, called Mike and Dolores.[4] Supposedly in Hawaii, performing a live sex-show in various nightclubs, Mike and Dolores are interviewed as if on a satellite link.

Unsurprisingly, there's something rather unconvincing about the characters. Despite Arthur's claim to be the best Elvis impersonator in the world, the girls observe that he doesn't even look like Elvis, and, when he addresses the audience as though he's in Las Vegas, they point out that they're actually in a crappy hotel in Birmingham. While the skeletons' minimalist gestural style nods in the direction of Noh, the awkward hesitancy of their action and speech suggests they are not really sure who or where they are, an uncertainty underscored by the ill fitting party-shop outfits they wear. Moreover, when Mike and Dolores recount their acts, they frequently contradict each other and their story changes continually.

The show opens with Presley rambling through a droll pastiche of an introductory routine to a nightclub act, while the girls loll about and occasionally interject or dance in a desultory fashion. After ten listless minutes, the skeletons emerge through the trapdoors. A half-remembered tale of love and separation unfolds, as a showgirl passes a microphone to and fro between them. The softly spoken language veers between the poeticism of classic Noh plays and incongruous 20th-century intrusions, as when Onatsu says her words 'fall away from me like swallows riding on the East Wind', but then announces, 'Look, I found an envelope of the strong tranquilliser Tranxene.' It turns out they have gambling debts which they must repay, or face execution. They disappear as abruptly as they emerged, and Presley and the showgirls dream of being in heaven – which is played out with the girls putting sheets over their heads and pretending to be spirits. They describe it as full of 'flowers and gardens, waterfalls everywhere'. They might 'squeeze some new thrills from this heaven crap' and one suggests, 'Normally our lives are full of physical pleasures like sex and drugs, but now we're up here we should try to find something more – esoteric.'

Returning to Earth, Presley's ramblings are interrupted by Mike and Dolores' appearance on the upstage monitors. As they take turns speaking to Presley, the effect is created of a microphone being passed to and fro between them – except, of course, it is notionally across the void that lies between the monitors.[5] Although their conversation is

Figure 16   *Some Confusions in the Law about Love*

banal, they inject some energy into the listless atmosphere that has reigned so far, with Dolores, wearing the blonde wig from *200% and Bloody Thirsty*, being particularly giggly. They enthuse about the bars in Hawaii, although it turns out 'one is rubble and the other just a shell', and the roof has blown off the Happy World, revealing the stars above. The pair are performing an act in which Mike names all the stars and Dolores calls out what they mean; for example, Persion 'stands for first loves and lost loves and for lovers who are lost and far away'. Asked whether they 'believe this stuff', Mike says, 'No, we only, um, we only use it in the act.'

After this brief introduction, Mike and Dolores are dismissed. The skeletons reappear and enlist the girls' assistance in mounting a fake suicide. Looking up 'past the faint galaxies', they say goodbye 'to the town with its new bridges and tow-away zones' and whisper instructions to Presley to do a big crying routine, as though some tragic death has just been enacted. The girls reappear, stripped to underwear and covered in talcum powder, and enact the lovers jumping into the lake. With Presley, now also stripped, they discuss the lovers' getaway and also look to the stars. On cue, to disturb the 'solemnity' of the moment, Mike and Dolores pop up on the monitors again. Presley enquires further about their routine, which has become more extreme: Dolores now shoots Mike. They describe how Dolores counts out the shots in Spanish and tell of a planned routine in which, 'Mike's going to dance naked til I come and then I'm going to dance naked til he comes.' Presley then tells a story of them supposedly having done some sort of disappearance/death routine in the Caballeros Bar, before dismissing them once more.

The identities of Mike and Dolores now start to fuse with those of the skeletons. Fearing that the lovers 'will die like the dewdrops falling from this blade of grass' (a common image in Noh), the girls look for the skeletons, and find them – but the performers are out of their skeleton suits and wearing the same shirt and dress as Mike and Dolores and their faces are covered in blood. Lost and fearing for their future, they reminisce about their first romantic meeting, in language that collides the celestial imagery of Noh with the crudity of the porno act:

> Seijuro: Your moon-shaped eyebrows rivalled in beauty that crescent held aloft in the festival parade. ...
>
> Onatsu: We used to fuck endlessly then and never tire of it. There was nothing but the taste and wet of flesh for us then.

They decide to die together. Seijuro makes a pistol shape with his hands and 'shoots' Onatsu three times, saying 'Bang, bang, bang' as she counts in Spanish. He then shoots himself, while she counts again. The comic shooting (with its echo of the Mike and Dolores act) is wittily at odds with the hesitant solemnity with which the performers play it, as though they really are in the tradition of tragic lover suicides.

When Mike and Dolores immediately reappear on video it emerges that their show, Sex Man Still Lives, is becoming even more extreme: they plan to copulate on stage and nine months later Dolores will return and give birth. Mike describes a past show in which everyone drank a love potion, and 'when they woke up they were all in love and no one felt sad. ... Well, it's not the kind of work we want to do anymore.' Dolores hints at the desperation behind their work: 'You know, I once read that the world is too small a place, no, no, too cold a place, for two lovers to be happy together all their lives.' Presley reminds them of touring in winter in England, but Mike and Dolores refuse to acknowledge the memory and disappear.

The extremes of romantic and pornographic love portrayed so far prompt the performers into their mock Symposium on spiritual and carnal love. The showgirls strap on rubber breasts, Presley attaches a rubber penis, and they decide to 'waste time by talking about love'.

Standing on the bed, O'Connor, paraphrasing and contradicting Pausanias in *The Symposium*, begins:

> Many great men praise those who love the soul and not the body; they say if you love the body you're stupid, ' cause you love the bit that doesn't last. They say as soon as the flower of the body dies and shit like that. But for me the best love is for the flesh and for fucking and the best lust is for kissing the skin.

Naden also rejects a stance taken in *The Symposium* (these are very learned show-girls!), arguing that 'the best love is quick and the best seductions are sudden and mercifully brief'. Presley makes a drunken interruption, like Plato's Alcibiades, but soon falls asleep, while the girls proceed to more panegyrics, to corrupt love and deceitful love.

Donning blindfolds, they then imagine their way to Graceland – where they encounter the skeleton performers again, but now identified as Elvis's bodyguards. In a gesture that both echoes a scene in *The Symposium* and evokes Mike and Dolores' Hawaiian locale, they put garlands around their necks. Having all supposedly jumped into a pool, they announce a last song (actually spoken in a flat, unmusical way): 'We're sick and tired of wandering about in the rain. ... Moan, moan, moan.'

After further paeans to different loves, Mike and Dolores make a final appearance on video; but this time their performers stand in the trapdoors and interview their video selves – looking at them askance, as though puzzled by their presence on the monitors. The giggles gone, they are drained of energy as they relate the latest news of their show, which has become even more Baroque in its imagining, with planned fatal orgasms and a Lie Detector Test for love. As Presley recalls an act in which 'a god and a goddess of love try to disappear ... and leave the shitty nightclub and head off together for islands in the dark', Mike and Dolores disappear.

Preparing to leave, the showgirls dream of 'new loves and of worlds that will stay still', and Presley addresses a last faltering homily about dreams coming true to the audience. The energy fades, the neon light is switched off, and the show moves towards an ending similar to that of *200% and Bloody Thirsty*, with the miked voices of Seijuro and Onatsu naming the morning stars, Persion, Entropy 10, and Capella:

> They say its path in the sky is romantic.
> They say it comes close to the earth and then turns away.
> They say it's romantic to turn and walk away and never to return.

As with the earlier show, lights, music, language and performance combine seductively to manipulate spectators towards a sentimental sympathy with the trashy romanticism of the ending, even as they recognise the manipulation at work.

Teasing out the work of video in the production, we might first note similarities with, and differences from, its use in *200% and Bloody Thirsty*. As there, individual portrait shots are shown on each of the monitors. The placement of monitors is also similar, although they are located inside the frame, as part of the room, rather than above the world of the play. Moreover, they are larger and their veiled light casts a continuing glow over proceedings – marking the greater integration of the videotaped figures in the development of overlapping narratives, as opposed to the mainly choric use of the videotaped angels.

Originally the show was to include a woman who held séances to summon up the ghost of Elvis. Although the séance framework was dropped, Mike, Dolores and the skeletons seem to bear traces of it – figures summoned from the dead to accompany Presley and the showgirls through the long night in their crappy hotel room, with the video and the trapdoors simply providing alternative ways of introducing them. (That Mike and Dolores might be seen as dead is also suggested by the way they ask Presley various questions about their past; furthermore, their final act is done in 'Paradise'.) It might then seem apposite that the representatives of a classic Japanese tale of tragic love be represented by the slow-moving live performers, while the tale of the trashy modern sex-show is beamed in as though on a tabloid television chat-show. The situation is complicated further by the gradual merging of the two couples. The suicides which link them are the culmination of the way their stories are portrayed throughout as flipsides of each other – romantic and pornographic, classic and contemporary, tragic and comic. The traditional high-culture narrative of star-crossed lovers, though estranged doubly by its Noh play setting and the awkward, unconvincing playing, is shadowed by, and eventually merges with, its darkly comic popular-culture version on video – although, again, it is one in which the performers seem to have grave doubts about who they are and what they've done. This playing off of one against the other is also reflected in the way the showgirls' chat about love replays in a bastardised fashion Plato's *The Symposium*. It is not only Presley, then, who is a 'third-rate copy', and not just the videotaped Mike and Dolores whose presence is mediated. All the figures are operating in gaps between various identifications and origins, as they explore their confusions, fears and desires associated with love and death.

Emanuelle Enchanted (or A Description of This World As if It Were A Beautiful Place)[6]

> More than ever our memories of things were utterly bound up with the TV news. In the miners strike of 1984/5 we had the weird experience of seeing things live in Sheffield and then seeing them reported later in the day. They always seemed more real on television. (Etchells, 1996, 82)

> Set on a crude wooden stage and backed by a curtain of electric stars, the performance space was framed by a rough, skeletal proscenium. Wooden rails draped with jumble sale clothes were suspended at each side, while a white translucent curtain runs across the front, leaving just enough room, once closed, for the performers to stand and address the audience. In this crude arena there was also a series of wheeled theatrical flats, with their plywood backs displayed to the front. There were two televisions on wheeled trolleys and a video camera rigged to pass images directly to the TVs. Beneath the clothes rails were stacked numerous cardboard signs bearing the hastily scrawled names of characters, both real and imaginary. (Set description from typescript of *Emanuelle Enchanted*)[7]

With its starry backcloth, the jumble shop clothes, the skeletal framing and video monitors, *Emanuelle Enchanted* contained many customary Forced Entertainment elements. Again, action takes place over a long night 'in the fractured landscape of the contemporary world ... the new and abysmal internationally co-produced soap called UNCERTAINTY' (Programme note). Again, the inhabitants operate with unstable identities in their struggle to survive, to dream, to love. And again, much of the imagery, textual, visual and performative, references a media-saturated culture. This time the substitutive dramatic use of video in the first two shows is replaced by live relay, with the production becoming as much about the framing and editing of performance and 'reality' as about the search for 'a beautiful place'.

Only a few of the fourteen scenes employ video. Five are what would be called in pantomime 'frontcloth scenes': the performers stand before the translucent curtain addressing the audience, while, behind, the stage is reset (but, of course, with the curtain being diaphanous, spectators can see faintly what is happening). There are also two 'cardboard sign' scenes – where performers walk or run across the stage holding cardboard signs bearing names of various figures; two 'newsroom' scenes – in which the performers are videoed while they read out dozens of phrases in the style of news headlines; three 'wall-moving scenes' – in which the mounted flats whizz about the place, hiding and revealing the performers; a long solo speech by one of the performers, and a parodic presentation of a film supposedly called *Emanuelle Enchanted*.

The performance begins with the curtain being drawn back to reveal the first cardboard sign scene. Accompanied by loud heavy metal music, the five performers throw on costumes from the rails, pick up cardboard signs, and move across the space, seemingly presenting the figure described on the sign. As performers reach the other side, they swap costume and sign and start again. The titles vary from the specific to the general, the real to the fictional, the plausible to the implausible: ELVIS PRESLEY, THE DEAD SINGER; A NINE YEAR OLD SHEP-HERD BOY; A DRUNK MAN SHOUTING AT THE MOON; PRINCE VALIUM; MISS DEEP FREEZE, and so on (the published text includes over 150 such titles). Sometimes, the performers run on the spot centre-stage while others place signs in front of them. Sometimes, through costume and demeanour, they apparently attempt to embody the figure named and invest it with an appropriate emotion, creating an evocative cameo moment. At other times costume and/or movement seem at odds with the named figure, even though performers present it to the audience as though they believe in their representation. With its loud music and frantic presentation, the sequence veers between the appearance of some bizarre identity parade that has fallen into chaos and a witty demonstration of the linguistic concept of the arbitrariness of signs. First time round, the sequence lasts about five minutes, while towards the end of the production it lasts twice as long, with the enactment of the figures seeming even more confused.

The opening sequence is followed by the first frontcloth scene. This starts with all five performers out front, and Lowdon reluctantly reading the production details of the movie *Goodbye Emmanuelle*, made in 1976.[8] Immediately, however, the cast switches to locating the coming action:

> In the summer when the earth changed and it rained for five months and on the night the rain stopped a silence fell like we'd woke up in a silence from a dream. We were in a city and on that strange night only the dead walked about in it, smiling and drinking halves of lager LIKE THEY OWNED THE FUCKING PLACE. ... This, as the poets say, is what happened next as the night unfolded. (Etchells, 1999, 147)

The curtain is whisked back as though to start another scene; but it is then hurriedly dragged across again as the scene is not yet ready. This happens a few times, with each speaker describing further the atmosphere of the city 'on the night the rain stopped', while accompanying parts of the account with a bizarre sign language. Eventually the curtain opens on a scene ready to go. This is the pattern of most subsequent frontcloth sequences: each time there is further description of the activities the inhabitants engage in, such as 'Closing Both Eyes Tight Whilst Driving Down A Road', or writing messages on the walls like 'Stop Playing Games Or I'll Fucking Kill Myself.' Each time there are false starts, as the performers apparently compete with each other to start or prevent a scene.

In this instance the scene revealed is the first involving video – the Newsroom scene. While the performers take turns reading lists of 'headlines' at a microphone on a centre-stage table, they are videotaped by a tripod-mounted camera downstage centre, with the images relayed to monitors on either side of the stage. The reading starts frenetically, accompanied by loud, insistent music. The 'headlines' are organised in lists of ten that the readers seem to grasp at random. Like the figures on the cardboard signs, they vary from plausible to implausible, and only a few take the shape of headlines: others resemble book or film titles, or evocative slogans, sometimes with a strong political undercurrent.

1. A porn magazine called CRUCIFIED WOMEN
2. 50 more years of bad news
3. At 12 am like in a fairytale
4. Lighthearted
5. A vision
6. The kids playing hide and seek in the back of the car
7. Noiseland – video arcade
8. Slander
9. HOW TO FILM A MASSACRE.
10. HOW TO FILM A MASSACRE FOR KIDS
(Etchells, 1999, 148)

Surrounding activity begins to suggest that the news is taking place against the background of some sort of violent disturbance. At one point Marshall is ushered on with a blanket covering her head, but reads her list nevertheless; at another, Lowdon wanders on with a towel bandaging his arm, looking as though he's strayed from a hospital drama onto the wrong set; O'Connor has a revolver trained on her while she reads. The music becomes quieter, almost sinister, while the readers slow down and speak more quietly, investing the atmosphere with a sense of hushed desperation. Eventually, Marshall breaks down sobbing in the middle of her reading.

Throughout, spectators can see both the live activity and the video-taped head and shoulder shots on the monitors. The close-up framing on the monitors intensifies the emotions of the readings; and it is the televisual framing of activities such as those involving the blanket and the revolver which effectively evokes familiar images from news coverage of revolutionary situations, when often the local television studio is an early target – as, for example, during the overthrow of the Ceaucescu regime in Romania two years before the production.

The subsequent frontcloth scene refers to 'magic acts' and 'party tricks' done on the night the rain stopped. Accompanied by Tom and Jerry style cartoon music, the performers then begin wheeling the stage-flats about the space, disappearing and reappearing from behind them. Initially it does seem like a manic magic act, but increasingly the performers revealed by the moving flats begin to look lost or in a state of panic. Sometimes they are in pairs, looking as though they are engaged in some melodramatic scene. Activity is

Figure 17   *Emanuelle Enchanted*

interrupted briefly by a further frontcloth scene, in which Naden describes how 'We practised TRANSFORMATION and LOSS. We rehearsed UPSET FOR NO REASON, and then became upset for no reason' (Etchells, 1999, 152).[9] The music becomes more quietly sinister as the walls begin to move again; sometimes performers team up to taunt individuals, as the walls circle around them, leaving them dazed and confused.

After the walls re-form momentarily at the back, O'Connor, accompanied by quiet music, delivers a long monologue, full of repeated questions:

> On the wild night the rain stopped we looked down at the city and said: / Wherefore is this night distinguished from all other nights? / We're in a PLACE OF CHANCE. / Wherefore is this night distinguished from all other nights? ... Why such a big city tonight? / Why so many people? / Why such a big city, why such a big world? (Ibid., 153)

Meanwhile, the walls move slowly about, revealing and dissolving evocative images: people are seen crouched next to walls, clinging to them, undressing, embracing, looking to the stars, and so on. Without using video, the atmosphere is very cinematic, recalling American artist Cindy Sherman's photographs of imaginary film scenes.

This is followed by the second, longer, cardboard signs scene, in which the whole atmosphere takes on a more forlorn, awkward air and the performers increasingly look at a loss. During the subsequent curtain scene the video camera and monitors are arranged for Scene Thirteen, The Kiss. Behind the curtains Lowdon and Marshall are filmed in close-up as they engage in a lingering kiss, which is relayed onto the monitors in front of the curtain. Their kiss is thus mediated by both a literal screen, the curtain, and by an electronic one. As they embrace, Naden, in the manner of someone explicating a film in a foreign language, stands by the monitor and apparently describes the action of *Goodbye Emmanuelle*. But the narrative is totally at odds with the screen image: she describes Emmanuelle waiting for a call from her lover, and then tells of conversations between Chloe, an ornithologist, and Gregory, a filmmaker. While the characters' names are indeed from the real film, their dialogue seems to be mostly Etchells', as when Emmanuelle says:

> What do the foes of melody know of melody? What do the foes of love know of love? What do the liars, fuckers and murderers know of anything except lying, fucking and murdering? Nothing. (Ibid., 154)

The discrepancy between the video images and Naden's account may seem disconcerting, but, in a way, it continues the previous play with the arbitrariness of signs. Despite their incongruity, both the doubly mediated kiss and Naden's narration gradually acquire a certain emotional power, aided again by John Avery's filmic music.

As Naden concludes, the camera slowly pans away onto the littered stage and the isolated figure of Arthur. He begins the ensuing Newsroom sequence, announcing:

> When morning came we were still alive Writing messages on the walls of our room. We did not weep though we had full cause of weeping. (Ibid., 155)

Thus begins a reprise of the sort of routine seen earlier, except that this time the readers break off after only a few items in the lists, and the camera, now hand-held, pans around the room, catching performers other than the reader. As more and more reams of paper litter the place, the effect is to suggest the collapse of attempts to frame and represent the world. This is reinforced by the recurrence of words such as 'unreadable', 'untraceable', 'uncertainty', and lines of computer-speak referring to errors, passwords being incorrect, and so on. Eventually, Arthur returns to the microphone and begins a long, final monologue, which, although it contains a kaleidoscopic picture of desolation and separation, is described by Etchells as an 'upbeat answer to Terry's WHEREFORE text' (Typescript, 24). The mix of emotions is exemplified in text such as:

> And heartless breezes and / born not with a hole but a war in my heart and / heaven street and / impossible scenes and / an illness that spreads via the telephone and / that illegitimate son of a bitch and / innocent and innocent again and / I'm floating and thinking: / that night they held the world in their arms and / innocent and / innocent to a fault and a man says: you're so far away, you're so far away, / you're on one side of the world and I'm on the other. (Etchells, 1999, 159)

Much of the impact comes from Arthur's (musically underscored) intense, emotional delivery, which moves through lyricism to urgency as he returns, towards the end, to the man who is 'so far away'. He repeats the man's speech four times, before reciting a final list, which paradoxically contains the line 'I am here to tell you I was happy.' As with previous shows, for all that the production has shown the performers' playing out, in an allusive, fragmentary way, 'the dark comedy of a broken down town in pieces and fragments', it returns to a redemptive vision of 'repeated escape and impossible survival' (Programme note).

While the texts themselves and the performances evoke both the chaos and the need to dream a beautiful place discussed in the Programme, another significant aspect of the production is to do with framing, representation and performance. The curtain immediately establishes one framing device. As it is whisked to and fro, with the performers often disputing whether it should be open or drawn, it becomes like an editing device, illustrating the point that what is normally seen on the stage is always controlled and framed. In typical Forced Entertainment fashion, this is both gestured to and undercut: with the curtain being diaphanous, we can often see shadowy figures and actions behind it. This (incomplete) framing is echoed in other framing devices. In the moving walls scenes, as the flats glide to and fro, they both reveal and conceal actions and figures, just like a camera shutter. The plethora of situations parallels the numberless characters indexed by the cardboard signs – where, again, the signs serve to frame (imperfectly) the way we view the performers at each point. These framing devices are then extended further by the use of live relay to frame the performers' readings of the fantastic lists. While the monitors show head and shoulder shots of the readers, in the conventional news programme style of the time, we also see onstage the surrounding chaos that such framing excludes. It is as though we are a studio audience watching a particularly hectic news programme being televised; we see the difference between what is happening in the studio and what the television viewer at home is allowed to see. In the later repetitions the camera roams about, showing the spilled papers, the scattered costumes, the readers' legs, inviting spectators to consider more closely the conventional 'head and shoulders' editing of the standard news programmes of the time.[10]

The notion of editing can also be seen as shaping the performances themselves. Just as the 'news' is represented by simple headlines and titles, the snapshot depictions in the cardboard sign and wall-moving scenes allow performers only a moment to suggest characters, emotions or situations – just as a cutaway shot in film or television demands instantaneous and momentary performance. Where normally stage actors have time and space to build a portrait of a character or situation, here the performers must work more like film actors. The staging description in the typescript even refers to the performers with the cardboard signs as 'performing as though to close-up camera', with the runners on the centre spot 'often motivated with details as though from narrative, or film' (Typescript, 6). It is as though we are witnessing a series of quick takes that have not been edited together to create the narrative coherence expected in a film or television drama. The fact that these snapshots often still produce a powerful effect, despite their lack of conventional editing, also underlines how contemporary spectators, inundated as they are by electronic imagery, rapidly draw on an enormous memory bank of conventional representations to respond almost instantaneously to certain images. And yet the very arbitrariness of their pell-mell presentation and the ambiguous, hesitant or incomplete ways in which characters are signalled underline the arbitrariness of signs.

This depiction of the arbitrary, conventional nature of signs is then carried through in the use of music and in play with vocal delivery – including the way amplification produces different effects. For example, the use of the microphone and close-up shots in the first Newsroom sequence, along with shifts in the accompanying music, allows the performers to explore a whole gamut of emotional atmospheres in their delivery. Without any narrative grounding, the delivery moves between suggesting urgency, self-consciousness, desperation, contemplation, and tragic loss. Although the overall scenario suggests a fragmenting city, there is rarely an explicit diegetic rationale for the moment to moment shifts in atmosphere. It is as though the performers are saying, 'Look how, with just a shift of tone or look, with a change in the music, or by coming closer to the microphone, we can manipulate your emotional response to what we say, no matter what it is.' As they occupy the different rhetorical positions worked through in both text and performance, the performers question the possibility of any position being more 'authentic' than any other and reveal them for the verbal and visual tropes they are.

In this, *Emanuelle Enchanted* illustrates more general points that become apparent when these three productions are examined more closely. Drawing attention to the initial surface of seemingly chaotic behaviour in Forced Entertainment shows, and taking account of how television feeds into the work, some critics portray the productions as though they simply replicate the randomness of television channel-hopping. The work is described as relying, in characteristic postmodern fashion, on depthless pastiche and encouraging simply the sort of distracted viewing we associate with television. Closer examination suggests that behind the apparently disorderly surface there is a closely structured exploration, not just of such thematic concerns as dislocation, love, sex, death, and faith, but of the very apparatuses of representation themselves. The use of video and of television-inspired figures and activities is central to this. In a passage which contains echoes of Foucault's discussion of heterotopias, Etchells has spoken of Forced Entertainment shows as evoking 'parallel performance worlds' which don't necessarily have surface similarities with our own, but which 'resonate down to our own without ever setting out to describe it or argue about it' (Etchells, 1989). As has been seen, the use of video and play with other types of mediation, along with the representational conventions of film and television, all contribute to the sort of anamorphic distortions of the world found in Forced Entertainment shows.

6   Live Films on Stage: The Builders Association

The work of The Builders Association straddles both the theatre of attractions tradition and the more critical Piscatorian tradition. Employing video dramatically, didactically, and in a choric way, as well as exploiting opportunities provided by live relay, computer animation and editing to work innovatively at the interface between live and mediated performers, the company's increasingly hypermediatic productions have led to them being seen as at the forefront of experiment in this area.

The company was established in 1993 by Marianne Weems, Jeff Webster, Jennifer Tipton and others, to present a version of Ibsen's *The Master Builder*.[1] Weems previously worked with Richard Foreman, Meredith Monk and Mabou Mines, and was Dramaturg and Assistant Director with The Wooster Group from 1988 to 1994, during which time Webster also performed with it. Tipton, an acclaimed lighting designer, has worked with The Wooster Group and Robert Wilson amongst others. Subsequently, another key collaborator has been video designer Christopher Kondek, who has also worked frequently with The Wooster Group, Laurie Anderson and Robert Wilson.

The company's handling of video initially shared some similarities with The Wooster Group's approach, but it quickly developed a distinctive style of its own, which both uses video technology more expansively and concerns itself more overtly with screen culture and the impact of technology on contemporary culture as a subject. Believing that electronic media can reanimate theatre, Weems argues that 'screen culture has become the dominant means of artistic expression, and if you're going to be a functioning artist in the world today you have to grapple with that on some level' (Interview, 2003).

The 'screen' here also encompasses the computer screen – which soon supplemented monitors and projection screens in the company's shows. While the first two productions reworked classic texts with live and pre-recorded video material delivered on monitors, thereafter, wide-screen video projection has played an increasing role, along with complex use of digital animation and rendering techniques. This shift has accompanied a move towards basing productions on 'real-life' stories rather than fictional texts. The focus of discussion here will be on these later productions. Weems describes the company as constructing them 'like a live film on stage ... you see the technicians and performers working in concert together, like a chamber orchestra, to create this overall spectacle' (ibid.). Much of the video material is mixed live on stage and the performers perform much of the time for the battery of cameras that relay their actions, confounding the sort of distinctions critics since Walter Benjamin have made between stage acting as being for an audience and screen acting for a camera (Benjamin, 1973, 222–4). In Builders Association productions performances are largely predicated upon electronic mediation. Weems rejects any suggestion that the performances are not also geared towards the audience, suggesting that the simultaneous viewing of the performers and the mediation of their performances provides spectatorial pleasure:

> All the actors have learnt to perform along this spectrum from naturalism to this mediated performing, where they're still very conscious of the audience. So that, though they're facing a camera, they're playing to an audience beyond the camera, out there, and that they pace things and use the camera to create different expressions under different circumstances. (Ibid.)

Although Weems describes the use of video in *Master Builder* (1994) as 'relatively primitive', the production was a striking response to the play. Using an abridged text and performed in contemporary dress, it was presented in an industrial warehouse in New York. The set consisted of a wooden house, sections of which were demolished during the performance, revealing the rooms within; eventually it was split in two. The gradual revelation and destruction echoed the dramatic movement of the play itself, as the secrets of the family and the disintegration of the relationship between Solness and his wife are uncovered. The house was wired with MIDI triggers which the performers activated, setting off various sound effects. Most rooms contained a video monitor. Reflecting the distance between them, Solness's wife spent much of the performance sitting alone, while Solness himself moved about the house, drilling and hammering. The performers generally spoke into hand-held microphones, with the intimacy of their speech backed by ambient music, while video showed close-ups of the speaker or shots of other occupants of the house. Pre-recorded film appeared occasionally: for example, when Solness tells Hilde how he used to imagine his earlier house burning down, the monitors moved from a close-up of the side of Hilde's head to displaying a clip from a black and white silent-era film showing a woman running out of a burning house – while over the dialogue a fire-station telephone operator could be heard.

Imperial Motel (Faust) and Jump Cut (Faust)

Master Builder was followed by *The White Album* (1995), created with students from New York University's Experimental Theater Wing. It overlapped the actions of a band working on some songs from The Beatles' *The White Album* with those of performers in a neighbouring studio recording Noel Coward's *Blithe Spirit*, with much of the action relayed onto three large monitor screens. The next production, *Imperial Motel (Faust)*, a co-production with Zürich's Theater Neumarkt in 1996, incorporated for the first time the large-scale projection that has characterised subsequent work. This was then reworked in the US as *Jump Cut (Faust)*, in which version it also toured Europe. While initiating a new phase in their handling of video, these multi-layered responses to the Faust myth also marked the end of the company's early phase of playing with classic texts.

Weems researched the Faust story extensively, exploring its irreverent handling in popular puppet shows of the 17th and 18th centuries, as well as the plays of Marlowe and Goethe, and film versions by Georges Méliès (1905), Friedrich Wilhelm Murnau (1926) and Gustav Gründgens (1963). Exploring Goethe's sources, she encountered transcripts of the 1772 trial of a chambermaid who killed her baby and whose story inspired Goethe's treatment of Gretchen. Weems commissioned John Jesurun to create a text for the show. Much of Jesurun's own work as a writer and director in New York since the 1980s also made use of video and Weems worked with him and Ron Vawter on *Philoctetes* in 1993.[2] The resulting text, seemingly set initially in a motel room on Highway 66 in Arizona, is a witty updating that mixes contemporary slang and references with echoes of Goethe and Murnau.[3] Its jarring shifts of tone may surprise spectators who associate the Faust legend with tragedy, but in fact recalls the way Goethe's version exhibits 'an overwhelming disrespect for etiquette' and 'abounds in doggerel, slang and jokes' (Kaufman, 1963, 4). Discussion here will focus on the *Jump Cut* version. The Swiss production included many of the same elements, but much of the dialogue was doubled in German (with there being two Fausts and Gretchens) and Mephistopheles was played by a woman. Weems saw the second version, which lasted just over an hour, as stripping out material from the first and creating a 'jump cut' version. Material relating to the Gründgens film was cut, with the Murnau film providing a spine around which the production was built.[4]

The production was structured around thirteen scenes, preceded by a brief prologue. The early scenes in which Faust summons Mephistopheles and makes his pact with him largely mimicked, and were interwoven with, footage from Murnau. Faust's subsequent adventures with Mephistopheles and Gretchen were based on Jesurun's texts, although they also incorporated imagery drawn from Murnau and others. In the spirit of Méliès as much as Murnau, the complex interweaving of the various sources played off the story's fascination with mischief, magic and transformation, while also bringing out thematic concerns with humankind's desire for knowledge and power over nature and the contemporary technological ramifications of this.

The set essentially consisted of bare stage-flats delineating a bare room, above which a large projection screen spanned the width of the stage; about six metres in length by two metres high, it consisted of three sections, each served by a video projector. With cameras dotted about the place and technicians working them and the visible mixing desks, the overall atmosphere suggested a television studio, signalling the way the production was creating 'a live film on stage'. The live relay of onstage action and its mixing with recorded material effectively drew spectatorial attention to the projected action for the most part, although this focus was in constructive tension with a viewing of the onstage performances feeding into the projections. Four scenes will serve to illustrate the production's layering of live and mediated, textual and filmic sources, and comic 'attractions' with more serious concerns: the opening scene, a Méliès-like drive through the heavens, a trial scene and the closing scene.

Murnau's (silent, black and white) film begins with a sense of looming destruction, with the (written) epigraph, 'Behold! The portals of Darkness are open and the shadows of the Dead hunt over the earth.'

While the camera travels around Faust's bustling city, Mephistopheles bets the Angel Gabriel that he can persuade Faust to surrender his soul. A dark cloud covers the city and plague descends upon it. Faust, despairing of finding a cure, burns his bible and summons the Devil to assist him. Drawing on the atmosphere of all this, Jesurun's prologue evokes a modern-day apocalyptic image, beginning with a letter being spoken by a man to his lover:

> Dear one, I'm writing to you from an airplane above your country. The computer breakdown is still affecting most of the hemisphere. (Jesurun, 2004, 98)

The writer goes on to report that her city has been destroyed and he assumes that she will not in fact receive the letter. (The atmosphere of impending apocalypse and the global computer breakdown here resemble the 1991 Wim Wenders film *Until The End of the World*.)

In The Builders Association staging, Jeff Webster stands, dimly lit, reading the letter aloud, while projected above is pre-recorded back-shot video of him driving along an open road – seemingly at odds with the description of him in a plane. However, as he describes his plane circling above the smoking city, the road gives way to images of swirling clouds. When Webster, in a long coat and a Mediaeval cap, begins to fiddle with some crucibles and test tubes, live relay of this alternates with footage from Murnau's film showing an old bearded Faust similarly occupied. This is flanked by Gothic script on either side: 'A knave like all the others he preaches good and does evil. He seeks to turn base metal into gold!' Webster holds a large book up and a wind-machine blows its pages, as he invokes the 'spirit of darkness'. As a voice whispers, 'Come forth demon of evil', this title, from the Murnau film, is projected on the upper screens – before they are filled with burning flames and Webster's image is superimposed. This composite image alternates with Murnau shots of Faust in a ring of flames. Immediately, the production establishes the way it will continue to collide together Mediaeval language, early cinema, and contemporary language, technology and imagery, and displays its underlying fascination with magic and transformation.

When Mephistopheles (David Pence) appears, Faust bargains with him for 'four and twenty years living in all voluptuousness'. As Faust cuts his arm to seal the bargain in blood, the upper screens show a close-up, before revealing the words 'Homo Fuge' (Flee, man) written in blood. When the aggressively cynical Mephistopheles tells Faust about how he was hurled out of heaven, Pence and Webster both play directly to onstage cameras and speak into microphones (rather than to each other), with their faces shown in alternating close-up on the upper central screen. Weems later reflected, '*Faust* was kind of hilarious, because we had something like six or eight cameras planted all over the stage; it was really about the actors learning to hit their marks and hold the mike out of the frame, and adopt this whole cinematic acting style on stage' (Interview, 2003).

The enlarged filmic doubling of the performers marks the way both characters adopt grandstanding rhetorical positions; this estranging of

Figure 18   *Jump Cut (Faust)*

the text is reinforced by the occasional projection of the text itself onto the screens. Mephistopheles promotes himself as the source of motion and energy in what would otherwise be a static universe. He complains that God punished him because he introduced the idea of love into the universe:

> And the universe moved. Galaxies shifted. Time began. Everything moved. You understand, it had never moved once since time began. It was a frozen beauty. I just put a little flame under it. How did I know it would melt into another reality? And was he pissed. (Jesurun, 2004, 101)[5]

The pastiched grand metaphysics of the opening pact are followed by the comic seductions of Gretchen (Heaven Phillips, in white miniskirt and boots) and her Aunt Marthe (Moira Driscoll, in voluminous Mediaeval dress echoing Murnau). Accompanied by techno music, the performers move into a comically stylised disco dance, while the projection above alternates between moments of live relay and moments from Murnau, culminating in Phillips swooning in Webster's arms, echoing exactly a Murnau shot.

The model for the following sequence is more Méliès than Murnau, as Mephistopheles takes the others on a manic ride across the heavens that recalls the celestial journey in *Merry Frolics of Satan*. The four actors assemble in front of a blue screen and mimic riding in a car, while the projection above mixes in scenery to show them first driving along a road ('the driveway to Hell') and then through the starry heavens, as they comment on various sights and passers-by. They squabble, knock down a 'hellhound', spot General Custer, John Lennon and Cleopatra en route, and almost hit a woman who turns out to be Faustus' secretary Rhonda Kindermörd. The irreverent atmosphere is underlined when Webster, thrown about in the speeding car, begins singing The Beach Boys' 'Help, Help Me Rhonda'.

The subsequent birth and death of Gretchen's child is preceded by Murnau's scene-title, 'And has borne a little child in the depth of winter'. In low light, and filmed in black and white, Mephistopheles pours flour through a sieve onto Gretchen, who has a cloak drawn up around her head and swaddling cloths in her arms: the projected shot reconstructs exactly Murnau's depiction of Gretchen stranded in the falling snow. The constructed pathos of the moment is both played and undercut through the revelation of the flour and sieve.

Figure 19 *Jump Cut (Faust)*

Goethe's scenes in which Gretchen is condemned and Faust visits her in prison are then given a bizarre twist. Drawing on the 1772 trial referred to earlier, a conflated figure of Gretchen and Rhonda Kindermörd (Child-murderer) undergoes an elaborate show-trial. Relayed live on the upper screens, Mephistopheles and Faustus stride and pose in the manner of television courtroom dramas; prosecuting, Mephistopheles claims the child was the product of a rape and calls on 'baby Kindermörd' to appear and testify – the baby is represented on video by a flickering light. Although Gretchen is eventually acquitted, Faust visits her in prison, as in Goethe's text. Where Goethe's Gretchen repents of the death of their child, Jesurun has Gretchen/Kindermörd thank Faust for getting her off the hook, admit to having killed the baby, and ask him to run off with her. As Faust attacks her, the video shows Gretchen's face morphing into Mephistopheles' face: Gretchen has in fact been Mephistopheles in disguise.

As Faust exits, the screens are filled once more with the opening image of flying through the clouds, while Webster recites a letter to Gretchen. The impression now is of a complete technological and political breakdown, a world in which 'There will be no tomorrow tomorrow. No today today.' Out of fuel, the writer's plane floats above 'the dissolving city', but he says:

> I think I've found a place where I know I can be forever. What this has to do with God or the devil, I'll never know. Surf's up. See you there. (Jesurun, 2004, 127)

As the clouds part, it becomes evident that the flyer is over a Mediaeval German city – but with a swastika on one of its towers. The film is an excerpt from Leni Riefenstahl's *Triumph of the Will*, the city is Nuremberg, and the plane is Hitler's, taking him to the infamous Nuremberg rally.

The complex intertextuality of this ending requires some unpacking. Contrary to Marlowe's tragic ending, where Faust is swallowed into Hell, Goethe ends with a host of heavenly angels saving Faust's soul from the Devil. Visions of his soul being carried through the clouds, which part to reveal the beauties of nature, lead towards Gretchen's appearance amongst a crowd of penitents. Faust and she are reunited in Heaven, while the last lines praise the 'Eternal Feminine that lures to perfection'. The videotaped flight through clouds and Faust's parting statement that the surf's up and he will meet Gretchen there become a compressed, irreverent echo of Goethe's final epiphany. However, the concurrent revelation of the identity of the city he is flying over (and a textual comparison with the destruction of Dresden in 1945) strikes a discordant note. Noting Kaufman's view of 'Western civilisation as a Faustian culture' (1963, 22) and recalling also how Stein's Faust symbolised the ambiguous gains of the Enlightenment project, the Promethean, alchemical, Enlightenment tradition Faust has come to represent seems, in contrast to Goethe's comic ending, to be presented here as leading to the horrors of the Nazis.

Although the compression and ambiguous tone is in keeping with the continual tensions played out between Mediaeval story, 19th-century text, early film and contemporary political and technological context, the injection of such political implications here may initially appear somewhat surprising in a production seemingly dominated by comic pastiche of its sources, and in which spectatorial pleasure largely derives from the portrayal of Mephistopheles as a cynical prankster and from the playful interweaving of the live action, its videotaped representation and Murnau's romantic film version. The reviewer for *Le Monde* overstates the case when suggesting, 'The myth of Faust is no more than a pretext for John Jesurun's verbal fantasies and for a layering game in which one is easily lost'(*Le Monde*, 25th March, 1998). Nevertheless, Weems seems to accept that the sort of postmodern playing with classical texts associated with The Wooster Group and with The Builders Association's early productions had played itself out, when she suggests her subsequent turn

> from canonical texts to works based on real phenomena in the wider world is based on my burgeoning interest in reaching a wider audience. There's often something inherently hermetic in starting out with a theatrical text that may mean something to people inside of theatre, but outside of theatre I think many of those facets have gone kind of cold. (Interview, 2003)

Weems here reflects a broader disenchantment in the 1990s with what some saw as the excesses of postmodern intertextual play; she also implicitly establishes an independent line of development for The Builders Association away from that of The Wooster Group. If the Faust productions' merging of live relay and pre-recorded film marked an important step on the path towards creating 'live film on stage', the next project, *Jet Lag* (1998), marked an even stronger shift in terms of the source materials used and demonstrated an increasing interest in the place of technology as a running theme in the company's work.

Jet Lag

A man sets out on a solo round the world sailing race, falls into difficulties, sails in circles for eight months, while creating a fictional account of a circumnavigation of the globe, before finally throwing himself overboard. A woman kidnaps her grandson and flies the Atlantic 167 times in six months, living in planes and airports, before finally dying of jet lag in mid-flight. Seen as emblematic of the distortions of time and space which have accompanied developments in modern transport and communications technologies, these real-life stories formed the basis of *Jet Lag*, a collaboration with architects Diller + Scofidio. The production played in contrasting ways with the means by which the central figures attempted, with fatal consequences, to escape from daily life into an almost virtual world of travel. It employed video primarily for scenographic purposes, but it worked significant variations on the conventional methods of doing so.

Part One was based on the story of Donald Crowhurst, a Briton who set sail from Devon in 1968. After a couple of thousand miles, realising that his trimaran would not get him round the world, Crowhurst began falsifying reports to race headquarters in Britain, while he sailed off the coast of Argentina for 86 days. All the while he kept two logs – one charting his real position, the other a fictional account of a trip through the Roaring Forties and across the Southern Pacific. Eventually, he headed home, reporting positions that showed him vying for first place. While the British media were celebrating his heroic voyage, Crowhurst, fearing his deception would be discovered and increasingly losing his grip on reality, threw himself overboard with his ship's clock, a few days from home.

The Builders Association changed the protagonist to Roger Dearborn, an American sailing from Nantucket, and had him concoct a video-diary of his supposed journey, while also maintaining his pretence in occasional radio-calls back to his wife. This allowed parallels to evolve between the way technology may be used to create a persuasively realistic fiction and the way Dearborn used technology to create a fictional persona and voyage. As Jeff Webster and the technical crew are shown creating the fictional Dearborn for the audience, so Dearborn is shown creating a fictional self-portrait for his audience. Here the making of a 'film onstage' formally echoes the subject matter of self-invention.

The set for this first part consists of three main elements: downstage, a long table fronted by a Liquid Crystal Display screen (able to switch from transparent to opaque), behind which three performers play a radiophone-operator, Dearborn's wife, a publicist, and a reporter; up-centre, a large projection screen; and centre-left, a stool in front of a smaller screen, along with a tripod camera and various sailing paraphernalia. The show begins with Webster casually organising props and video equipment as he prepares to assume the role of an intrepid sailor. A video seascape is rear-projected onto the small screen behind him, as he sits and begins speaking to camera. The resulting composite video, seemingly of a sailor at sea, is projected onto the large screen, while Webster talks about the anticipated trials and tribulations of eight months at sea. During the rest of the performance the small screen provides changing backdrops for his video diary. At one point, Webster asks the technician, 'Do you have, like, a stormy sea? Dramatic, that's it.' As crashing waves appear, accompanied by appropriate sound effects, Webster dons wet-weather gear, sprays water over his face, and rocks about on his stool, creating a convincing picture on the main screen of a storm-tossed mariner – while also producing spectatorial pleasure at the divergence between what we see of his onstage activities and the dramatic video he creates.

Figure 20   *Jet Lag*

The production continually plays with such analogies between Webster's job as an actor and Dearborn's 'performance'. Interspersed with his speeches to camera while supposedly sailing, the radio-calls to his wife (Heaven Phillips) move between awkward intimacies and banalities about supplies. While carefully orchestrated sound effects of radio static effectively suggest a sense of the difficulties of communication across a supposed distance of thousands of miles, the fictional picture thus created is counterpointed by the onstage presence of Phillips lit behind the screen only a few feet away: again, the production draws attention as much to its processes of construction as to what is constructed.

The story concludes with a report that Dearborn is feared lost at sea, only days before completing his voyage. On the large screen a red line tracks down a map of the Atlantic, plotting his actual course, while the reporter tells of growing suspicions about Dearborn's reports. Lit behind the LCD screen, his wife and publicist describe how the tapes and documents on his abandoned boat revealed his deception. The reporter delivers a damning epitaph, 'To put it bluntly, he never even did it.' While there is a certain dramatic pathos in this as a comment on Dearborn, in the context it might also be interpreted as a metatheatrical comment on the gap between what is purportedly presented as a 'picture of reality' on video and what actually goes into the making of such representations.

The second part of *Jet Lag* draws on the story of Sarah Krassnoff, a 74-year-old woman who, in 1971, flew continuously with her grandson to and fro between New York and Amsterdam, in order to thwart his father's attempts to gain custody. Although based on this story, what little dialogue there is provides no exploration of the originating dispute or the feelings of the boy. Instead, the focus is on the experience of constant travel and the airport as a site. Airports are, of course, a favourite topos for writers about postmodernity: the overwhelming plethora of continually changing screens, signs and announcements in different languages; the cloned shopping malls; the estranging sense of suspended time, as people wait in places where time is both all-important (getting to the gates on time) and yet distorted, as food outlets simultaneously serve breakfasts and dinners to travellers whose body clocks are at variance with 'local' time; the way they operate as a transient 'non-places' of arrival and departure, populated fleetingly by a stream of passengers whose flights may be the locus of diverse desires and aspirations.[6] All these are grist to the mill of theorists and Paul Virilio is cited in the Programme for *Jet Lag* as describing Sarah Krassnoff as a 'contemporary heroine who lived in deferred time'. One can hardly imagine what it must have been like to spend six months moving in and out of airports and planes, yet, in the space of half an hour, this section of *Jet Lag* effectively evokes the disorienting atmosphere of air travel, mainly thanks to its use of CGI and a complex soundtrack.

The comparatively simple technology of the first half, with the almost 'home movie' feel to the creation of the fake video-log, gives way in this part to much more hi-tech imagery, as wide-screen CG images of the interior and exterior of a trans-Atlantic jet and an airport dominate the space and the performers. Where Webster actively engages in the creation of Dearborn's fictitious account, Ann Carlson and Dale Soules (as the renamed Doris Schwartz and her grandson Lincoln) are more like puppet-figures set against a constantly changing and disorienting backdrop. While their minimal exchanges create a sense of the exhaustion and monotony of their lives, it is the animated scenery that stars here. The scale of the projection comes into its own, recalling Svoboda's large-scale projection in shows such as *Odysseus*.

When Doris and the boy use a moving walkway, he stands behind her
'pushing' her wheelchair while they talk: they are, in fact, standing
still, while the diorama-like video creates the impression of passing
walls as they supposedly move along. They take an escalator, and the
video tracks up past the adjacent windows to the outside world, showing planes taking off. At another point, they arrange themselves on a
set of chairs while the video shows enlarged CCTV-style footage of
them creating a temporary encampment in an actual airport. All the
time a soundtrack of plane noises, airport announcements, and insistent electronic chords, contributes to an atmosphere of dislocation and
dissociation.

The final moments of the production double the sense of alienation that pervades the presentation of the story. An announcer
reports Doris's death in mid-flight from New York, while the screen
fills with the sort of route-tracking map found on planes, showing
the path of her flight (and echoing the earlier route-tracking of
Dearborn's boat). The screen switches to a huge CG image of the
plane's interior, while a pair of airline seats, raised up on a jack-like

Figure 21   *Jet Lag*

contraption and carrying Doris and the boy, is hauled on in front of it. After a brief conversation in which Doris is clearly in some confusion, the boy sinks back into his flight simulation game.

After the complex interplay of historical film material, mimicry of such material and making a 'live film onstage' in the Faust productions, the principal use of video and CGI in *Jet Lag* may seem more straightforward in its harking back to one of the earliest proposed uses for film in theatre, as a scenographic tool. We can see, however, that in both sections its employment goes beyond simple scene-setting. In their different ways, the real life models for Dearborn and Schwartz broke with the everyday regimes of time and space. As they attempted to suspend time and live in 'non-places', they entered a sort of virtual time-space symptomatic of the distortions of time and space experienced in postmodernity. In both sections, then, the virtual nature of the projected settings, and the interaction of the performers with those settings, reflect the production's general concern with such virtualisation of time and space. Moreover, the use of CGI for much of the second section establishes a parallelism between the flight simulation game of the boy and the simulacral nature of his and his grandmother's existence; the 'non-places' in which they lived the last six months of Doris's life is for the performers literally a non-place, a virtual setting produced by the electronic images.

XTRAVAGANZA

The programme for *XTRAVAGANZA*, printed in the style of a 19th-century Music Hall bill, includes a subtitle, 'Ten Acts Displayed with Moving Pictures'. It lists titles for each of the ten 'Acts' and the fourteen 'episodes' with which they are interwoven – episodes in which the main action is, indeed, mostly portrayed by 'moving pictures'. The programme declares: '*XTRAVAGANZA* looks back at theatrical forms which preceded much of what is now called multimedia performance.' Noting the multimedial nature of 19th and early 20th-century forms of variety show, it asserts, 'Multimedia is not something which emerged with the experiments of the 1960s or even the advent of television.'

The production plays with the history of what Weems sees as early American experiments in multimedia performance, starting with the Wild West Shows mounted by Buffalo Bill Cody and the subsequent work of three figures who worked with him: the producer Steele

Mackaye, the dancer Loie Fuller, and showman Florenz Ziegfeld. Added to these is Busby Berkeley, on whose first film Ziegfeld collaborated. Episodes charting their activities are interspersed with the ten Acts: mostly song and/or dance routines, some of which are built around a 'show rehearsal' narrative. Drawing on movies such as *42nd Street* and *Gold Diggers of 1933*, this portrays two chorus-girls coming to New York and becoming involved in a musical, culminating in one being plucked from the chorus to sing 'Broadway Rose'. Other Acts include performers adapting contemporary club dance styles in routines that are then relayed live, with the images manipulated spectacularly by an onstage VJ.

The production is a highly entertaining, self-reflexive exploration of recent traditions of spectacle. The ambitions of these pioneering figures to expand technology's capacity to dazzle audiences are highlighted through readings of letters and diaries, backed by visual material. Mackaye, for example, writes about his plans for a spectacular new 'total theatre' and his patenting of a floating stage and a device which could expand and shrink the proscenium arch – technologies that would provide theatre with the sort of scenic and focal fluidity cinema would soon make possible. Fuller became famous in Paris as the Electricity Fairy: she experimented continuously with developing more dynamic lighting for her shows and worked with slide projections. Berkeley rhapsodises about his shift from stage to screen, 'You can take the camera any place, you can do anything with a camera.' Film footage illustrates how he flies, tracks and zooms his camera above and around his precisely drilled choruses. The production acknowledges, and exploits in a double-coded way, the seductiveness of their spectacles, but also touches on the industrialisation of art and commodification of the performers in the work. It also reveals how each practitioner was prey to insecurities, artistic and financial, and each ended up in personal and financial ruin of one sort or another.[7] Through interaction between the onstage performers and the diverse projected material, links and contrasts emerge between what was done with lighting, cameras and editing (and lots of performers) in the earlier period and what modern electronic media can achieve with a far smaller troupe, provoking reflection on issues around 'live' versus 'virtual' spectacle.

It is only possible here to provide selective examples of the constant interaction between live performers and projected material. Video and CGI fell into a number of categories, sometimes overlapping in individual instances: historical, 'factional' historical, illustrative, and spectacular.

Much was pre-recorded, but there was a considerable amount of simultaneously edited live relay, with the technicians given latitude to improvise on the night with the materials available. Much of the impact of the live relay sequences came from spectators seeing the relatively minimal choreography of the performers transformed via cameras and computers into stunningly dynamic imagery. Weems describes how, paradoxically, an expansion of the company's technical capacities allowed the production to operate in a more 'live' way:

> It was the first time we got enough money to get enough computer power and space to store all the information, so that the music and video were really being played nightly like the performers were playing. It was set up to be like a vaudeville show where things could be shuffled from night to night, and there were moments for improvisation between the video and the sound guys. (Interview, 2003)

Recalling Piscator's early productions, a large projection screen traversed a wide platform, with no attempt made to disguise or soften its presence. Open steps up to the platform allowed the screen below platform level to be illuminated at certain points. Two Foley sound effects tables attached to swinging metal arms flanked the platform. Occasionally a set of glittering, rouched, theatre curtains were drawn across to provide a backdrop to a production number – as in the finale song. As usual, technicians and technical equipment were openly visible on either side of the stage.

The opening episodes illustrate well the integration of all these. The show begins with a spot-lit Webster as the director of the 'play within the play' Broadway show, standing in front of full theatrical curtains giving a pre-rehearsal pep talk. The curtains sweep back to reveal the other glittering curtains. Heaven Phillips as Dolores, a Marilyn Monroe look-alike in a flared white dress, dashes on and pulls these back to reveal a tableau of five other performers who, accompanied by high energy music, embark on a show-dance routine. As the music grinds to a halt, they all exit. A swirling CG title for Episode One appears, 'Buffalo Bill's Wild West Show directed by Steele Mackaye, Madison Square Garden 1885'. The performers reappear and stand looking up at a picture of Mackaye. Two take up positions at the Foley tables that have swung into view. Footage of Buffalo Bill's show plays – Native Americans riding and dancing, cowboys shooting, and so on, while Webster at a downstage microphone reads a letter by Mackaye outlining his plans to mount the show in Madison Square. Interspersed with the archival clips is video of Webster in the guise of

Buffalo Bill riding towards the camera, doffing his cowboy hat and adopting a heroic equestrian pose. Through this and the following two episodes the VJ improvises, playing it as a sort of scratch video, with the imagery frequently repeating (in particular Webster's heroic ride). Meanwhile, performers use the Foley effects and a few props to support the video material: coconut shells create the sound of horses' hooves; gunshots ring out to synchronise with the video cowboys' shots; mention of sharp-shooters is accompanied by one performer raising and lowering a target, while another takes aim. The witty montage of text, demonstrational action and rapid editing quickly evokes the early Western spectacles – while also drawing attention to the onstage construction of its own spectacle.

Episodes Two and Three, 'Florenz Ziegfeld Jr Runs Away from Home, Chicago, 1883' and 'Loie Fuller Joins the Wild West Show, 1881' follow a similar pattern, as photographic projections support readings of passages which outline their early involvement with Buffalo Bill (Ziegfeld performed as a crack shot and Fuller played a 'prairie waif'). Music, sound effects, the repeating imagery, and the final moments of a train roaring across the prairies, accompanied by a percussive rhythm, contribute to an energetic, compressed picture of the way in which Mackaye, Ziegfeld and Fuller became caught up in the spectacle of the West, described by Cody as 'a grand show going on for the entertainment of the East'. Yet the relatively detached reading and actions of the performers lend an air of distance to the proceedings: this is a demonstration of the rise of these figures and their part in developing a spectacular theatre.

The subsequent Act introduces the 'chorus girl makes good' narrative as Dolores and friend attend an audition. A combination of performance and video ingeniously highlights the way in which a dancer's legs become almost independent objects of spectacle in musicals. Webster and the two girls begin a dance number. While the girls dance upstage of him, Webster sways to the music, holding a square panel in front of his lower body. This serves as a screen for projection of a pair of legs doing a soft-shoe routine – the sort of close-up found in Fred Astaire movies. The comic disjunction between the two halves of this cyborgian figure develops more critically when Webster calls for a new dance. Four other performers provide backing for Dolores and Queenie. Each pair holds a 'dancing legs' contraption – a bar with four legs dangling from it, which the performers kick up in time with their own legs. Meanwhile, the rear screen shows a Busby Berkeley chorus routine: two converging lines of kicking legs, shot from the thigh down. While the Berkeley routine is seductively spectacular, and the interplay of stage action and video is highly comic, it also highlights how the camera is used to fetishise the female leg in musicals, effectively turning the performers into mechanical objects.

The implied critique is developed in the following Episode, 'Busby Berkeley's Hollywood Debut 1930', where Berkeley is shown on film insisting that the low back of a dancer's dress be cut even lower. As he extols the camera's capacity to 'go anywhere' we are shown a zoom shot down through a long line of female legs, followed by a series of classic Berkeley routines in which crane shots from high above the circling female dancers produce his signature geometric patterns: the women become mere architectural components. Spectacular footage of sixty women playing neon-lit violins follows: again, the women effectively disappear, as only the lit violins and bows are picked out in the darkness and shot in kaleidoscopic patterns. Simultaneously, Phillips 'remembers', 'We had violins with neon lights, and we had helmets, hats made out of metal that looked like helmets; so all the time we were doing this we were getting shocks, little shocks.' While the video material seems illustrative for the most part, its juxtaposition with the stage action in these episodes functions in a Piscatorian choric fashion. A feminist critique emerges through montage rather than through explicit textual statement.

Returning to the show's broader development, Episodes Four to Eight focus more on Mackaye's and Fuller's careers, with video providing illustrative material. Fuller is depicted through her letters as very much a woman in control of her own presentation, choreographing her dances, experimenting technically and designing her own lighting.[8] Video combines with live performance to evoke her early performances. As she recounts her triumph in Paris as the Electricity Fairy, the screen is bathed with film of star-like lighting, which then 'melts' down the screen, providing an effect of a waterfall of light for the ensuing Act. A female performer, accompanied by techno-music and a cheering crowd, dances in front of the screen while manipulating large cloths in the shape of butterfly wings. While for most of the show projection is from the rear, front projection here allows the performer to be caught in the waterfall of light, tying her into the projected picture, which echoes a previous still image of Fuller herself.

Subsequent episodes trace the decline in the fortunes of Mackaye, Ziegfeld, Fuller and Berkeley, interspersed with acts from the evolving rehearsal narrative and other dance routines.[9] In one routine Dolores and Queenie stand either side of the stage in white hooped petticoats and carry out simple rhythmic motions with their arms and upper bodies, which are picked up by the cameras; their images are then multiplied in such a way that the projected effect is of dozens of women doing a spectacular Berkeley routine. In another, Brahms 'Bravo' La Fortune, a well known dancer on the New York house-music scene, does a relatively simple solo dance which is filmed from above and turned through computer animation into the sort of kaleidoscopic imagery often projected onto the walls of clubs.[10] In such sequences contemporary technology is shown doing the work of Berkeley's roving cameras and huge drilled choruses.

The production culminates in Dolores finally singing 'Broadway Rose', in a wry mimicry of a show-stopping Broadway finale. Wearing a sparkling gown and white-feathered headdress, Phillips stands before the rouched curtain, flanked by two performers with similar headdresses holding large feather fans to cover seemingly naked bodies. All seems set for a nostalgic climax, but then we notice one of the chorus girls is in fact a man; and when the other comes forward to adjust the microphone stand, she drops her glamorous fan, revealing very unglamorous underwear behind it. As Phillips embarks on the

Figure 22 *XTRAVAGANZA*

song, her voice is amplified, creating the effect of it echoing through a large theatre, and falling stars fill the projection screen. But house music begins to infiltrate over her song, and the chorus, which has been doing desultory swaying movements, is joined by a suited man and a woman in a simple dress, each holding a fan and swaying along. The act thus becomes an ironic rendering of the spectacle it mimics, a fitting conclusion to a production which continually plays off a tension between nostalgic homage and a critical archaeology of the use of technological spectacle.

Weems describes the production as originating in the experience of technology at club events:

> It was obvious that this was a modern day use of the magic of spectacle – with walls of video monitors and really sophisticated sound systems. ... But the sad part of the story of techno is that it became immediately co-opted also, and whatever subversiveness and experimentation there was became a Volkswagen commercial within two weeks of any record coming out. So there were a lot of complicated ideas in play between that whole idea of spectacle, its commodification and its seductiveness, and also the failure of it. (Interview, 2003)

The ambivalence expressed here reflects the productive ambiguity of the production and is typical of the company's overall outlook. Much of the show depends on a sort of double-coding which both exploits the seductiveness of the spectacular tradition it explores and acknowledges its shortcomings. Like much postmodern work, it operates 'inside yet outside, inscribing yet contesting, complicitous yet critical' (Hutcheon, 1989, 158). This also extends to its demonstration of the capacities of contemporary technology. While it plays with the way the NATO software can produce spectacular equivalents of the Ziegfeld and Berkeley chorus-lines with a minimal cast, the production also evokes a sense of loss: for all the energy of the music and appeal of the few live dancers and the magic of their replication on screen, spectators are conscious of the absence of the sort of massed chorus lines which made such productions so visually seductive.

Alladeen

The company's next project *Alladeen* (2003) aroused debate over the extent to which its stunning technological effects may seduce spectators rather than engage them in critical reflection on concerns to do with globalisation and cyborgian existence in the space of technology that are implicit in its subject matter. *Alladeen* was produced in collaboration with the London-based company **moti**roti. Founded by Keith Khan and Ali Zaidi in 1990, **moti**roti regularly works across a range of art-forms, from theatre and film through to large-scale carnival events, installations and music videos.[11] Exploring experiences of the South Asian diaspora in theatre productions such as *Moti Roti, Puttli Chunni* (1991), *Maa* (1995) and *One Night* (1997), they employed film and video alongside live performances that drew on diasporic South Asian cultural forms as well as Bollywood movies and contemporary club culture. The stage production of *Alladeen* is one of three manifestations of the collaboration between the two organisations, with the others being an interactive website (www.alladeen.com) and a music video for MTV Asia. The website describes the project as exploring 'how we all function as "global souls" caught up in circuits of technology, how our voices and images travel from one culture to another, and the ways in which these cultures continually reinterpret each other's signs and stories'.

The expression 'global souls' derives from Pico Iyer's argument that the explosion in international travel and communication in recent decades has created

a kind of migratory tribe, able to see things more clearly than those imprisoned in local concerns can, yet losing their identity often as they fall between the cracks. A Global Soul is a ventriloquist, an impersonator, or an undercover agent: the question that most haunts him is 'Who are you today?' (Iyer, 2000, quoted in the Programme for *Alladeen*)

Weems and dramaturg Norman Frisch initially explored with Khan and Zaidi how they might employ the Aladdin story to explore such issues as this and the ways cultures borrow from and cross-fertilise each other. The transformations in the story as it moved from its original Persian and Indian contexts into Western literature, theatre and film were seen as analogous with the way people function as global souls. A further analogy was drawn between the magic role of the genie of the lamp and the place of technology in contemporary life. This led to the decision to examine the way in which Western banks, airlines and other service industries have begun to outsource call-centre operations to India, and in particular, Bangalore. Nowadays, callers in Britain or America seeking telephone advice more often find themselves speaking to operatives in Bangalore, rather than Bristol or Boston. For the collaborators,

> The fantasies which lie at the heart of the story are instantaneous wish fulfilment, endless wealth, and total personal transformation. In the call centres of Bangalore we found a setting in which such transformations are being constantly and routinely enacted – culturally, socially, and economically – on both ends of the fibre-optic phone lines. (Programme note)

The creative team visited call-centres and interviewed operators. They witnessed operators being trained to sound American or British and studying aspects of American or British popular culture, so that they may chat more casually with customers, and they listened to Western callers seeking assistance. Although they acknowledge the neocolonial nature of the underlying economic and cultural relations involved, they felt ambivalent about the effects of the jobs on the operators' lives. On the one hand, the anti-social hours (synchronising with British and American time-zones) and the demand that they adopt Western identities for work purposes place a constant pressure on operators; on the other hand, being well-paid by local standards, the operators see the jobs as helping them fulfil their material aspirations and providing them with skills which will enable them to advance further – often, in fact, they dream of moving to the US, like the many Indian IT workers recruited by the American computer industry.[12]

The whole matter of outsourcing such operations is rife with contentious political issues to do with economic globalisation and neo-colonialism. The divided reception of the resulting production was perhaps shaped as much by differing political expectations of its subject as by concerns about what was seen by some as a technological excess which undermined its potential political contribution to debates around globalisation and technology.

The production is indeed one of the most technologically demanding and visually complex works studied here; conversely, the story-line and interactions of the performers are relatively simple. While the multiple streams of video and CGI recall the polyscenic approach of Piscator and Svoboda, Khan and Zaidi themselves suggest their design was inspired by the look of Indian television, where 'there were always at least three things going on: the image in the middle, subtitles in two or three languages, and then you maybe had other little bits that gave it another identity' (Wessling, 2002, 34). The other clear, and particularly pertinent, parallel is with the multiple windows of computer screens.

The production consists of three Acts, with the first and third (set in New York and London) effectively book-ending the much longer central Act portraying the operations of a Bangalore call-centre. It opens with a striking use of CGI to locate the scene. On a large, stage-width screen and a further scrim in front of it, like blocks falling into place in a game of Tetris, projected segments of the façade and interior of a Virgin Megastore slide into place to create a virtual setting. The same device later sets the third Act in London. The Megastore stands as an image of homogenised international consumer culture, with only a couple of local signifiers superimposed to differentiate the two cities: a hot-dog stand, fire hydrant and a New York bus-stop; for London, a red post-box, red telephone box, and rain. The virtuality of the images also reinforces the sense of the simulacral nature of such stores as we encounter them in any corner of the world, cloned offspring of global capitalism.

Onto this set walks Tanya Selvaratnam, clutching a coffee and with her head glued to her mobile phone, as she fields four calls in quick succession, an image of contemporary cyborg existence. A model global soul, she is planning trips to Las Vegas (the Aladdin Hotel), Hong Kong and London. She abruptly cuts off an attempt to hire a car, saying she can't understand the operator, and takes another call, switching effortlessly to speaking Mandarin with her flatmate. Then, almost as soon as it has arrived, the virtual setting is whisked from view again; suggesting the rapid pace of life for such figures, the whole scene lasts only four minutes.

The scene switches to Bangalore. Initially, an interview with a supervisor at one of the call-centres is projected onto the screen: recalling Piscator's didactic mode, video is used to expand the spectators' understanding of the world of the play to come. As the supervisor describes how operators are trained to neutralise the impact of their mother tongue on pronunciation, five seated performers slide into view in front of the screen. While they enact a training session, large-scale projection shows footage of just such a session occurring in Bangalore. Lip-synching with the tape, they recite a catechism of American place names, one gives a lecture on American football, and another gives a talk on the television series *Friends*. The class is interspersed with excerpts from videotaped interviews about the need for operators to be 'culturally sensitised', to give the impression they have lived in the US all their lives. One interviewee suggests that after 9/11 many Americans would be unhappy if they knew they were talking to an Indian and tells of operators being asked if they are Muslims.

The relationship of mimicry established between live performers and documentary video here functions to suggest the authenticity of the representation of call-centre life that is to follow. This effect is reinforced by the transition from the training session into the next scene. As the words 'CALL SPAN, BANGALORE, OPERATORS LOADING' appear on the screen, head-shots of a dozen Indian operatives gradually appear; they each give their Indian names and their adopted American names, and then begin greeting callers under their aliases. As this builds a choric effect, the screen is raised half way, revealing the live performers now at computer workstations around the stage. They join in, announcing themselves to callers with their *Friends*-derived aliases, Phoebe, Monica, Joey and Rachel. The overlapping strategy and subsequent occasional insertions of extracts from the video interviews all work to authenticate the picture being presented and perhaps even suggest the production operates in a documentary way. Yet, in fact, the dialogues, phone-calls and evolving relationships of the subsequent scene are a dramatised view of call-centre life, scripted by Martha Baer.

Subsequent action is structured around a series of phone-calls and occasional lulls between them, during which something of the operators' circumstances and aspirations is revealed. The operators deal with

Figure 23   *Alladeen*

requests for travel reservations and assistance with computer problems and route-finding, they attempt to sell medical supplies and insurances, and one even operates as a 'spiritual adviser'. Performers play not only operators, but also their American callers: they step into narrow illuminated booths on either side of the stage to make the calls. The callers' shadowy, almost disembodied, presences suggest the depersonalised, distant nature of service industries communication today. The three South Asian and two white performers play a range of characters, British, American and Asian. Weems and Khan 'wanted to have Indians playing white people and white people playing Indians, that the discussion of the flux of identity should be carried to that level' (Interview, 2003). So, as well as adopting white 'masks' for their operator identities, the South Asian performers play a range of American callers, including one who is clearly African-American. In terms of the vocal performance involved, this is not, in fact, very different from the way in which the South Asian performers, who all live abroad, themselves perform an 'Indian' accent when they play the operators.

Opportunities for linguistic misunderstandings abound as a gallery of characters and situations is created, including a confused elderly woman who can't work her computer and understands 'cookies' literally, a doped-out woman trying to fly home to 'Philly' on Christmas Day because her sister is about to come out of the closet and another who has won a 'gazillion smackeroonies' and wants to go to Vegas.

All this is accompanied by a panoply of visual effects. Minicams on the operators' computers and two cameras on tripods feed live coverage into the production crew's computers, which are on both sides of the stage. They mix this material with pre-recorded video – various film versions of the Aladdin story, airline schedules, route maps, and images of the characters in *Friends*. The resulting mix is projected onto the screen which traverses the upper front of the stage and onto six discs suspended upstage of the performers. Additionally, along the foot of the stage an LED display runs, sometimes showing scene-titles (like hi-tech Brechtian placards), sometimes showing a range of wishes culled from those of the real operators.

Several streams of material appear simultaneously on the upper screen: for example, it may show the logo of an airline, a changing airline arrivals board, images of the *Friends* cast, material from an Aladdin film and a close-up of the face of an onstage operator. Particularly striking is the way head-shots of operators are morphed with images of the *Friends* cast: for example, when Jasmine Simhalan speaks to a customer, her video image mutates between her own face and that of Monica, becoming an image of her cyborgian identity.[13] Occasionally the upper screen is filled with cinemascope-like projection across its whole width. For example, when Selvaratnam is guiding a caller who has become lost in a cave, the screen is filled with diamonds slowly falling. This video is then further layered with an image of Rizwan Mirza riding an undulating magic carpet consisting of printed flight details; onstage we see him in fact slowly swaying on top of a desk, but the DinoVision software enables the technician to mix video of this action with animated images of the flight numbers and so create the magic carpet effect.

Generally, the projected Aladdin films serve to suggest the fantastical, 'magical' nature of these intercontinental proceedings – while, paradoxically, the audience sees the technicians hard at work constructing its fantastic representation and witness the various transformations the performers continually put themselves through. Sometimes clips from the film and animated versions echo something of the ongoing narratives. For example, one operator, Joey, accumulates a large credit card debt (mimicking the world of the callers he deals with every day) and asks his supervisor for an advance, only to be sternly told that this is not possible; above, we see the Magician admonishing Aladdin, while below, the words 'The Magician counsels Aladdin on the acquisition of wealth' flicker across the LED.

This episode exemplifies the occasional insertion of more personal narrative moments within the routines of the call-centre, moments where operators lapse into Tamil or Hindi or more heavily accented English and chat with each other. Some back-stories are built around individual operators: for example, Joey unsuccessfully attempts to make a date with Satya and Satya is shown in conflict with the supervisor over the extent of 'mother tongue' influence on her accent. While some critics have suggested these are 'half-hearted attempts at character development', it is arguable their rare and fleeting appearance reflects the pace and pressure of working in such environments.[14] Weems herself asserts, 'I'm not really interested in dramatic development in terms of the characters. ... It's not so much about the life of the individual people; it's about the life of the call-centre' (Interview, 2003).

That said, even the phone-calls, when the operators are performing their adopted identity, are sometimes revealing. One, in particular, poignantly suggests the contradictions in which such identity play may catch the operators. In this, Phillips plays an operator speaking to an Indian engineer from California's Silicon Valley who is booking a flight to India to attend a wedding. When he comments on 'how long these

Indian weddings go on', she doesn't reveal she is Indian – she's supposedly Phoebe from Phoenix, now living in New York. He speaks of
Silicon Valley as a land of opportunities. When she expresses interest
(and asks if he's travelling alone), he asks why she doesn't just move out
there. When she tentatively asks what if someone was not from New
York, but from India, he cuts her short and says to get back to the flight
reservation. All the while the video close-up on Phillips brings home to
the audience the quandary in which her character finds herself.

Her situation is immediately juxtaposed with divergent conclusions
to the Joey and Satya narratives: Joey's success in sales wins him a trip
to a conference in California, while Satya is sent back for further language training to eradicate her mother tongue traces. At this, the scene
ends, with the five operators gathered around two computers while
the descending screen is filled with their morphing faces.

The final scene begins with a London version of the first scene, with
Selvaratnam on the phone once more, planning to go to a karaoke bar;
this time she switches to Spanish for one call. As the Megastore graph-
ics disappear again, the rising screen reveals an anonymously chic bar,
with its hi-tech feel established by a line-up of flat-screen monitors on
which images of cocktails appear. Mirza sits at the bar working on his
laptop, his Aladdin-like wish to travel fulfilled, while Simhalan and
Selvaratnam dance on dance pads next to the glass booths. During the
subsequent scene projections on the screen above alternate between
captions such as 'BITTER MAGIC Be Careful What You Wish For' in
the graphic style of film-titles, and Bollywood-style images of 'exotic
Eastern princesses' and Aladdin. In turn, Webster, Mirza and Phillips
perform karaoke versions of Donovan's 'Season of the Witch',
Steppenwolf's 'Magic Carpet Ride', and Karen Carpenter's 'Superstar',
while Simhalan performs a disco dance that draws on the angular arm
and leg movements of classical Indian dance. The lyrics have overt connections with the production's concerns. The Donovan song begins
with the lines, 'When I looked out my window / Many sights to see /
And when I looked in my window / So many different people to be.'
And 'Magic Carpet Ride' contains such lyrics as,

> Why don't you tell your dreams to me? Fantasy will set you free.
> Last night I held Aladdin's lamp, so I wished that I could stay.
> Before the thing could answer me well someone took the lamp away.

Moreover, the setting of this as a karaoke bar where people adopt
other people's voices, underscores the themes around ventriloquism

and desire for transformation. The atmosphere of the ending is quietly melancholic: as Selvaratnam makes her final call and the performers drift off, the LED display runs with a series of wishes collected from the Bangalore operators:

> I wish I could click my heels and instantly be transported anywhere in the world – I wish people would wish for the world and not for themselves – I wish to obtain a leadership position in the company of my choice – I wish I could meet my daughter and still be friends with her mother – I wish there was a magic lamp. ...

As this account suggests, *Alladeen* employs electronic imagery in a more complex, continuous way than any other production discussed so far: this is neo-Baroque hypermedia writ large. Although some of Svoboda's Laterna Magika productions included continuous film throughout, film there generally alternated between scenographic, dramatic and rhetorical uses: it set the scene, continued the narrative, or highlighted aspects of a scene through the use of close-ups or POV shots. In *Alladeen*, the range of materials, functions and modes of delivery is far greater, and there is more simultaneously on display at any one time. In this, and in the political thrust of some of the material, some of Piscator's later shows, such as *Hoppla!* and *Rasputin* provide a closer parallel – recall, for example, the simultaneous use of three film sources in the latter. But Piscator did not include such a continuous display of film material that related to the onstage action in such disparate ways, and the available technology gave him a more limited palette.

Many reviews agreed with Mark Swed's assessment of this fusion of live action, video and CGI as 'a glossy multimedia spectacle full of dazzling technology that actually works' (*Los Angeles Times*, 5 March, 2004). Nevertheless, some critics argued that the production's technological flair and the complexity of its references militated against its political potential. It was suggested that the parallels drawn between the operators' and callers' experiences and desires, and between the identity confusions experienced by operators and jet-setting global souls alike, were not grounded in a sufficiently differentiated understanding of the power relations that condition different people's experience of globalisation and technology. Instead of the projections providing a straightforward Piscatorian dialectical elucidation of such differences, the multiplicity of imagery and information seemed overwhelming. Tom Sellar suggested:

> *Alladeen* can't seem to decide whether it's revealing the multiple faces of globalization or evoking an insidious, superficial monoculture. ... the production may

rely too much on the technology of global capitalism to critique its effects in fresh terms. (*Village Voice*, 10–16 December, 2003)

For Harries, spectators risk becoming fascinated by the mass of material:

> For some viewers ... *Alladeen* might occasion a sort of swerving between the poles of Brecht's *Verfremdungseffekt*, described by Lefebvre as 'an externalized judgement', and an immersion in the image proposed. For many others, however, the piece may occasion a hi-tech forgetting, an alienation through fascination and a loss of 'externalized judgement'. (Harries, 2003)

Harries echoes the more general fear, discussed in the Introduction, that spectators of intermedial work, accustomed to the proliferation of reified montage in contemporary media, might fail to move towards a dialectical interpretation when confronted by too much simultaneous material. The risk of this with *Alladeen* was perhaps increased by the design, which almost replicated the appearance of a flat-screen television or computer monitor. Framed by the LED running below the action, the wide screen above, the discs behind and the booths to the sides, the live action appeared to take place on the same plane – with little use of the depth of the stage beyond a couple of metres. The live performance is thus framed – and possibly absorbed – by the digital, rather than being foregrounded in the way that it can be when projection operates more like a backdrop or when video is delivered on a monitor. Just as it is impossible to keep up fully with the pace of the ever-changing material on a CNN screen for any length of time, so, with *Alladeen*, as the performance rushes on, it is difficult to keep so many streams of material in view or to read particular actions or images against each other. The temptation may be to retreat into immersion in the images or to focus on only one or two streams of activity and treat the rest as simply moving wallpaper.

Weems rejects such reservations as underestimating contemporary audiences, arguing that the opportunity to choose what and how to watch is enabling:

> We're gearing this towards a smart audience, who's computer-literate, who's used to taking in several streams of information all at once, and are able to jump between them and synthesise whatever they choose to. ... I think there's a certain amount of anxiety about people not being able to see everything at the one time: there's too much going on. Well, welcome to the world. Again, I don't think that replicating that structure is celebrating it. It's taking it as a given and using it as a tool. What's placed within the structure is the critique. (Interview, 2003)

From this point of view, critics of the show's multiplicity of imagery miss the point, locked into nostalgia for a perspectival representation (or at least a simply dialectical presentation). Weems would argue that such an approach is no longer appropriate for spectators used to negotiating and forming judgements about the range of information, events and impressions that they encounter on a daily basis.

The ubiquity of information technology informs the latest show mounted by the company, *SUPER VISION* (2006), produced in collaboration with the digital animation company dbox. Again, large-scale virtual settings reinforce the exploration of the datasphere in which it suggests we all live now, with the production's punning title reflecting the ambivalence many feel about this development. The production interweaves three stories. In one, a man supports his American Dream suburban lifestyle through a complex web of computer identity fraud that finally catches up with him, but only after he has amassed half a million dollars debt in his son's name. In another, a Ugandan Indian travels in and out of America, confronting a series of customs officers whose computers seem to know everything there is to know about his history – and more, given there are erroneous entries in the system which keep dogging him. In the third, a US-based Sri Lankan keeps in touch with her grandmother in Colombo over the internet and tries to build up a picture of her life through a box of photographs and records she has been sent.

In a distant echo of Burian's interwar experiments, episodes in each of the unfolding stories take place in a narrow performance corridor between a rear projection screen and the front of the stage, where five transparent screens glide to and fro to create different configurations for front projection. The figures are literally caught up in the virtual world created by the projections. As with *Jet Lag*, the digital scenography does not just aim at the sort of illusionist scenery of productions such as *The Woman in White*; it becomes emblematic of the broader thematic concerns. So, for example, for scenes involving the fraudster and his family, a cleverly digitised 'dream home' slides into view on the rear screen, while David Pence and Kyle deCamp perform in front of it. At times, a virtual child appears and interacts with them. The acting style adopted by Pence and deCamp, who are both miked, is slightly distanced, even hollowed out at times, as though their characters are almost as virtual as the projected child. The episodes take on the air of ghosting conventional domestic drama, as husband and wife discuss their family affairs. As the fraudster moves into his den to work on his web dealings, the front screens slide across to show pro-

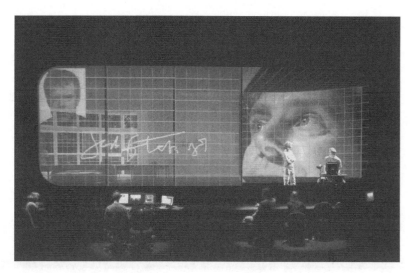

Figure 24   *SUPER VISION*

jections of a huge grid – onto which are then layered further images of Visa cards, computer records, close-ups of his face, and so on.

Similarly, in the customs scenes, the front screens slide fully across, so that Rizwan Mirza is caught between them and the rear screen. On the latter, various grid-like patterns and computer data are projected, while Josef Silovsky's image appears as the customs officer on the front screens. Silovsky himself spends the performance seated at a computer in front of and below the stage, performing for a minicam.[15] Mirza's traveller, therefore, always interacts with a projection of the officer. Interrogating him, Silovsky reads off from the screeds of computerised information about his life that appear on the screen – his travel history, medical records, family and business links. Again, projection assumes a metaphoric function – Silovsky's projected officer is just the inhuman human face of the data stream that shapes his actions and controls the traveller.

The interaction between Angelos as the Sri Lankan grandmother and Tanya Selvaratnam at one level replicates the sort of communication now available over internet video telephony systems such as Skype. While Selvaratnam potters about onstage, moving between computer screen, scanner and mobile (in a reprise of her model cyborg of *Alladeen*), Angelos, filmed at her computer, appears in enlarged projection on the front screens. Old photographs and maps of

Colombo are also projected, as Selvaratnam tries to assemble a picture of her grandmother's younger life. There is a suggestive contrast between the paper-based identity construction here and the computer-based data identities of the other characters. It gradually becomes clear that the grandmother is showing signs of dementia – the phone-calls seem to be partly an attempt to keep her mind and memory active. As the grandmother's mind falls into confusion at times, the image on screen breaks up.

The three tales illustrate diverse responses to the datasphere. The traveller's tale evokes the paranoia that might well be felt in the face of its pervasive presence (the grounds for which are heightened in his case by his Muslim identity in a post-9/11 world); while the fraudster is caught up in the suburban fantasy, he does attempt to subvert the datasphere, to use it against itself, although eventually he flees to the Arctic to escape its clutches; the grandmother's story acknowledges more positive possibilities provided by modern communications, although at the end she appears to suffer a collapse in isolation – her only contact thousands of miles away at the end of a fibre-optic cable, unable to help. As with its previous shows exploring contemporary technology, while the company happily takes full advantage of the possibilities it offers for dazzling presentation, and indeed promotes this aspect on its website, the production itself adopts a more ambiva-lent view: while it shows a political concern at the intrusiveness of ubiquitous data-gathering, it is neither a Luddite call to put the genie back in the bottle nor a simple celebration of interconnectivity.

Reviewing the company's development over the past decade, the intermedial nature of the work has moved from being more concerned with the possibilities it offered for experiment with received texts to employing increasingly sophisticated technology as a means of explor-ing the impact of communications technologies on contemporary senses of identity and ways of being. As such, it is part of a wider trend in experimental work concerned with the place of science in contem-porary society; amongst many potential examples, we might cite per-formers such as Stelarc and Orlan with their concerns with the post-human body, Survival Research Laboratories' interests in robot-ics and artificial intelligence, and the Critical Art Ensemble's explo-rations of information technology, biotechnology and genetic research.[16] Like these, the company has actively engaged with the tech-nologies it is critiquing, rather than imagining it can adopt a stance outside the technological realm, so that the interaction between live performers and the mediated is emblematic of this underlying concern of the work. Inevitably, the seductive visual appeal of the more recent productions has brought charges that its work succumbs to the spectacle it claims to critique. This does not, however, do justice to the double-edged way in which that visual appeal is constituted and implicitly interrogated.

7 Crossing the Celluloid Divide: Forkbeard Fantasy

Once video projection became widely available and the quality of image improved, film came to be employed less in theatre, apart from occasional use for large-scale projected settings, or, at the other end of the scale, for performance art events. One notable exception has been the work of Forkbeard Fantasy, a company that pioneered British work in this field in the 1980s. Founded by brothers Chris and Tim Britton in 1974, the company initially operated along, and blurred, the borders between site-specific performance, experimental film, sculptural installation, and eccentric comedy of a particularly English kind.[1] They acknowledged influences as diverse as the nonsense verse of Edward Lear, Dadaism and Surrealism, *The Goon Show* (a radio show popular in the 1950s and 1960s, famous for its zany comedy), Happenings, and Tadeusz Kantor (in particular, his notion of object-actors). Along with these, the brothers' childhood involvement in their father's amateur filmmaking activities sparked a passion for early cinema, including the work of Méliès and the nature documentaries of Painlevé (whose Surrealist affiliations showed in his focus on the more bizarre aspects of the natural world).

Much of their early work was presented at performance art events or in outdoor locations (often at the alternative fairs and festivals that sprang up in the 1970s). In their first fifteen years they created numerous highly visual performances and events, many of which featured eccentric figures (often deranged scientists or bureaucrats), ingenious sets and mechanical contraptions, such as *The Human Mousewheel* (1982), *The Library SSS-Show* (1983) – with a set comprising three tons of books built into teetering stacks, and *The Brontosaurus Show* (1983), with spoof lectures on Palaeontology delivered from inside a huge brontosaurus skeleton. The shows often included animated figures, motorised marionettes or inflatable dummies, notably a huge inflatable 'Blue Woman' and Tellywoman, a cyborgian figure with a television for a head, which invaded the set in *Myth* (1986).

Alongside such performance work, the Brittons created short 16mm films that were shown after performances, or, in a throwback to the days of early cinema, as part of an alternative music-hall style of event, mixing performances, readings and showings. These often involved pastiches of various genres: natural history films (e.g. *Night of The Gnat*, 1982, a 'documentary' on two intrepid gnat-hunters which would have been at home in *Monty Python's Flying Circus*); horror films (e.g. *The Bonehunter*, 1984, in which a spoof Indiana Jones type searches for angel skeletons and a missing archaeological expedition); and public service education films, as in *Boxmanship* (1988), a hilarious animation about making everything in the world box-shaped, as it would be more convenient and more efficient for business.[2]

The move to actively incorporate interaction between live performers and film was perhaps inevitable. *Ghosts* (1985) was set in a supposedly 'inside-out' house, with the floors radiating outward from four walls in the centre. Through a cobweb-covered 'window' (screen) in one of the walls, spectators could see a (filmed) field that was apparently inside the structure; a ghost hunter was seen running across this field, knocking on the window and then crashing into the 'house' – which meant, of course, out of the central walled structure onto the floorboards. The whole sequence inverted normal logics of architecture and perception. At that time the Brittons also began developing a pair of characters, called the Brittonioni Brothers (Timmy and Chrissy), grotesque caricatures of avant-garde film directors, who supposedly would fly in from their latest appearance at the Cannes Film Festival to present their films. This led to increasing comic interaction with the films.

One of their earliest experiments in merging performance and film more fully was *Who Shot The Cameraman?* (1988).[3] As the Brittonionis, they initially presented several films, including *Boxmanship* and *Rollerblind* (which created a vertical diorama effect, against which Chrissy performed). They then showed a spoof murder mystery about a supposed pioneer of early cinema, Harry Cunliffe, inventor of the 'Cunliphone', a combined camera and projector. Initially, the pastiche of an early silent film rolls along smoothly, with dialogue bubbles, jerky movement by figures with exaggerated moustaches, and a plot to do with a Royal Visit by Queen Victoria. Then, abruptly, a strange figure in a hooded anorak appears in a field and begins running towards the camera and waving – a sudden intrusion from today into the early 20th-century narrative. Bewildered, the Brittonionis debate how this could have occurred; finally Timmy tells Chrissy to climb into the film and eject the intruder. Protesting that this is impossible, Chrissy sticks his head behind the screen; his filmed head pops up on screen (matched up exactly with his onstage body), and he turns it towards Timmy and the audience to express his amazement.[4] Once he has jumped fully into the film, he attempts to expel the interloper, but becomes caught up in a strange horror tale atmosphere and phones Timmy for help. As the filmed Chrissy dials, a telephone rings onstage and they hold a telephone conversation across 'the celluloid divide'. Timmy then enters the film, entrusting the projector to the audience. After discovering the skeleton of Cunliffe's cameraman, clinging onto the only surviving Cunliphone, they crash their way out of the screen and burst into the playing space with the Cunliphone in their hands.

The play between the conventional 'here and now' of the stage and 'there and past' of film was extended in another performance which sometimes followed *Who Shot the Cameraman?*, called *Experiments in Contraprojection*. In this the brothers also chased each other in and out of the film world; again, a glitch occurs, leading to the multiplication of dozens of ever tinier images of them inside the film. At another point both are seen standing 'inside' the film apparently holding up the very screen on which they are projected; as the filmed Timmy cuts up through the screen, Tim Britton (from behind the screen) does indeed cut the real screen in two. This leads to a confounding moment in which the real Britton gradually replaces his filmed image next to the jagged-edged screen that is still showing Chrissy trying to hold it up.

The comic personae adopted by the brothers and the spoof nature of the plots contribute to the sense that this is all just a comic romp in the tradition of Méliès and the theatre of attractions. But it is a very witty, knowing romp, in terms of the pastiche styles adopted. Close attention is paid to the music, camera shots and editing, and, although the work plays with an anarchic surface, there is a precise orchestration of the interaction between stage and screen. Moreover, they play very self-consciously with the way in which such interactions transgress the norms of time and space associated with film and theatre. Where some early examples of film in performance employed transitions between the stage and film worlds, extracting a certain humour from them, but almost taking for granted a shift between the two different media for presenting the story, these early Brittonioni performances mark the

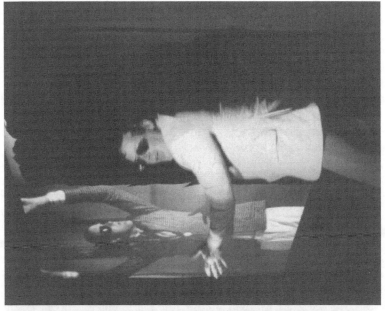

Figure 25 *Experiments in Contraprojection*

fact that the performers are in a sense going back in time to enter the film. Through the various exchanges that surround the transitions, the Brittons draw attention to the fact that the film is a manufactured object, something which has been made in the past. Yet they contravene logic by somehow re-entering the past: the live performance functions almost like a time machine, through which they can go back and alter what is already 'in the can'. (We know, of course, that literally they cannot, but that is part of the fun.) Entering the film to deal with a problem and evolving a new plot out of their incursion moves beyond the sense in earlier work that there is simply a change of media as narrative and performers slip between theatre and film.

The final screen-cutting also exemplifies the way Forkbeard Fantasy continually plays with the materiality of film and the mechanics of its presentation in these and subsequent shows, such as *The Bloopies* (1991), *The Fall of the House of Usherettes* (1996, revived 2005; hereafter referred to as *Usherettes*), *The Barbers of Surreal* (1998), *The Brain* (2000), *Frankenstein* (2001) and *Shooting Shakespeare* (2004). In *Usherettes*, for example, spools of film and film cans litter the set and performers openly handle film-strips and operate the projectors arrayed down the front of the stage. In all the productions the many projectors used are shown on the set. The company notes in the Programme for *Frankenstein* that 'they're noisy and mechanical-looking. We like them to be seen and heard as much as for what they are there to project.' In that show five film projectors and a video projector are used; even where projectors are used for rear projection, the revolving set ends up revealing them.[5] Little attempt is made to absorb or naturalise the presence of screens or other projection surfaces onstage. While occasionally *trompe l'œil* effects are achieved through incorporating a screen as a window, as in *Ghosts* and *The Barbers of Surreal*, generally attention is actively drawn to the projection surfaces through playing with their shape, size, and nature. This, of course, challenges the conventions of normal cinematic viewing, about which David Wills notes,

> The forms of punctuation in use in the cinema are designed to perpetuate the occlusion of the screen, of the cinematic frame. The fade and the dissolve always prevent the screen from being perceived in its blankness. ... the screen functions as a window rather than a solid and obvious fourth wall. (Kuenzli, 1987, 92)

Wills also notes how this window effect, along with the grammar of film, contributes to the illusion of 'the real which supposedly exists behind it' (ibid.) In contrast, Forkbeard productions often show the blank screen and play purposefully with it. In *Usherettes*, for example, the show begins with the performers inflating plastic posts that support a screen. As the opening film draws to a close, the character depicted in it fights his way through the screen onto the stage, crumpling it about him. Subsequently, when film is used to depict long, menace-filled corridors, the screen onto which it is projected is narrowed down, to create the effect of the film itself being a vertical rectangle, thus rotating the conventional horizontal rectangle of the

Figure 26   *The Fall of the House of Usherettes*

cinema screen. Towards the end, in a scene that pays homage to Méliès, film of a character's head is projected onto an inflating weather balloon; as the balloon expands, so does the head, until it reaches monstrous proportions and explodes. Through devices such as these, the company continually draws attention to the spatial dimensions of film and its constructedness.

Such playing about also challenges the way in which the practices of the dominant entertainment industry have effectively naturalised its means of presenting film in cinemas or on television. In the Programme for *Usherettes*, a show created to mark the centenary of cinema, it is noted that after the experiments of cinema's early years, the consolidation of the film industry 'led cinema to settle down and enjoy its comfortable development in auditoriums and picture palaces that have changed little in design in a hundred years'.[6] Recalling alternative cinema of the 1960s and 1970s, the work highlights the way in which commercial cinema, for all that it has sought ever more spectacular special effects within films themselves, has tended to limit the ways in which film is generally presented. At a time when we are increasingly habituated to all sorts of electronic reproduction and manipulation (and the spectacular in cinema), the work also once again reminds us of the 'magic' involved in film – it reminds us of the 'uncanny' experience involved in manufacturing and playing with images of ourselves.

Turning to the ways film functions in the work, it is often used to carry forward the narrative of individual productions (each show does revolve around a coherent, even if bizarre, story). Sometimes films shows characters in other locations (often notionally adjacent spaces), but much of the time it allows a small company of performers to present a wider range of characters. This often leads to dialogue between filmed and onstage performers, with an onstage performer sometimes seen speaking to himself in another guise on film: a large part of the spectatorial pleasure arises from watching a performer going off to 'enter' the film in one guise and then reappearing onstage in another guise to interact with his filmed self. Sometimes film may be used for particular rhetorical effects, such as exaggerated close-ups, or to show 'impossible' events or figures (such as a tiny homunculus in a bird cage in *The Barbers of Surreal*). Always there is close attention to styles and genres evoked, from gothic melodrama and *film noir* through to scientific documentary and children's fantasy. Such genre pastiches are supported by close attention to the effects of various types of shot, from well-done illusionistic realism to deliberately shaky hand-held tracking shots, expressionistic zooms and iris-shots, and self-conscious breaking of conventions around the line of shot. (Although Tim Britton's detailed cartoon-like storyboards for individual productions already indicate the strongly citational ways in which film operates, much of the effect derives from Thorburn's and Jobling's knowing contribution to film and sound.)

Unsurprisingly, as with *Who Shot the Cameraman?*, several productions revolve around plots based on cinema. *Usherettes* brings the three witches from *Macbeth* into a situation lifted from Poe's *The Fall of the House of Usher* (which itself is probably best known through films such as Roger Corman's 1960 version). The 'house' is in fact a derelict cinema, *The Empire*, in the bowels of which is hidden a huge archive of early film, guarded by three decrepit usherettes and their drug-hazed brother Roderick; amongst its treasures is the only surviving example of the fantastic 'liquid film' – through which action was filmed and stored in a liquid that was then sprayed, rather than projected, onto screens. *Frankenstein*, while it brings attention back to the thematic implications of Mary Shelley's original novel and presents a comic version of its inception in the Villa Diodati, makes much play with the various film versions of the story. The inspiration for *Shooting Shakespeare* was the British Film Institute's release of a video containing samples of early Shakespeare films. Forkbeard Fantasy created a comic murder mystery (crossed with *The Tempest* and a 'separated siblings' plot of the kind found in *Twelfth Night*), in which Dame Theatre, under attack from Kid Cinema, loses her voice – before eventually finding it again.

Although film is used extensively, the performances are highly theatrical and depend on the performers' ability to combine the technical precision required to synchronise exactly with various filmed moments with a comedian's seemingly spontaneous, out-front performance style. The Brittons and Jobling have defined performing personae and play off strong physical differences between them. They usually play a couple of characters each, often crossing gender, with the performing style being presentational – the audience is always conscious of the performer behind the boldly drawn comic characters. This is reinforced by costuming: big wigs, patently fake moustaches, and outrageous outfits drawn from the world of pantomime and farce. As in those genres, a strong sense of complicity is built between performers and spectators through open address of the audience and use of asides – overturning the claims of critics who argue that the use of film in theatre necessarily obstructs such performer/audience relationships.

Acknowledgement of the audience is not just found in the performing style itself but is also scripted in metatheatrical ways that contribute further to the self-reflexive nature of the work. Characters show awareness of their presence in a play or film and comment on how a scene or action is being handled. This is especially the case in *Usherettes*.

The Fall of the House of Usherettes

This homage to the gothic opens with a brief prologue scene in which the Brittons and Jobling establish their identities as the outlandish usherettes – in voluminous black Edwardian costumes and high wigs. Spouting a pastiche of 'When shall we three meet again' from *Macbeth*, they concoct a liquid-film mixture in the crypt of *The Empire* cinema (accompanied by appropriate thunder and cinema organ atmospherics). A film appears on the 'liquid screen' that they have inflated. With a combination of model shots and location shooting, done with a shaky hand-held camera, Tim Britton, as Bernard von Earlobe, a 'tomb-robber from the National Archive', is shown approaching the ruins of a cinema through a misty wood. His voiceover draws on Poe's opening:

> During the whole of a dull dark and soundless day in the autumn of the year I had been passing alone through a singularly dreary tract of country when at length, as the shades of evening drew on, I found myself within view of the melancholy façade of the Empire Picture Palace.[7]

Echoing Poe further, he describes the 'sense of unutterable gloom' that pervades his spirit as he looks upon 'the filthy brackish tarn' that surrounds the cinema. As the camera moves from close-ups of his horrified face to shots of the 'glooping oils' of the tarn and the derelict landscape, he comments,

> I lurched from frame to frame as on the half-developed emulsion of some film. I felt as though I was superimposed upon a model landscape, and as each cut increased my mounting tension, so each dissolve heightened the effect of mystery.

Struggling out of the screen onto the set, von Earlobe soliloquises about the smell of celluloid that envelops the place. During a bizarre encounter with one of the Usherettes he is introduced to the history of liquid film, through a cartoon film that crosses the history of early cinema with the sort of family history found in Poe's story. As he goes off searching for Roderick, he resumes his past-tense commentary. The three sisters then gather (with Tim Britton doing a quick costume change to return as one) and debate how to deal with him. Opening the curtains, Nancy (Chris Britton) reveals a (filmed) corridor, into which she steps. A comic sequence of doors opening and shutting, and missed meetings ensues as she searches for Earlobe. Echoes of Cezanne's *Card Players* and films such as *The Fly*, *Doctor Mabuse*, *Don't Look Now* and *The Shining* appear fleetingly. As Earlobe resumes his voice-over commentary, using the past tense once more, the watching Deirdre and Lucy are thunderstruck:

> *Deirdre*:   Oh tis awful! It's Earhole. He useth the first person past tense narrative – to make believe he's in control.
> *Lucy*:   The fiend! But he's only just arrived!
> *Deirdre*:   Yet talks as though he's been and gone.

This self-reflexive guying of the rhetorical tropes of cinema pervades the piece and is combined with a developing sense that the characters themselves (and beyond them, the performers) are caught up in a world of repetition, the filmic analogy of which is the loop. When Earlobe and Roderick plan their escape from the sisters (who keep Roderick in a drugged state to protect their liquid film), Roderick asks,

> Don't you ever get the feeling you've been through all this before? ... That dreadful sinking feeling? When the bottle tips and you know it's all about to start again?

To Earlobe's consternation, Roderick apparently thinks they are in a film and babbles about intending to steal it:

> We're going to edit out all the bits with you and me in them. Then we'll get a clean bottle and all the necessary chemicals and put ourselves in a really positive and uplifting movie, with lots of romantic interest.[8]

This leads to a hugely entertaining piece of theatrical business that is also emblematic of the fusion of life and film in the surreal world of *The Empire*. Roderick and Earlobe spot Deirdre in the (filmed) corridor, blocking their way. Grasping the central set-structure (which contains the screen along with reversible flats, all on a small revolve stage), they begin spinning it around, attempting to eject her from the corridor/film. As they push the set round and round, the audience alternately sees them circling around and the increasingly dizzy Deirdre wobbling about in the onscreen corridor. Eventually, she spills out onto the stage, while Roderick and Earlobe fall into the corridor/film. Subsequently, however, Earlobe becomes caught up in a loop down in the vaults of the cinema. Much hilarity ensues as his filmed figure is shown running towards the audience and trying to break through, only to bump up against an invisible wall (coincident with the screen) and bounce back. Being in a loop, the sequence is, of course, repeated several times (with the onstage Deirdre looping the film through the projector). Earlobe finally escapes only when hair from Deidre's wig falls into the projector, thus breaking the loop and allowing him to escape from the film/vault. When he reappears, he seems to have had a revelation about being caught up in a life of repetition, but says he's determined to escape such a life and 'live the way I choose to live my life'.

Before he can escape – after further mishaps, including the explosion of Roderick's head referred to previously, *The Empire* is rocked by a spectacular explosion. Two four-metres-high articulated statues on either side of the set collapse, limb by limb, to the accompaniment of a symphonic finale. Out of the ashes the sisters emerge to sing a song – about meeting again. The implication is that the performance, like the film, will be played again.[9] At one level this seems a comic riposte to Earlobe's imagining that he can escape repetition. But also, from their work in the performance art field the company is well aware of the sort of debates about repetition which surround discussions of performance, theatre and film. Here, when the cataclysmic finale is being staged in such comically spectacular fashion, the promise of another appearance not only continues the existential comedy initiated by the characters' sense that their lives are caught up in repetition, but also provides a witty comment on the repeatability of live performance.

The Barbers of Surreal

> Many of our shows have been concerned with human vanity constructing its own ultimate come-uppance, man-made creations running wildly out of control, the unknown engulfing the known, tinkerings and tamperings with the natural order of things. (Programme for *Frankenstein*)

Just as *The Empire* comes tumbling down around the usherettes' ears, so in *The Barbers of Surreal* and *Frankenstein* fanciful scientific ventures come to disastrous ends. While both shows abound in pastiche, both employ their surreal comedy ultimately to touch on darker themes to do with science and technology, abuses of the environment, genetic engineering and cloning.

The Barbers of Surreal combines a number of the Brittons' long-standing interests: the prevalence of magic and fantasy in early film and the links between such work and Surrealism; fantastic children's literature, especially Lewis Carroll's Alice stories; and their concerns about science and the natural world. It is rife with allusions, verbal, visual and filmic, to artists and filmmakers such as Dali, Magritte and Buñuel, while also introducing the Gryphon and the White Rabbit from *Alice in Wonderland* – although this two-metres-tall rabbit smokes and speaks in the hard-boiled language of *film noir*.

The plot draws on the extremes to which people go to mould their appearance, pandered to by the cosmetics industry. Its barbershop location derives from the historic association of barbers with medicine and surgery as well as cosmetic experimentation. The central characters are a barbershop trio: bug-eyed, slick-haired Salvador, who dreams of building a 'follicular empire' with his invention of an organic wig and experiments on other bodily prostheses; his brother Flabberjay, who has returned from mixing with poets and artists at the 'Jean Cocteau Institute of Beauty' in Paris to carry out mysterious experiments in genetic engineering – physically, it is he who more resembles Dali, with an elongated moustache on one side of his face and a toupee with a will of its own; and Salvador's son Yacob (subsequently revealed to be his clone), who arrives like some biker of the Apocalypse in full motorcycle gear, only to disrobe and reveal a lilac priestly robe which makes him resemble an extra from an amateur production of *The Magic Flute* – he has been 'up on the Downs' engaging in some sort of cultic practice.

The barbershop looks out onto a village square through a 'window' that is in fact a screen. Throughout the production film reveals the comings and goings in the square: children visit the neighbouring Museum of Childhood, Little Red Riding Hood and an ancient Alice in Wonderland appear, as do a pack of hunting hounds and riders, and several human-size rabbits (which we discover are laboratory animals released from the Institute of Anthropomorphism). Characters visiting the barbershop are shown approaching through the square, and characters exiting the shop reappear in the square: superb timing, along with precise attention to scale and depth of field in filming, makes the transitions between the two worlds baffle attempts to distinguish between the real and the recorded. Apart from a couple of brief spells, when a blind covers the window, the film runs continuously, thus setting a challenge to the performers to maintain the timing necessary to synchronise with the activities in the square. On the upper rear wall of the barbershop there is also a strange 'looking glass' which keeps misting over and into which the barbers peer anxiously at various times; sometimes it appears to mirror them and a chequerboard floor that recalls Tenniel's classic illustration of *Through the Looking Glass*, but at other times it shows, in the style of Magritte's 1937 painting *La Réproduction Interdite* (*Not to be reproduced*), the rear of their heads rather than their faces.

Before the mayhem begins, the show opens with a ten-minute film (projected onto a frontcloth) that makes clever use of tracking shots and suspense to suture the spectator into the production. The film shows a grotesque uniformed warder, accompanied by rising chords and echoing footsteps, lumbering towards the audience down a long corridor – seen from the point of view of a (presumed) inmate looking through a barred door. A comically sinister atmosphere develops as he leads the unseen inmate down eerily lit corridors populated by 'mad scientist' figures bobbing in and out – all shown in a shaky tracking shot from the inmate's POV. Provided with 'a standard issue survival kit' and twenty cigarettes, the inmate is finally freed, accompanied by triumphant choral music and a blaze of white light. As the film resumes, a bus comes along a country lane, pulls up and takes on an unseen passenger. On the side of the bus are scrawled the words, 'Ceci n'est pas un autobus', echoing Magritte's famous painting of a pipe, with the words 'Ceci n'est pas un pipe' – a play on the difference between actuality and representation. As the bus pulls out an old crone is seen in close-up gesticulating at it: her costume recalls Tenniel's illustrations of Alice. The film ends with a shot of a helmeted figure on a motor-scooter riding through a village.

Although the helmeted figure then appears onstage as Yacob, the spectator is left in suspense about the other events in this prologue: that the inmate was a released laboratory rabbit (who is addicted to nicotine) and that the old crone was Alice in search of her lost reflection only becomes clear much later in the show. In the meantime, it all contributes to the creation of an uneasy atmosphere for the opening scene onstage. Here the nature of Salvador's hair experiments is revealed, as is the fact that he and his brother have taken over the defunct Museum of Childhood next door in order to carry out their genetic engineering projects.

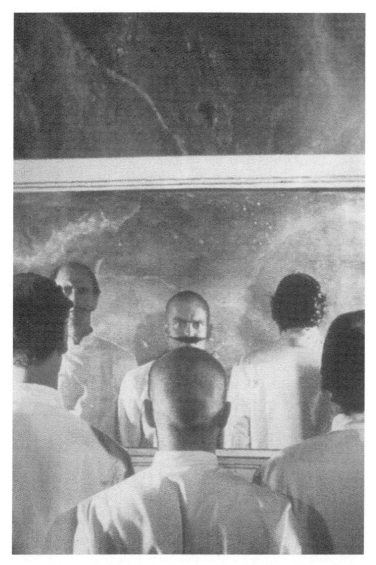

Figure 27   *The Barbers of Surreal*

Through deft doubling acts, aided by the use of film, in the next section of the show Jobling and Chris Britton play both Yacob and Flabberjay and two clients of Salvador. Appropriately named Madame DeRange and Squigglehair, they come to have their bizarre organic hairdos tended. In a sharp satire of the cosmetics industry, Salvador settles DeRange in, saying 'Let us use the creatures of this earth and turn them into fine scents, sweet ointments, powders and shampoos.' He wraps her head in a hot towel 'steeped in exotic scents of Tibetan dung-fly glands and a rare Japanese orchid', before giving her a new implant, 'a tussock from an SSSI (Site of Special Scientific Interest), a wild flower meadow on the route of the new by-pass'.

Play with film during all this allows some highly amusing sleight of hand. For example, Jobling exits as Yacob to carry out business in the square; while Yacob is seen through the window/screen, Jobling returns as DeRange. Then, while he is supposedly in the chair having his wig done, Salvador's business with the towel momentarily masks him, allowing him to be substituted by a dummy so that he can slip out and return to the shop, once as Yacob, and then as 'Mr Jobling', a warder from the lab seen in the opening film. During an exchange with Squigglehair he even asks where Yacob is – wittily drawing audience attention to his own disappearing act. By the time Salvador finishes the hair transplant he reappears once more in the guise of DeRange – with new hairstyle. Soon afterwards, Chris Britton also goes into the square as Squigglehair, only to appear on film and chat through the window with himself as Flabberjay – having reappeared onstage in that guise. This builds up to a comically congested window scene in which the boundaries of the real and the filmed are playfully blurred. In a production that explores genetic engineering and cloning and where strange creatures are being sighted around the town, the performers themselves are seen to multiply and change appearance at the drop of a hat.

As Flabberjay's experiments begin to make the surreal real and the world of the barbers more like Wonderland than they might wish, film plays a key role. When the ancient Alice appears in the courtyard, she approaches the window and peers in; a momentary zoom creates the effect that everything has suddenly grown in size, before the zoom out restores things to normality. A package arrives from Paris and writhes about in Yacob's hands before falling to the floor. Salvador scoops the contents up and pops it into a birdcage on the wall: it appears to be an homunculus. It is, in fact, film of a naked man, rear-projected onto a mini-screen, to create a very disturbing image for the rest of the show – as the tiny creature paces about in his cage like a zoo animal,

Figure 28 *The Barbers of Surreal*

an ongoing comment on treatment of laboratory animals. Then the giant rabbit arrives and lights up; when Salvador grabs his cigarette, everyone stops as if in freeze-frame and the rabbit delivers a (recorded) voice-over commentary on the shop's inhabitants. He is then sent outside to clean the window. As the characters congregate around the window and Yacob protests that he doesn't 'know what's real anymore', a strange-looking black creature (like a giant toucan) suddenly flies across the window/screen, giving rise to a typical self-conscious exchange. Asked what it is, Flabberjay responds, 'Just a little German symbolism, that's all: Max Klinger, 1881, Die Entfuhrung. Big influence on De Chirico actually.'[10]

The bird's appearance is indeed a harbinger of things to come. Rumours spread about rhinoceroses roaming the town (an echo of Ionesco), and Flabberjay reports a catastrophe in his laboratory:

Lost control, fell apart, total chaos, whole bang shoot, gone berserk ... it was the bladder set it off ... Hieronymous Bosch, a Mediaeval bagpipe with a face.

Ghastly thing. Smells. Cornered the Dali, the great masturbator. Called him pretentious. A Miró popped the bladder, with a sharp point. Pandemonium. Cave paintings fighting cartoons.

When a group of townspeople (life-size puppets) come to protest, Salvador claims to be a qualified genetic engineer and berates them for trying to hold back the future, launching into a Gilbert and Sullivan style song and dance vision of scientific progress:

> I can meddle, intermeddle, / interpose and intervene. / We can tinker, tamper ... / we can dehumanise and barbarise, / decivilise, denaturalise, / and jumble up whatever comes our way. / We can distort and warp, / deform, pervert, / corrupt the very principles of life.

Further mayhem ensues, including a huge Gryphon crashing its way about the shop, and Alice reappearing at the window, in search of her lost looking glass. Again, precisely synchronised use of several films contributes to a piece of theatrical 'magic', which is once more framed in a self-reflexive fashion. As Rabbit confronts the Gryphon, the filmed Alice gestures to one of the onstage projectors. Rabbit comments:

> I got up and took a look. It was a 16mm Bauer projector, with a 10mm lens – that's very wide I thought. She made a sign which I interpreted to mean, 'Turn it on'. I did.

While Rabbit goes off to smoke, Alice looks into the room and suddenly leaps. Accompanied by triumphant choral music, her image reappears on the wall below the looking glass. She then leaps up into the looking glass and starts spinning around and around; as she does so, she sheds her years, until she finally ends up as Tenniel's Alice. When Salvador and Flabberjay subsequently reappear, the Gryphon attacks Flabberjay, leading into a climactic finale, in which film projected onto the width of the set shows a bizarre stampede of animals, led by a herd of plastic rhinoceroses and mixing real animals with figures from cartoons and children's stories, such as The Mad Hatter. The performance ends with the barbers being driven out, as the world of Alice's looking glass has taken over and science (and film) have turned surreal fantasy into 'reality'.

Frankenstein

The company's subsequent show *The Brain* revisited earlier concerns with natural history, while again managing to combine a madcap visual

and performative inventiveness, pastiche scientific film, and more serious exploration of scientific investigations of the brain. The ongoing
interest in contemporary science was crossed with more reflexive interests in literary and cinematic history in the following show *Frankenstein*.
Adopting a clever deconstructive approach to the myth of Frankenstein
as it has mutated through hundreds of theatrical and cinematic adaptations, as well as exploring the story's allegorical combination of science
fiction and horror, it became a comic meditation on what we might see
as the Frankensteinian nature of film itself.[11]

The typically convoluted mock-horror plot involves 'David G
Scrivener, the world's leading expert on Frankenstein' visiting a village
near Ingoldstadt in search of the 'Spark of Life' used by Frankenstein
to bring his creature to life. Having discovered it, he is held captive in
a dilapidated inn run by the strange Count Obladee; here he falls into
a time warp, appearing at the Villa Diodati to observe Mary Shelley
conceiving her novel and encountering a reincarnated Frankenstein's
Creature, who confuses him with Frankenstein and demands that he
make him a mate. (The Creature is accompanied by a comic grotesque
Igor, despite the fact that, as Scrivener asserts in a lecture on
Frankenstein films, 'the most extreme travesty is the invention of the
myth of Igor – who categorically never existed'. He appeared for the
first time in Bela Lugosi's 1939 film.) Horrified at first, Scrivener eventually attempts to harness modern biotechnology to produce a female
creature, all the time making a film which he dreams will bring him
worldwide fame. At the film's premiere, as he throws a switch to bring
his fantastical creation to life, an explosion inevitably occurs, destroying his creation and Igor.

The production takes place on a revolving two-tier wooden set,
designed and lit in a way that recalls the distorted sets of James
Whales' 1931 film and Expressionist films such as *Dr Caligari's
Cabinet* which influenced it. The front is initially used for Scrivener's
room at the inn and the reception area below, but locations become
very fluid as the twisted plot unfolds, with the same rooms becoming
the Villa Diodati and Scrivener's laboratories. Revolutions of the set
reveal the supporting framework and rear projectors which supplement the front projectors: a customary acknowledgement of the technology which sustains the work. Projection surfaces vary from a plate
to a full frontcloth that fills the proscenium (a co-production with the
Hammersmith Lyric and the Bristol Old Vic, *Frankenstein* mostly
toured to large proscenium-arch theatres).

Two sets of blinds that pull down in front of the rooms are used
ingeniously in an early example of crossing the celluloid divide that

sets the tone for much of the piece. At the end of an expository scene involving Tim Britton's seedy Scrivener, the latest in his line of bumptious eccentrics, and Chris Britton's sinister Count Obladee (with red wig curled up into two high horns on either side of his head), Scrivener is left alone. Having heard that the local mob is rioting because of the theft of the Spark of Life, and unable to leave the inn, he ponders the gap between his subservient relationship with his boss back in London and his grandiose self-image. He pulls down a blind across the front of his room; initially, his silhouetted figure appears behind it striding up and down, but after he approaches the blind directly a large eye appears projected onto it. This expands into a picture of a shadowy figure flitting through the room and then closes down to a close-up of Scrivener's terrified face. The camera then pulls back to show a life-size Scrivener pacing in the room, imagining a future documentary he might make, 'Frankenstein, the man, the monster, the myth ... a ten-part series ... even a film'. At this point the film shows a hand emerging from the bed and summoning Scrivener. Approaching the bed, Scrivener is swallowed up by it. As the film shows his head struggling to stay above the bed's enveloping force, Scrivener's (real) legs are seen dangling down through the (real) ceiling of the room below and then dropping into it. As the live Scrivener appears in the lower room, Obladee appears in the upper (filmed) room and begins searching it. Downstairs, Scrivener pulls down another blind/screen. While the film on the lower screen shows Scrivener again pacing up and down, Tim Britton delivers a lecture on the Frankenstein myth. Meanwhile, Obladee is sucked down into the bed (on the upper film), to be followed by Scrivener's being swallowed by the bed on the lower film; this leads to a wonderful visual trick, whereby Scrivener's legs are eventually seen falling through the ceiling of the upper room, while his head and torso are still visible in the bed on the lower film. He then appears in the upper room, still droning on about the film he dreams of making. As he perseveres, both films switch to shifting location shots that play comically off his monologue.

Apart from the hilarity it provokes and the way it quickly introduces spectators to the ever-fluid boundaries between live and filmed in the show, the movement to and fro between live performer and screened performer becomes a figure of the cyborgian nature of the story it treats (after all, Frankenstein's creature might be seen as one of the first literary cyborgs). Moreover, the placing of the retractable blinds/screens one on top of the other, the way in which images are duplicated with variation, and the doubling of the 'live' room and its

Figure 29 *Frankenstein*

objects and inhabitants by the filmed room and inhabitants, all bring home the constructedness of film and its projection.

The way in which bodies are split across two screens and Scrivener's imagining a film begins to conjure up a film also take on a certain Frankensteinian aspect. This is brought out more graphically when Scrivener describes the monsters that have been depicted in theatre, film and comic book versions of the story: rapid sequences of various mismatching torsos and lower bodies (mixing human performers, animation, drawing, painting, film images, and so on) roll down the two blinds/screens. Film thus echoes Frankenstein as it brings together the assorted mismatches into ever more monstrous combinations. Doing so, it implies that film itself is a Frankensteinian process: editing, after all, involves gathering and cutting up images of humans and sticking them together in the editing suite to create the 'living' characters we see in action on the screen. This notion is reinforced by Scrivener's subsequent doubling as both a film director and a (misidentified) Frankenstein, whose attempted projects – the creations of a film and of a mate for the Creature, merge. In drawing parallels between the film director and Frankenstein, the production echoes Mary Shelley's own paralleling of her role as the writer of *Frankenstein* with Frankenstein's role as creator of the Creature in her 1831 Preface.

As the production unfolds, interactions between live performers and film become increasingly ingenious, while the way that cinematic monsters play a role in society's dealing with its anxieties about science and technology is developed as a running theme behind the frantic comedy. So, for example, when Scrivener is invited to dinner by the Count, he enters into a filmed dinner party attended by various figures from science fiction. He also encounters Mary Shelley, whose *Frankenstein* is seen as the founding story of the genre. Afterwards, in a voice-over, Scrivener, unseen, pontificates about Mary writing the story, while the live Mary reappears on the upper level and sits in front of a vanity table with a revolving mirror. She soon complains to her 'reflection' about this 'horrid little man droning on and on', and asks if he is inside the mirror with her. Meanwhile, the set revolves, revealing Tim Britton sitting beside the projector that is producing Mary's 'reflection' on the mirror/screen and reading the voice-over. When the revolve returns to Mary's room, she flips the mirror over, revealing on its reverse side film of Scrivener; as she turns it again his image is inverted and, with appropriate fading scream, he tips out of the mirror, to be replaced once more by Mary's reflection. Proceeding to choose her clothes for the evening, she carries on a filmic interior monologue with her reflection, continuing further the scene's comic play with filmmaking conventions.

When Mary goes down to a multimedia burlesque of the Villa Diodati gathering, Tim Britton becomes Percy Shelley's head attached to a foppish half-size puppet figure of him, and Byron is seen as a circular projection of his head on a plate – literalising the notion of the 'portrait shot'. Byron and Shelley are shown as a grotesque double-act pumped up on drugs, booze and Romantic machismo, patronising Mary, and refusing to listen to her story of Frankenstein. This leads into a wonderful *coup de théâtre* to close the first half. Mary goes upstairs to write. As cinematic music swells, the lights fade and leaves begin to fall, to be replaced first by (real) pages of paper blowing about, then, as the frontcloth drops, by filmed pages blown about in the wind – they gradually fall into the shape of a man.[12] With the creation of Frankenstein's Creature thus reclaimed for Mary Shelley, again playing off her own analogies between literary and scientific creation, the following action becomes a compressed figure of her creation's co-option by the film industry. The shadowy shape rises from a prostrate position to produce a huge silhouette, surrounded by a circle of light, as at the end of silent movies. While horror music builds to a climax, the silhouetted figure becomes ever bigger; meanwhile, the frontcloth is pushed from behind, creating the effect of the monster trying to claw his way out of the cloth/screen and reach us in the audience. Such play with the boundary between screen and the live audience recalls, of course, the techniques of early cinema 'trick' films, where often the impact derived from having someone or something hurtling towards the audience, threatening to escape the screen.

In the second half the focus falls less on metatheatrical play with film and more on the live interaction between Scrivener, Igor and the Creature, a stitched-together cyborgian assemblage of body parts and plumbing played with comic pathos by Chris Britton. Albeit in a comic fashion, the monster comes to represent society's rejection of the Other, the demonising of difference, just as he does in Shelley's novel. In contrast with Shelley's Frankenstein, however, Scrivener, under some duress initially, ends up overcoming his initial revulsion and attempts to make the Creature a mate. (Scrivener effectively accepts the role of Frankenstein thrust upon him, even referring to himself as a 'pale student of the unhallowed arts', echoing Shelley's description of Frankenstein.) During his attempt at creation, the whole set is bathed in swirling film of bacteria under microscopes ('these are the new monsters'), followed by distorted images of jars full of glands, muscles, veins and such like. A pastiche scientific documentary film shows a crew following Scrivener around, as he gives orders to a gallery of caricature boffins. The whole section, live and filmed, plays off the ambitions of contemporary biotechnology and genetic engineering to find a way to create life. It draws parallels also between the function of the Spark of Life (electricity) in 19th-century fantasies of creation and discoveries today about the role of electricity at the subatomic level of biology; and, of course, cinematic creatures are equally animated by electricity.

At the end, when the Creature's mate explodes and Igor is killed, the Creature exits through climbing into Scrivener's suitcase. Having decided they had become his only friends, Scrivener tries to follow, but can't. He is forced to accept that they were all just fancies of his imagination, and that he will need to face the real world without them. He declaims defiantly, 'I can do it. I don't need any monsters. There are no monsters.' As he departs, however, there is a typically Forkbeard comic sting in the tail, as another of Penny Saunders' giant inflatables crashes through the back of the set.

While the parting image casts some ambiguity over Scrivener's final assertion, in many ways this reflects a tension found in the portrayal of the Creature in Shelley's original work. On the one hand, his creation by Frankenstein is a figure of scientific over-reaching, as man tries to play god, but on the other hand, once he is brought to life his treatment does become a figure of how society creates 'monsters' out of anyone who appears to be different, as his rejection and persecution leads to isolation and ultimately a violent response. Scrivener's eventual friendship with the Creature and Igor – and his recognition that they are only projections of his own fears and insecurities – reverses the original Frankenstein's rejection of the Creature, but it still reworks Shelley's insights, which had been lost in much of the film tradition. On the other hand, the emergence of a new monstrous apparition becomes a figure of the way science still tries to master nature, even more so in the age of genetic engineering when Frankensteinian hybrid creatures are an actuality, no longer a fantasy.[13]

With shows such as *Frankenstein*, *Shooting Shakespeare*, and the 2005 revival of *The Barbers of Surreal* touring to major theatres, Forkbeard Fantasy has successfully crossed the barriers usually operating between the experimental theatre and performance circuit and mainstream venues. Their brand of grotesque comedy has played a major part in their success, with their Surrealist-inspired outlook having become more viable in a period when everything from mainstream drama series and music videos to television advertisements employs watered-down Surrealist approaches. Nevertheless, insofar as it is possible for work to resist such reification of Surrealist devices, Forkbeard's work has remained true to the radical spirit of its forebears. It manages still to create a degree of displacement amongst spectators that incites them to look afresh at how pictures of reality are constituted and how humankind interacts with the 'natural' world. Their particular approach to fusing live and recorded performance has been an important factor in this: I have sat near blasé teenagers and grey-haired pensioners and witnessed the delight experienced by both as the first crossing of the celluloid divide occurs in a performance. There is a palpable sense of spectators grappling with the uncanniness of what is taking place before them. Examination of the work suggests, however, that while it may continue a theatre of attractions tradition, it also contributes to a critical interrogation of the way film and the film industry function and challenges common assumptions about the relationship between theatrical and cinematic performance and between these and the performance of identity.

There is, of course, a tremendous paradox that lies behind the success of their playing across the celluloid divide. Perhaps more than any other practitioners discussed here, Forkbeard performers are seemingly locked into the machine of the performance by the way they interact with the recorded material. Rarely does film just serve as a setting or carry on a narrative by other means. Continually, the images on the screens are incomplete without the live performer's interaction with them – whether through having his head in the right place in relation to a torso on the film or through engaging in a conversation with an onscreen character. The almost continuous running of the film in *The Barbers of Surreal* illustrates this at its most extreme. The live performers' timing must be precise to the split-second and their blocking and gestures exact – no mean feat when one considers the amount of doubling and quick-change routines that occur and the general anarchic atmosphere that apparently reigns in the shows, along with their use of complicated 'magic box' sets. All this should surely militate against any audience sense of the performance being 'created as we watch'? Surely we should feel that the performers are in danger of becoming cogs in the machine of the performance? Yet paradoxically, although they are caught up in the system of repetition that informs most theatrical production, a fact cheekily acknowledged at the end of

Usherettes, their upfront performing style and open playing with the mechanics of the production, as performers allow the audience to sense the risks they run of it all falling apart, combine to create the sense that the performers are in control of it, rather than it of them.[14] This produces a greater 'liveliness' to the way the performers work their various relationships with each other, the characters they adopt, the films and their audiences, than is often found in theatrical productions that attempt through conventional illusionistic devices to sustain the belief that the action is actually taking place in the here and now of the performance.

8 Quantum Theatre: Station House Opera

Although Station House Opera has been creating an idiosyncratic abstract theatre that draws more on art and architecture than conventional theatre for 26 years, it was not until 1998, with its show *Snakes and Ladders*, that it moved into working with video. Nevertheless, its two subsequent productions *Roadmetal Sweetbread* (1998) and *Mare's Nest* (2001), both of which have been revived frequently, generated a great deal of interest in the way they fused live and videoed action: in both, continuous projected video showed doppelgangers of the live performers existing in a sort of parallel world. They recall Gunning's argument that the true subject of Méliès' films was 'the process of appearance, disappearance, transformation and reappearance', along with Mitry's suggestion that 'the real is nothing other than a form of the fantastic to which we have become accustomed'. Playing with synchronicities and discrepancies between live and videoed action in a way that extends the experiments of Whitman and Blossom, they also seem initially to play with the type of contrast between the Conscious and the Unconscious espoused by R. E. Jones. But they soon move beyond the clear dialogue Jones suggested between a filmic Unconscious and an onstage reality, to suggest something more like a quantum view of several possible worlds co-existing at any one point in time. They have been followed by two works, *Live from Paradise* (2005) and *Play on Earth* (2006), which used video-streaming over the internet to bring together performers working simultaneously in three different venues, again, if less successfully, showing actions in the onscreen and onstage worlds apparently impacting on each other, across continents and time-zones.

The company was founded in 1980 by Julian Maynard Smith and Miranda Payne, who had previously worked with Ting Theatre of

Mistakes. Ting created abstract, task and rule-based work, using what founder Anthony Howell described as 'functional chorography' (Martins and Sohn, 1983, 185). For example, in *Homage to Morandi* (1980) the performers' task was to carry out several different rearrangements of a table, two chairs, a book and two jackets – with the way in which they moved about the space, lifted chairs, changed jackets and so on governed by various rules. During the course of it, 'Items of furniture are not used as "props" but as partners in the work – the manipulators and the manipulated become exchangeable. Performers arrange and are arranged in turn' (Howell, in ibid., 174). The minimal dialogue consisted of brief clichéd phrases that bore little relationship with the task in hand.

Although Maynard Smith and Payne established Station House Opera partly because they wanted to 'do something a bit looser and freer', Ting's 'sculptural way of dealing with bodies in space and time' remained a major influence (Maynard Smith in Kaye, 1996, 194). In a show such as *Ultramundane*, the world was turned upside down, with carpets and furnishings attached to the ceiling, and in *Cuckoo* the space was filled with furniture, some of which was suspended from the ceiling. Performers sawed furniture up, were nailed to it or trapped in it. For *Drunken Madness* five tables were suspended from the Brooklyn Bridge, with diners sitting at them. Waiters on counter-weights moved up and down serving them. Chaos began to reign as the performers threw plates down, fought with each other, stripped and hung upside down from the tables, in a performance that was as comic as it was dangerous. In such shows the environments and objects created constraints with which the performers had to work, as they tried to maintain some equilibrium amidst the disorder that appeared when the environment was disturbed. Although there was generally not a conventional plot and dialogue was minimal, various mini-narratives emerged momentarily from the performers' inter-actions, which often involved repetitive play with slightly distorted versions of everyday behaviours. The performers operated with personae that avoided both the full-blown psychological characterisation of much theatre and the claims to authentic presentation of self found in some performance art. Maynard Smith 'found it productive ... to play with representation, with narrative – in a kind of fractured sense – to deliberately court that, to use those sorts of ambiguities' (ibid., 203).

While the interactions often produced a bizarre comedy, there was also a darker, crueller aspect to the behaviours and conditions depicted, which suggested a metaphoric aspect, to do with the 'disparity between inner and outer states, between thoughts and actions, individual desires and social demands' (Kent, 1998, 135). In early works where characters and sets fly – and usually crash – the flying emerges out of a formal ambition, with Maynard Smith citing Baroque painting, and the way it filled the canvas, as an inspiration:

> We wanted to occupy every part of the theatre – if it was a proscenium, every part of that rectangle, every part of the whole space, equally. ... We've always tried to make theatre out of the physical limitations of the form. So we don't walk off in the wings. We're always physically stuck in the space. (Kaye, 1996, 202)

He suggests the metaphoric aspects:

> All this escaping by flying – all the hanging tables – is precisely using the dual nature of what one might imagine is the ambition to fly. It's like the mental world of fantasy or ambition, and what happens when it come crunch up against the physical reality. (Ibid.)

In similar fashion, the company's eventual recourse to video allows it to play with both expanding the stage picture beyond its conventional limitations (to go 'off in the wings' while staying onstage) and with the potential metaphoric relations between video and the 'mental world of fantasy'.

Works including video such as *Roadmetal Sweetbread* and *Mare's Nest* resemble earlier productions in their play with repetition and ritualised behaviour, their variation of mood and atmosphere, and their apparent oscillation between formal games-playing, a movement towards enacting narratives, and their play with disparities between inner and outer states, desires and realities. Like them, they have taken on different configurations as they have been remounted in various venues.

Roadmetal Sweetbread was first presented in 1998, and in 2006 it was still appearing around the world, with a different cast. Maynard Smith explains the puzzling title as suggesting a world in which things are not what they seem: 'Both words ... sound like something they are not. Sweetbread isn't sweet and it isn't bread, it's brains or organs of animals and road metal is Tarmac, it isn't metal at all' (Jones, 2001). The performances are effectively site-specific, since much depends on *trompe l'œil* play with the relationship of video to site; hence, although the basic pattern of movement and games-playing remains similar, performance and video must be made anew for each site. The following account draws on the company's video of a performance at

London's Hoxton Hall, a small Victorian music-hall theatre, although I first viewed the show in a very different setting, a wood-panelled Victorian parish hall in Glasgow, where, to my mind, the video doubling of the location was more effective. The performance consists of an almost ritualised, wordless, series of interactions between a man and a woman, in which the fantasies, desires and hostilities that lie behind the façade of relationships emerge through the interplay between live and videoed action; it plays a lot with games of appearance and disappearance, which function at one level as simple pieces of theatrical 'magic', but also resemble some Freudian game of *fort/da*, through which the loss and recovery of a loved one is symbolically explored.

After a brief initial video image of a man and woman standing side by side, looking blankly out, the performance opens with the familiar trope of video showing a performer arriving and looking for the performing space. It shows Maynard Smith walking through the corridors of the venue and entering the auditorium at the rear. In Hoxton the projection was onto the wall above a narrow platform to the rear of the raised stage, above which there was also a gallery walkway. This meant that the projected material was generally above the performers (except when they performed on the platform). In Glasgow the projection filled a rear wall on the same level as the performers, so that when the video subsequently consisted mostly of action performed in the room, there was a deceptive, almost hallucinatory, layering of the video image of the room against the real space itself: videoed door lay over real door, videoed skirting over real skirting and live performers stood alongside video doubles, eliding usual distinctions between the real space in which theatrical performance takes place and the fictional space represented therein.

The opening sequence establishes a pattern for the games played between live action and the videoed. Having entered the auditorium, tracked by the video, Maynard Smith, a gaunt, lugubrious-looking figure in an overcoat, moves slowly about examining a table and chair and taking in the scene. The video projection shows the same actions – the synchronisation between live movements and videoed is such that a spectator might initially suspect it is live relay, but small discrepancies soon reveal it as pre-recorded. Susannah Hart enters the space through an upper door in the rear wall, steps down off the raised platform, and walks briskly past him, down off the stage and out of the theatre. The sequence is then repeated on video, then live, and so on, four times; Maynard Smith stands watching. Both perform in a quite impassive manner, reinforced by the soundtrack of a slowly ticking metronome. As often occurs in the company's productions, a pattern is established so it can then be disrupted. During the fourth video crossing of the stage both the live Maynard Smith and his video double stick a leg out and Hart stumbles over it onscreen. Recovering her balance, she carries on walking out. A laugh runs around the audience at the sight-gag involved; another live pass occurs, followed by another video pass – with a trip again raising a laugh. The laugh is killed next time round, however, when the actions are enacted live and Hart falls down more heavily, tumbling off the stage. She picks herself up and exits. Maynard Smith sits down at the table. When Hart reappears on video, stops and looks down at him, he and his video double both fall down behind the table – as though withering under her look. She goes up to the table, looks at it and exits.

The sequence gives a foretaste of subsequent patterns and issues:

- Boundaries between live action and videoed action begin to blur, as the live performer 'does' things to the videoed and vice-versa. There are parallels with Forkbeard Fantasy's crossing the celluloid divide – but in a more stylised context, and with the videoed action and performers doubling (with variation) onstage action and performers. There is a matter of fact quality to the appearances in and out of video and to the play with aspects such as the videoed performer looking down at the live performer. Nevertheless, there is occasionally a certain deadpan humour to the way it is employed – as in the tripping sequence.

- As action is played and replayed with variation, live and onscreen, the variations and discrepancies create a tension between the live and the videoed, in which neither has priority over the other. Although Hart initially moves into the space live, and this is echoed by the following video sequence, the tripping sequence first appears on video – perhaps suggesting that Maynard Smith's subsequent live action copies the video. Initially, spectators may be tempted to employ such temporal and causal logics; but as the performance evolves notions of original and copy or of real and imagined rapidly dissolve, as do distinctions between the past of recorded and present of live action.

- Discussing his work more generally, Maynard Smith has remarked, 'Existence carries on. ... There are no resolutions, there's no catharsis. The problems always return, the misery seeps back in. What else is life, but nice sunsets and bits in between?' (Kent, 1998, 134). It is not surprising, then, to find an almost Beckettian tragi-comic play with physical routines in the production, with the repetition with variation also recalling Beckett's work. Here we might note how the initial trip brought laughter, the second brought it again, but a bit less this time, and the third, 'real' trip met with silence: suddenly an 'act' seems to turn into something 'real'. A similar pattern operates subsequently, as performers treat each other quite violently.

- The video marks the fact that this is, after all, a performance. The frequent moving in and out of the theatrical frame, as Hart leaves and re-enters the room, along with the way in which the video seems to track her and Maynard Smith when they leave the stage – showing the localised offstage environment of the theatre – combines with the metronome and the relatively mechanical nature of the performing to forestall the temptation to establish conventional character-based identification with the performers. This steers the spectator towards a more detached viewing, as though watching a demonstration, even while the picture of relationships that emerges is bleak.

The play of appearance and disappearance and how it slips between game and metaphor may be illustrated through two scenes. In the first Hart holds a stage-flat next to her on the upper platform. She then slides it in front, revealing a video image of herself holding the flat. Maynard Smith watches impassively again from the lower platform. As she varies between sliding the flat across and sometimes slipping herself across behind it and emerging on the other side, a rhythm builds up and the whole action takes on a hallucinatory quality, and we lose track of which is the real, which the videoed Hart. At one level this operates as a simple 'turn', but at another it does, through repetition, push towards potential metaphoric interpretations about absent and present selves, the real or projected self. A similar sequence occurs later, when the performers exit through a concealed door in the wall: there follows a long sequence of reappearances and disappearances which vary between the live and the videoed. It becomes a *tour de force* of synchronisation between live performers and video as they or their videoed selves pass through the door (or the videoed door), looking for, but always missing, each other – until eventually there is a struggle in which Hart's video double appears to push against the real door which is being opened by the real Maynard Smith. What starts as a comic play with apparitions gradually becomes a savage game, an image of chasing phantoms of each other.

The action oscillates between such routines and something more like a Pinteresque exploration of psychosexual games. (It recalls especially Pinter's 1963 play *The Lover*, in which a married couple spice up their relationship through playing at being each other's fantasy lover.) At one point while they sit opposite each other, Hart's video persona fetches a hammer and smashes Maynard Smith over the head; as his video double ducks the blow and falls to the floor, Maynard Smith echoes the move onstage. On the floor, he begins kissing and caressing Hart's foot, until she kicks him away; while he crawls around to lay his head in her lap, his video double carries on caressing her foot, before then echoing the onstage action. Soon the onstage Hart slides under the table. Although the video shows Maynard Smith kissing her and beginning to make love to her, the onstage Maynard Smith wanders offstage. Returning soon, he discovers Hart rhythmically moving her body under the table as if she were making love. Subsequently, she kneels next to the table, while he watches. As a soundtrack of him howling plays, the video shows her in the same kneeling position, while a naked man approaches and begins caressing her. He then places a collar on her neck and leads her off by a leash – with the onstage Hart echoing her video movements. She then returns to the stage and punches Maynard Smith in the stomach. As he exits, the video shows him making his way along to a cafeteria and picking up two plates of food. On his return, they begin feeding each other with a spoon – sometimes live, sometimes on video. This ends abruptly as Hart slaps Maynard Smith on video, while onstage he slaps her. The slaps are then returned – with slapper and slapped again inverted on video. Onstage, Maynard Smith retaliates by picking up a chair and throwing it off the platform into the lower area, while on video he picks Hart up and throws her down. In turn, Hart drags Maynard Smith down to the lower level, while on video she drags the table down. (In each instance the actual movement sequences very closely resemble each other, it is just the object or person being dropped that is different.)

This sequence is followed by a further complex interplay of live action and video involving Maynard Smith seemingly having a meal with another woman (recognisably Hart in a different dress, sunglasses and scarf). When the couple depart on video, onstage Hart 'follows' them out through the real rear door – leading to the second appearance and disappearance scene already referred to. After they re-emerge onstage, Maynard Smith prepares a cup of tea. Hart, however, fetches a hammer and smashes the cups and saucers; Maynard Smith carries on indifferently eating toast. The scene eventually culminates in Hart's onscreen double smashing Maynard Smith's skull with a concrete slab and scattering the stage with clothes; when the onstage Maynard Smith walks off, Hart arranges the stage picture to match up with the onscreen picture of the 'murder scene'.

Figure 30   *Roadmetal Sweetbread*

Towards the end, the two reappear on the upper gallery above the projection area. An attempted rapprochement is played out, with the video again echoing, but in inverted fashion, the live behaviour. While on video Hart moves towards Maynard Smith, her exactly echoing move on the walkway takes her away from him – and vice-versa as the action repeats. While initially this discrepancy creates a comic effect, it leads eventually to a final video image of them standing next to each other – echoing the opening image of the show, while up in the gallery they are standing well apart, staring into the abyss below.

While at first sight, this may appear simply to suggest a distinction between a 'real' separation, and an aspired to togetherness, the continual ambiguity about what is 'real' action and what is imagined, desired or remembered, and the way they seem to interact with and influence each other, casts doubt over attempts to find such a neat resolution. Instead, the production seems to imply the co-existence of several possible worlds or relationships at any one moment, with there being no grounds for privileging supposed 'real world' events or behaviours over supposedly imagined, desired or remembered events or behaviours – or vice-versa. All feed into the flux of the relationship and how it is prosecuted and experienced, and what is apparently visible at any one moment is exactly that – *apparently* visible; what may not be visible is no less 'real' or significant. The refusal to separate the portrayed action into two realms, 'real' onstage and 'imaginary' onscreen, seems indeed to signify an attempt to overthrow such polarities and to embody a quantum approach to psychology – in contrast with the simplified Freudian model that lies behind R. E. Jones' model for how live action and film might portray the Conscious and Unconscious.

The production's setting, with its overlaying of the site with video of itself, also might be seen as embodying the notion of 'hypersurface' explored by Stephen Perrella and others in the context of how architecture reflects and contributes to the contemporary experience of mediatisation and the implications of this for disturbing conventional dichotomies between form and image, real and virtual, conscious and unconscious. For Perrella, 'hypersurface considers ways in which the realm of representation (read images) and the realm of instrumentality (read forms) are respectively becoming deconstructed. ... Hypersurfaces are an interweaving and subsequent unlocking of culturally-instituted dualities' (1998, 7). Drawing analogies with the way the surface of contemporary buildings is so often a site of signs as well as form, and noting how this has been incorporated into designs which confuse conventional inside/outside binaries (as with the Centre Pompidou in Paris, with its escalators and large video screen on the outside of its glass walls), Perrella suggests:

> Prior to experiences with the contemporary built environment, one is already affected by the media complex. This techno-existential condition situates us in an inescapable relation to media. ... Activity in the contemporary milieu triggers associations that resonate within a partially constructed subject. The co-presence of embodied experience superposed upon mediated subjectivity is a hypersur face. The manifestation of this construct in the built environment is a reflection of this. ... Hypersurfaces appear in architecture where the co-presence of both material and image upon an architectural surface/membrane/substrate is such that neither the materiality nor the image dominates the problematic. Such a construct resonates and destabilises meaning and apprehension, swerving perception transversally into flows and trajectories. (Ibid., 14)[1]

For Perrella, such hypersurfaces reflect the way in which 'Categories of the Real and the Unreal ... are insufficient today because each is infused within the other' (ibid., 8). Applying this to Station House Opera's work, one might see a similar permeability or blurring of the boundaries between the supposed real and the supposed virtual, not just in the setting, but in the interactions and identities of the figures who play within it.

In many ways, *Mare's Nest* continued in a similar vein, but a doubling of the size of cast brought more potential complications – in keeping with the title, a phrase generally applied to a complicated or confused situation. It makes ingenious use of the combinations and permutations of interactions between two male and two female performers and their life-sized video-projected doubles, again ambiguously evoking the aspirations, fantasies and fears that characterise a spiralling series of ritualised encounters between them, encounters that extend from the banal to the erotic, from the gentle to the violent.

The complications are compounded by a setting which again plays with the notion of hypersurfaces. Performances are staged in venues which allow spectators to move about the central set element. This is a large (c.5m x 3m) double-sided partition/screen placed along the middle of a narrow platform stage – effectively creating a small stage on either side of it, in addition to the ground-level playing space on either side, where performers and audience move about on the same level. Different non-stop video tracks are projected on each side of the screen. The videos sometimes contain footage of the localised offstage space – they show, for example, performers arriving at the theatre, exiting to pursue a quarrel outside, or moving about in an upper gallery space. Sometimes they function as a sort of window into a featureless room, in which the performers are seen carrying out various actions with each other or with a bizarre group of naked figures with elaborate white-feathered masks engaging in some kind of Baroque Bacchanal. Often, the videos duplicate the performing space itself, either doubling the live action taking place in front of the screen or showing a variant version, or showing an apparent close-up (as with *Roadmetal Sweetbread*, it is, in fact, all pre-recorded).

Performers go to and fro between the two sides, sometimes moving around the screen, sometimes passing through a door in it. A performer going through the door might be seen 'entering' the screen action on one side, while s/he simultaneously emerges on the other side to take part in live action (where, again, his/her behaviour occurs against a backdrop of recorded action) – an amplified embodiment of the Player's reference to 'every exit being an entrance somewhere else' in Stoppard's *Rosencrantz and Guildenstern are Dead* (1967, 20). The screen functions as both form and image, a liminal place of transition between both physical playing spaces and virtual playing spaces, with the performers functioning simultaneously as material and immaterial beings, an interweaving that confounds attempts to distinguish between real and unreal. With the audience free to move about watching action and video on either side, some stay for the most part on one side or the other, others move backwards and forward trying to catch the different phases of action. The consequence is that very few spectators see the same events, and no spectator can see the whole show in any one viewing. Any post-performance discussion of the supposed actions and relationships, and indeed any documentation, is conditioned even more than usually by the spectator's choices of what to attend to.[2]

Action once again is accompanied by a metronomic ticking, although occasionally music is heard. Again, with two brief exceptions, there is no dialogue, and the action is based around repeated series of actions and interactions that are more or less abstracted versions of everyday actions. Sometimes these may be relatively mechanical action sequences which seem to contribute little to any sort of narrative. Early in the show, for example, Mem Morrison begins an exhausting routine in which he continually rushes around from one side of the space to the other, picks up various objects (including a ladder), and rushes through to the other side to deposit the object, before rushing back around again to pick up another object. As he varies between running around the side of the screen and through the door, with his actions always synchronising exactly with video of him doing the same thing, it becomes mesmerising to watch. At other times action is more mundane, and the synchronisation is accompanied by variation. So, for example, at various times performers carefully set a table and serve drinks. Such action may be carried out fairly neutrally at times, at other times the manner of doing it seems more laden with meaning. Thus, at one point, while Maynard Smith and Hart are shown on video having a drink, live in front of the screen Maynard Smith goes through the same scene with Morrison; meanwhile, on the reverse of the screen, video shows Morrison and Katye Coe drinking, while in front Coe plays the scene live with Hart. In a similar way, at one point, Morrison tugs at Coe's arm, while Coe resists, her other arm outstretched; meanwhile, behind them video shows Hart pulling the outstretched arm. The echo with variation has a darker side in moments such as when Maynard Smith holds an ash tray out for the seated Hart to drop her cigarette ash, while the video shows Maynard Smith lying on the ground and Hart dropping ash into his open mouth. In this and other scenes, the sado-masochistic undertones of the Maynard Smith / Hart pairing found in *Roadmetal Sweetbread* seem to recur. Elsewhere, a sort of sexual rivalry seems to be played out between the women. While various aggressive behaviours are portrayed sometimes, at other times there are moments of reconciliation, with video and live playing out of variant versions: in one instance, the video shows Coe approaching Maynard Smith, trying to make things up with him, while in the performance space the same actions are played out by Maynard Smith towards her.

According to *The Oxford English Dictionary*, the origins of the title phrase lie in earlier use to denote a deluded belief in something which is in fact illusory. We might see this as applying both to the way in which the various figures in the performance see or interact with each other and to any spectator who imagines that s/he has some grip on 'what's really happening'. As with *Roadmetal Sweetbread*, the spectator's desire to come to a unified understanding of the actions is both teased and frustrated. It may be tempting at first to read the screen action as a sort of sub-text to the live, revealing the unconscious of the performers, or to read certain behaviours in a fixed way: for example, one might easily read the tug of war sequence over Coe as representing her being torn between past and present relationships, or between a male friend and a female friend. But the multiplicity and apparent incompossibility of the actions and the impossibility of attaining any

Figure 31 *Mare's Nest*

complete sense of them forestall initial spectatorial attempts to fix particular readings or to decide what are 'real' characters or relationships, or even what might seem to be fantasy as opposed to likely real behaviour. Instead, the fusion of video and live action allows several 'presents' to co-exist, encouraging the sense that at any one time characters and relationships might operate simultaneously in multiple and contrasting ways, without any grounds provided for disentangling the motives and emotions which underlie them. While the behaviour patterns exhibited may suggest something of the psychopathology of everyday relationships, the form of their presentation also draws attention to the partiality and virtuality of our constructions of reality in daily life.

In *Live From Paradise* and *Play on Earth* casts of three in three different venues were linked by video streamed over the internet – for the former, the venues were first in Amsterdam, and subsequently in Britain, for the latter they were in Newcastle, São Paulo and Singapore. In each instance performers played in one space, while their action was videoed and shown on screens in the other venues; for *Play on Earth* three screens (each approximately two metres squared) were suspended next to each other above the playing space, so that spectators in São Paulo, say, could watch their own performers as well as simultaneous webcast of that and the performances taking place in Newcastle and Singapore.

The scenarios involving two male and one female performer in each venue depicted a melodramatic love-triangle; each set of performers (wearing similarly colour-coded, but different, outfits) carried out the action in their own way, but there were occasional moments of congruence between the actions in the different venues, as well as occasional overlaps of dialogue. (There was more speech than in productions previously considered – in Portuguese, Cantonese and English.) For example, when the two men in Singapore fell into fighting with each other, as they shoved each other to the side and off-screen, an image of two men in Newcastle 'fell' into the screen, pushing and shoving. At another point, the woman in Singapore walked around one of the men, trussing him up with a rope; as this was shown onscreen, one could see the Brazilian woman similarly walking around with a rope (but without the man visible). Eventually, the trussed and gagged man was thrown to the floor, and simultaneously in Brazil a trussed-up man was dragged in and shown onscreen. Occasionally, items were 'passed' from one screen to another, and towards the end a very long table covered in red cloth was constructed onscreen by coordinating filming of a table in each venue. At this point, there was a rare sustained playing with coordinated simultaneous action between all three venues, as a man and woman in each venue carried out similar actions, such as one bringing flowers to the other, caressing one another, dancing and so on. In the venue itself, spectators saw two of their own performers live, but also saw how their action became part of a larger group action as the images on the three screens were matched up.

The approach to performance and the use of screens was a further development from the company's previous projects, but it also recalls earlier (and perhaps more successful) experiments in 'telematic performance', such as Paul Sermon's *Telematic Dreaming* (1992). In this durational performance over several days a performer lay on a bed in one room while video of this was projected onto another bed in another room. With the beds functioning as hypersurfaces, combining form and image, spectators could become participants as they could sit on the second bed and interact with the videoed performer, who in turn was receiving video streaming of the spectator's actions and responded to them. Variously intimate and threatening encounters which confounded distinctions between real and virtual ensued. Susan Kozel (1994) has written powerfully about her experience of being the performer in an Amsterdam version of the piece, exploring, among other things, the challenges it posed to her sensation of space and her own body, issues it raised about relations between the real and the virtual, and the ethical issues posed by the virtual intimacy it created between strangers.[3]

In some ways, the concept was perhaps more intriguing than the execution in the case of Station House Opera's attempts to create such telematic performance on a larger scale. Technical difficulties led to drop-outs and time-lags which impeded the degree of synchronicity between live and videoed action that was characteristic of *Roadmetal Sweetbread* and *Mare's Nest*. In *Play on Earth*, for all that there were parallelisms in the scenarios enacted, the links made between the different performances rarely enhanced the viewing of the individual local performances, and indeed often the demands made by attempts to link them to the others disrupted the rhythm of these, as one Singaporean commentator noted:

> For the most part ... the actors marched around robotically trying to get in front of the right camera at the right time, and then buggered off outside for a while, leaving us with an empty stage. ... This wouldn't have mattered so much if we were left watching meaningful or interesting stuff on the video screens, but all too often what we saw there was disparate (random juxtapositions of interior and exterior views) or banal (the Green Voyeur in close-up watching the other screens). (Lyon, 2006)

While creating a confusion of the material and the immaterial across continents and time-zones may have seemed attractive conceptually as an image of global mediatisation, along with the opportunity to multiply exponentially the sort of interactions seen in earlier work, it required much smoother delivery in practice to effectively produce the confounding experience associated with the earlier shows or with other telematic works such as Sermon's. The placement of the screens above the performers, along with the disparate material that appeared on them at times, prevented the sort of slippage through a hypersurface that characterised the earlier work, leaving those conjunctions of live and video activity that were successfully achieved to appear simply as constructed tricks.

This is not a question simply of botched illusionism or a failed attempt to achieve suspension of disbelief. With the earlier productions, it was not a case of suspending disbelief and believing that the performers and the videoed figures were really operating in the same realm. It was more that the spectator's sensory experience was of the worlds fusing, leading to a tension between an awareness of the mechanics of what was occurring and the sensory experience of it. The abstraction of the routines, along with their repetition with variation and the precision of their performance, also contributed to the spectator's sense of disorientation. Coming out of them, one needed to decompress, to reorient oneself to the material space one was re-entering. In the case of *Play on Earth* this sort of disorientation was rarely achieved, and in the absence of the sort of hypersurface relationship between videoed and live found in earlier work, the spectator was left to contemplate the relative flimsiness of the scenario and routines; it became like watching three rather awkward pastiches of television soaps shown on poor quality televisions. Although there was an attempt to herald these shows as the beginnings of a new sort of international performance, it might be argued that they showed up the potential pitfalls of such work rather than a way forward.

Here an informative contrast might be made with some recent work by a young company called *mouth to mouth*. Describing itself as a dispersed performance collective, it comprises performers, dancers, musicians, a sound designer and a videomaker who came together as postgraduate performance students in 2004. Having collaborated on a couple of projects and sharing a vision of how they wished to develop site-specific theatre, they came up against a problem: their members were from Italy, Korea, Bosnia, China, Switzerland and Britain, and once their student visas expired the non-Britons had to disperse to their various countries. Determined to carry on working together, they use a combination of mail, Skype, blogging, and MySpace to exchange developing ideas and images for performances. With Kate Craddock and Lynnette Moran as co-directors based in Newcastle and London, they have devised some short performances in a number of British cities and in Canada.

As part of an ongoing project begun in 2006 called No Fixed Abode they drew on material related to a site on London's Isle of Dogs; the performers in the other countries responded to the material and investigated potential parallel sites in their own countries which had similar resonances and atmospheres. Songs, stories and movement were developed and scratch performances presented, with live performers in Britain linking up via Skype with the other performers around the globe. During a performance at the Whitechapel Gallery, they performed as a virtual band, with a cellist, violinist, dancer and singer in different countries performing together. They also invited the audience to join in the song, continuing a process whereby the absent, videoed performers engaged directly with the gallery audience at times. Actions and objects seemed to pass from one site to another. Live web streaming of performers in their own domestic surroundings in

Beijing, Basel or Seoul was streamed in, inviting the audience into the bedrooms, kitchens and living rooms of the videoed performers. Projections sometimes depicted part of the virtual performer, rather than revealing them fully, playing with the webcam's ambiguous role in contemporary internet activity. Images of the internet performers were projected onto various surfaces including the bodies of the live performer, screens, walls and boxes. When performers encountered problems with the technology, it was they who tackled them and discussed them openly with the audience, so that any glitches became a figure of the fragility of the technical apparatuses which support their staying connected.

While this all has obvious similarities with previous telematic performance, and it does play around with notions of presence and absence and live/virtual interactions, here the global nature of the performance is driven by a desire to explore and overcome geo-political boundaries – bypassing the passport controls and regulations which keep these performers separate. The conjunction of live and mediated performers, of the real with the virtual, both signals the separation that political structures impose and marks a way of challenging such separation and creating a positive virtual communion, with the use of everyday connections such as Skype being emblematic of the role such technology plays in their remaining connected as a group.

9 Electric Campfires: Robert Lepage

Since first attracting international attention with *The Dragons' Trilogy* (1985) and his solo show *Vinci* (1986, both with Théâtre Repère), Canadian theatremaker Robert Lepage has become a controversial figure in contemporary theatre, arousing vociferous support and vitriolic criticism in equal measure, hailed as a theatrical magician or condemned as a gadget-obsessed purveyor of empty spectacle. Like Svoboda, Lepage has restlessly experimented with a range of technologies, including kinetic scenery, lighting, and various types of projection, to create productions that, even when they do not use video extensively, frequently have a cinematic feel to them. Sometimes accused of imprisoning himself in technology, he argues that 'it is a tool that allows me to explore things' (Ouzounian, 1997). Lepage's handling of video is eclectic; unlike some companies previously considered, it would be difficult to identify a particular developing avenue of experiment, and individual examples of how he manipulates video are not in themselves particularly innovative. Nevertheless, the overall structure and look of his productions have led to him being identified as a leading proponent of a video/theatre hybrid.

The strong differences in critical opinion have partly been in response to his experimental approach to production. Lepage develops productions over many months, and early showings of 'works in progress' have sometimes seemed scrappy. The early three-hour version of *The Seven Streams of the River Ota* in 1994, for example, was described by one of the performers/devisers, Marie Brassard, as 'a catastrophe' (O'Mahony, 2001), but its final seven-hour version was widely celebrated as a masterpiece of contemporary theatre. Heavy technical demands have even sometimes led to last-minute cancellations, as when a snapped bolt prevented the premiere of *Elsinore* at the

1996 Edinburgh International Festival. The divided response also, however, reflects broader critical ambivalence about the emerging forms of hybridised theatre exemplified in this study. Due to the paradoxical nature of Lepage's engagement with technology and the effects on performances in his shows, he has become something of a lightning rod for criticism of such work.

Echoing charges sometimes made against companies already examined here, Lepage's productions have sometimes been described as formalist exercises and his own performing as emotionally cold. Rejecting what he sees as the emotionalism of Method-derived acting, Lepage himself acknowledges a certain coolness in his approach (derived from self-confessed shyness). Nevertheless, he asserts that the work is concerned with emotions and relationships, suggesting that much of it has responded, if indirectly, to traumatic events in his own life, such as deaths of family and friends and relationship breakdowns.[1] Moreover, he suggests video helps him achieve intimacy:

How do you maintain a sense of intimacy with a thousand people? You have to rely on technology to magnify you, to change the scale on which you work. With *Needles*, we were successful in creating a sense of intimacy in a big space and in general it works quite well. (Charest, 1997, 111)

While his mixing of media and 'high' and 'low' cultural forms, his play with fragmented identities, and his eclectic appropriation of stories and forms from different cultures have led to him being seen as an exemplary postmodernist,[2] Lepage has been described by former director of the Royal National Theatre Richard Eyre as a 'very traditional theatremaker' (Hauer, 1992). He himself talks about the need for theatre to revive the sense of communality associated with storytellers spinning their tales around the campfire (Charest, 1997, 124).[3] For him, film is an extension of shadow puppetry, a development from the shadows cast while sitting by a fire telling tales, and his shows often combine shadow puppetry with other forms of object-theatre associated with storytelling traditions. And yet the sets also spin and fly about the place, along with the performers sometimes. As someone who trained in physical theatre and Commedia dell'Arte, he frequently argues that actors must recover the idea of playing, but the technical apparatus with which he fill his stages often demands split-second coordination between technician and performer, as the latter is flipped backwards through a revolving door or rises above a screen to match his real upper body to a screened lower body.

Although Lepage has directed films successfully, his career has been dedicated more to theatre than film. He argues that the coming of film 'liberated theatre' and that contemporary audiences have a 'sophisticated narrative vocabulary' that must be acknowledged when creating theatre (Ouzounian, 1997). Finding the constraints of the film industry inhibiting, he prefers the possibilities of continual experiment in theatre and values the live contact with an audience. In *Polygraph* (1987) he explores what he sees as the voyeuristic nature of film, with its one-way gaze, contrasting this with the interactive gaze of the live performer and spectator. (Note that he prefers to speak of spectators rather than audiences, seeing the latter term as suggesting a focus on text at the expense of theatre's visual aspects.) Nevertheless, he is excited by the visual emphasis, free play with time and place, framing capacity and syntax of film, seeing devices such as close-ups, flashbacks, dissolves and cross-fades as facilitating a mixture of epic scale and intimacy of individual moments. (Although Lepage generally uses video projection, his work is informed more by film and film genres than television.) Even when not using video, he employs equivalents of these devices, structuring productions through the dynamic montage of the equivalent of cinematic shots, in such a way as to give his productions a cinematic look. He advocates a new hybrid form of theatre and film:

There's not a lot of hope for theatre as it is today and there's not a lot of hope for cinema in the direction it's going right now ... And there's a place in the middle, I think, and there's a form of art and I don't know what it looks like and I don't know what's going to happen ... but I am sure it's going to happen. (Dundjerovic, 2003, 5)

Although Lepage has acquired individual fame as a multi-talented performer/deviser, his working methods derive from his early exposure to exploratory, collective theatremaking; he still develops projects, even his solo shows, through a strongly collaborative process. After training in the late 1970s at Québec's Conservatoire d'Art Dramatique, where he was alienated by a dominant Method approach to acting and became more interested in physical and visual approaches to theatre, he undertook further training in Paris with Alain Knapp. Knapp aimed to develop performers' writing and scenographic imaginations. He expected students to produce texts out of performance investigations, rather than interpret pre-written texts, and emphasised using intuitive rather than rational processes. Returning to Québec, in 1982 Lepage joined Théâtre Repère, a company that employed Ann and

Lawrence Halprin's RSVP Cycle approach to artistic creation (Resources, Score, Valuation, Performance). Through a collaborative devising process beginning with a range of materials – visual, textual, filmic, objects, or memories drawn from the performers, the company aimed to 'discover' a performance rather than set out with a specific narrative or theme in view. Lepage became convinced that literal and metaphoric transformations (for actors, materials, spaces and audiences) lie at the heart of theatre and rejected a theatre that treats 'plays like intellectual problems that need to be solved and only focuses on their socio-political or intellectual value' (Charest, 1997, 161).

During eight years with Théâtre Repère he was involved in creating works such as *The Dragons' Trilogy*, *Polygraph*, and *Tectonic Plates* (1989), and the solo shows *Vinci* and *Needles and Opium* (1990). In 1994, along with several former members of Repère, he established Ex Machina in Québec City. It is based in La Caserne, a creative complex that combines a performing studio with facilities for sound and video work, and offices for various artistic collaborators on Ex Machina projects.[4] The company's name, Lepage noted, 'evokes machinery. But for me, machinery is not only the harness that makes Cocteau fly in *Needles*, it's also inside the actor, in his ability to speak the text, to engage with the play; there are mechanisms in that too' (ibid., 27). Lepage has also directed productions for many other companies internationally, such as the Royal National Theatre and the Opéra National de Paris, as well as undertaking the staging for Peter Gabriel's 1993 *Secret World Tour*.[5]

Certain recurrent figures and tropes are often linked with how Lepage wields both video and broader stage technologies, especially in his devised work. Many of his productions include characters involved in the arts: artists, photographers, filmmakers, actors, dancers, writers. Issues to do with representation and the role of the artist often circulate around them. The characters often embark on journeys – geographical, cultural and personal, providing opportunities for disorienting cultural and linguistic encounters. In *Vinci*, for example, a Canadian photographer travels to Britain and Italy (with Lepage playing the photographer and the characters he meets); in *Tectonic Plates* characters move between Canada, the US, Scotland and Italy, while the title derives from the geographical phenomenon of the separation and subsequent collisions of the continental shelves of Europe and North America, with attendant analogies about cultural collisions; and in *The Seven Streams of the River Ota* characters move between Canada, the US, Europe and Japan. In most productions there is a mix of

English and French, but other languages such as Chinese, Japanese, Italian and American Sign Language appear. All this partly responds to Lepage's own ambiguous linguistic background and the broader cultural and linguistic tensions and opportunities arising from Canada's Anglo-French history and its relations with the US.[6] It is also symptomatic of the phenomenon of 'global souls' discussed in my account of The Builders Association – and which Lepage explored further in his 'techno-cabaret' *Zulu Time* (2000). Lepage himself also speaks of the need to go elsewhere the better to know oneself and to understand one's home culture. Discussing productions such as *The Dragons' Trilogy* (set in Canada's Chinatowns) and *The Seven Streams of the River Ota* (mostly set in Hiroshima), he states that the encounters with East Asian cultures therein are less concerned with revealing something about them than with showing the non-Asian characters discovering something about themselves.[7]

Lepage links all of this with the notion of *décalage* or displacement. In *Vinci* a British bus-driver tells his French-Canadian tourists that they will experience this when driving on the 'wrong' side of the road. It is also a term applied to jet lag. The general sense is of feeling dislocated, even to the extent of nausea or dizziness, as the familiar is removed or confused.[8] Many characters in Lepage productions undergo such displacement and its associated feelings, especially those who may be seen as alter-ego figures for Lepage himself.

Such recurring character types, narrative patterns and thematic concerns, along with a fragmentary approach to narrative structures, are all significant factors in Lepage's handling of kinetic scenery, lighting and reprographic media (from OHPs, mirrors and slide projection through to video and live relay). Although the look and feel of his productions is different, Lepage recalls Svoboda's interest in how such technologies may contribute to a sense of dynamic polyscenicness. The shifting scenery and frequent use of mirrors, as much as the use of video or live relay, continually reframe characters and actions, producing new ways of viewing them. As with Svoboda, such devices also facilitate the prevalent fluidity of location in his work, with a rotating screen or a projection of some sort often being used to signal a shift of scene.[9]

Literal transformations – as walls and floors dissolve – function metaphorically in tandem with the existential instabilities and transformations of the characters and their identities. Lepage himself sees transformation – of actors, characters, scenery and props – as 'the whole basis of the work', suggesting that 'people come to the theatre, often unconsciously, to witness a transfiguration' (Charest, 1997,

134–5). Lepage's inventive handling of scenery and video is echoed in his play with objects. A row of shoeboxes or books may quickly establish the image of a Chinese neighbourhood or the Manhattan skyline, a grand piano represents a continental shelf or a gondola, and an ironingboard becomes a fitness machine or a motorbike.

When such openly acknowledged transformations are combined with inventive, yet simple, video usage, as when a glass porthole in *The Far Side of the Moon* (2000) becomes in turn a washing-machine door, the window of a space capsule and a fishbowl, Lepage's productions turn into a celebration of the empowering 'magic' of the imagination in theatre, a further development in the theatre of attractions tradition. Yet we should note that attention is usually drawn to the fact of such magic being created. As Bunzli notes, 'Story and telling coexist, giving a special focus to the interaction between creators and creation' (1999, 95). Lepage productions usually include open acknowledgement of the spectators, of the transformations that occur, and of the technologies that contribute to these, thus bringing the spectators in on the act, including them and their imaginations as co-creators in the transformations.

We will also see, however, that sometimes the embrace of technology and the cinematic may run the risk of turning the productions into displays of trickery. To illustrate both the inventiveness with which Lepage combines kinetic scenery, object theatre and the use of projection, and the danger of technological display sometimes taking over, discussion here will focus on three of his solo shows, *Needles and Opium*, *Elsinore* and *The Far Side of the Moon*, and his epic *The Seven Streams of the River Ota*.

Needles and Opium

Lepage employed a brief section of video alongside cinema-style title projections in *Polygraph*, a production which had a cinematic atmosphere and structure (with flashbacks, flash-forwards and close-up effects). *Needles and Opium*, however, was Lepage's first production to use video more comprehensively, along with film-like projections and shadow puppetry. A solo show drawing on Lepage's personal experience and the lives of Miles Davis and Jean Cocteau, the production combines breathtaking performance with imaginative, if essentially simple, uses of technology to produce an atmosphere in which '*décalage* is everywhere' (Bunzli, 2000, 29).

As often with Lepage, it evolved out of a kind of archaeology of a particular place and time: his 1989 trip to Paris to do voice-over work for a documentary about Davis's 1949 visit there. Flying over, he read Cocteau's *Letter to the Americans*, written in 1949. Once there, Lepage stayed in a room in the Hotel Louisanne, which had previously been occupied by the performer Juliette Gréco, who appeared in Cocteau's 1949 film *Orphée* and with whom Davis had a brief, tempestuous relationship. Davis and Cocteau were further linked by their addictions to opiates: Cocteau's followed the death of his lover Raymond Radiguet, while Davis took to heroin on his return to New York after his affair with Gréco. Lepage drew parallels between their addictions and his relationship with the lover he left behind in New York during his own trip forty years later. Moreover, Lepage acknowledges more general affinities with Cocteau: his collagist approach, his use of popular culture in 'high' art-forms, his movement between different art-forms, including film and theatre, his fascination with transformations, appearances and disappearances, his espousal of a 'poetry of the theatre', and his exploitation of his personal life within mythic frameworks. Lepage suggests, 'he was criticised throughout his life for the same things as I am. He was considered an acrobat, an aesthete without substance, a formalist' (Charest, 1997, 164).

In *Letter to the Americans*, Cocteau describes himself as training his soul 'to be as well built and graceful as an acrobat'. The structure and scenography of *Needles and Opium* is shaped by this image, the use of mirrors in *Orphée* (where the poet walks into a mirror to enter Hell), and the fact that Cocteau wrote his letter while flying from New York, 'in this atmosphere which the plane ravages with its propellers ... profit[ing] from not touching the soil of any territory but being able to write in the nocturnal sky where there still exist realms of free expression'.

With Davis's music creating a moody atmosphere, the performance largely alternates between Lepage's readings from Cocteau's letter, elliptical evocations of the Davis/Gréco relationship and Davis's battle with drugs, and sequences in the hotel room where 'Robert' tries to reach his ex-lover on the phone.[10] When not in the room, Lepage spends much of the performance as Cocteau suspended in a harness from the flies, between two rotating 'propellers' (large ceiling fans, tilted to face the audience). Beyond the flying equipment, the setting is simple: a chair, a hanging light bulb, and a large suspended Lycra screen which tilts or revolves to create different wall-effects and onto which various projections play. Some are straightforward illustrative projections: a starscape; the effect of Venetian blinds for the hotel room; an image of Cocteau from *Life* magazine; and place and time titles throughout.

More complex, almost filmic, shadow-play images are ingeniously created with an overhead projector located behind the screen. Much of the Davis story is imparted through such shadow-play. Scene Five, for example, consists of parts of a trumpet being placed one by one on the OHP and then being assembled to form a trumpet; the sharp silhouette of these is then balanced by a more shadowy Lepage moving up to the screen and standing with a trumpet. Scene Fifteen illustrates Davis's addiction and its effects in stunning fashion. While Davis's music plays, OHP-produced shadow images of a watch and a trumpet being

Figure 32   *Needles and Opium*

pawned appear; then a spoon, a packet of heroin, and finally, a huge syringe. The silhouetted figure of Lepage steps up to it and is seemingly injected by a syringe twice his size – with the liquid spilling out over the screen.

Equally powerful, and proto-filmic in the style of early Forkbeard Fantasy, is the use of the OHP to show Cocteau seemingly ascending the exterior of a New York skyscraper. Suspended in mid-air, Cocteau describes New York as 'a tall giraffe, spotted with windows'. A coloured, hand-drawn sketch scrolling across the OHP appears on the screen behind him, producing the effect of a camera panning up a building. Having revelled in critics calling him an acrobat, Cocteau says that his work would 'give you such a vertigo that you would never forgive me'. At this, Lepage goes into a series of somersaults, while the OHP transparency is rapidly rewound, creating the vertiginous effect of Cocteau hurtling towards the ground past the windows of the building. (The technique recalls how Méliès filmed the tumbling horse and carriage in 1905.)

Compared with such inventive quasi-cinematic devices, the actual use of video in the production is relatively straightforward. It is used primarily in relation to the Davis story. After Cocteau's somersault, film footage of Gréco appears as one of her songs is heard. As the romance begins, further filmic shadow-play produces the effect of a bird's eye shot of hands meeting over cups of tea and cigarettes. In a scene entitled 'Miles Crosses the Atlantic', video shows an underwater swimmer playing a trumpet, creating an effect that is both sensuous and bizarre. As the swimmer heads for the surface, Lepage rises up behind the screen, to match up with the screened image. The video then moves to a collage of jazz performers. Subsequently, after the syringe shadow-play, a projected title indicates that Davis and Gréco only met again a few times, on the set of Louis Malle's 1957 film *Elevator to the Gallows*, for which Davis wrote the score; a sequence from this duly appears on the screen.

Video also appears briefly at the end of a sequence in which Robert speaks about his low self-esteem to a hypnotherapist (addressing the audience, in fact). After recounting the Orpheus myth, he links it with his own grief over the loss of his lover and talks of seeking a balm to heal his wounds. Implying that the hypnotherapist rejects this, telling him instead to open up his wounds, 'open the gates of Hell', he asks how to do this. The screen fills with video of circular patterns that gradually resolve into a spinning spiral pattern recalling both Marcel Duchamp's Rotoreliefs and the use of such spirals in hypnotism. As the screen tilts backwards and eventually flips, Lepage falls into the spiral and disappears – echoing Orpheus' descent into Hell in *Orphée*. Images of Cocteau are then projected onto the whirring propellers, before the text describes his experience of opium and the hellish effects of attempting to detoxify. The production's restless use of the technology to evoke the dream-world atmosphere of Cocteau's films reaches its culmination in this fusion of Robert and Cocteau's poet. Nevertheless, behind the pyrotechnics and the surrealist effects, eventually it resolves into a powerfully emotional evocation of lost love, as it concludes very simply with Robert sitting alone in his hotel room writing a letter to his lost lover. Structurally paralleling Cocteau's letter, its poetic, imagistic language also takes on echoes of Cocteau and the Orpheus myth, while his reference to himself as a Romeo banished from his 'dear Juliet' recalls Davis as much as Shakespeare.

Elsinore

Lepage saw his next one-man show, *Elsinore*, as 'a sketch, prior to one day creating the real painting':

> ... the technology available to me this time has enabled me to 'X-ray' certain passages of *Hamlet*, and while the action apparently takes place only in the protagonist's head, it occasionally has the look of an electro-encephalogram. (*Elsinore*, Programme note, 1996)

Lepage, who by this time had also mounted productions of *A Midsummer Night's Dream*, *Romeo and Juliet* and *The Tempest*, wanted to reintroduce playfulness into Shakespeare:

> I don't pretend that I can offer the absolute Shakespearean experience. On the contrary, *Elsinore* is more a statement of the playfulness of *Hamlet*. Shakespeare's play uses Players, they do a play – there's a Player King, a Player Queen – it's all about playing. (Eyre, 1997)

Lepage compressed the text greatly, relying on assumed audience familiarity and arguing that such compression into key scenes and speeches reflects the dynamics to which audiences are accustomed by television. Although described as a work in progress, the complex set and multimedia approach, which required over twenty collaborators in design, video, multimedia and so on, hardly suggested a modest experiment. For many reviewers of its first tour, in which Lepage himself performed, *Elsinore* seemed to show him at his best and at his worst.[11] Staged on 'a set that is a cross between a Ferris wheel and the Berlin Wall', full of 'technical dazzle', for many critics it was all show and no substance, 'wizardry without enchantment, stage management, not theatre', 'hollow, offering nothing more edifying than the chance to watch an admired director show off'.[12] The combination of kinetic scenery, video projection and straightforward sleight of hand provoked frequent comparison with magic shows. Responses took on the air of a personal assault on Lepage and the sort of marriage between theatre and video he had been pursuing:

> As he delivers the great soliloquies with all the passion of a robot you realise that this is the theatrical equivalent of a pop video, hip, clever and meaningless. Are you moved by this *Hamlet*? No. (Spencer, 1996)[13]

The cinematic aesthetic and video usage led Lyn Gardner to think, 'Hell, why didn't he just have done with it and make a movie of *Hamlet* rather than a theatre piece that looks like a film?' (Gardner, 1996)

Such responses were not confined to newspaper reviewers or to Lepage's performance. When Peter Darling performed at the Brooklyn Academy of Music in 1997, Tamsen Wolff in *Theatre Journal* claimed 'events are scrambled to no foreseeable end' in a 'magic show designed to display one conjuror's mastery of illusion' (1998, 237). For her, 'this family album of rapid-fire snapshots of *Hamlet* remains almost baffling in its emotional blandness' (240).

Underlying much of the criticism is a suspicion not just of the technology, but also of the whole exercise of directing and performing a one-man *Hamlet* (something Robert Wilson had also recently undertaken). Lepage's resolutely anti-psychological playing (and his unlyrical, French-accented delivery of Shakespeare's poetry) was the antithesis of what critics seemed to desire from productions of *Hamlet* – with the performing virtuosity of an Olivier or Gielgud being replaced by technological virtuosity, and a unified interpretation of the play seemingly supplanted by a fragmentation of text, action and character. Yet in many ways the production harked back to Edward Gordon Craig's notion of playing *Hamlet* as a monodrama, in which other characters are effectively figures inside Hamlet's head, and Lepage's use of mobile screens even contained distant echoes of Craig's 1912 Moscow production. Steen and Werry also argue that his anti-psychological approach and the playing with technology multiplied possible ways of interpreting the play and challenged conventional attempts to constrict it to an 'authorised' meaning, suggesting, 'the avowed and visible presence of technology highlighted the process and production of simulacra, of proliferation of image and sign' (1998, 146). As with other productions discussed in this study, the use of video contributes to more metatheatrical reflection on the way in which action, characters and imagery are always already mediated even in productions which make no use of electronic media.

Although *Elsinore* employed nine slide-projectors, six cameras and four video-projectors, Lepage claimed it was 'extremely low-tech. It looks extremely high-tech, and there's been a lot of high-tech in the workshops and in the rehearsal room, but I've replaced traditional shadow-play by simple live video work. It's very, very basic' (Eyre, 1997). At its simplest, Lepage's handling of projection recalls how companies such as Forkbeard Fantasy employ film to allow one performer to play several characters. Lepage's movement between playing Hamlet, Claudius, Gertrude and the others is often aided by video and slide projection. For example, in the second scene, featuring Gertrude and Claudius, images of the outer elements of Queen and King playing cards are projected onto the set – with Lepage adjusting his pose and occupying the central position in the 'card' as he plays them. Video is also used for scenographic purposes, for depicting Hamlet's father's ghost, and for rhetorical emphasis through devices such as close-ups and freeze-frames.

The way live relay is manipulated also assumes a broader metaphoric function. In a production where Hamlet's first words are 'Denmark's a goodly prison in which there are many confines, wards and dungeons', the set and live relay combine to create an effect that recalls Michel Foucault's parallels between a society under constant surveillance and Jeremy Bentham's Panopticon prison:

at the periphery, an annular building; at the centre, a tower; this tower is pierced with wide windows that open onto the inner side of the ring; the peripheric building is divided into cells. ... All that is needed, then, is to place a supervisor in a central tower and to shut up in each cell a madman, a patient, a condemned man, a worker or a schoolboy. By the effect of backlighting, one can observe from the tower, standing out precisely against the light, the small captive shadows in the cells of the periphery. They are like so many cages, so many small theatres, in which each actor is alone ... constantly visible. (Foucault, 1995, 200).[14]

The shifting walls and floors of the set create not just an image of the instability, the *décalage*, that unsettles Hamlet's world and mind, but also frequently produce a sense of confinement; and the projection onto them of images filmed from both in front of and behind the set (as if by CCTV) conveys the atmosphere of spying and intrigue pervading the Danish court.

The central feature of Carl Fillion's set is a 5m x 5m steel structure, called the 'monolith' by the production team. It contains a revolving circular section, in which there is a further removable rectangular panel (referred to as the 'portal'). Supported by four aircraft wires, the monolith can swing into many different configurations in relation to the stage floor and two further mobile screens that flank it. It can become a sloping floor, a wall, a roof, and a ship-deck, with the portal operating as a door, a window, a table or even a grave-mouth. When the monolith is vertical and aligned with the screens, together they form the battlements of Elsinore and become a projection surface (with dimensions similar to that of a cinema screen); at the beginning, for example, stonework projections are overlaid with projections of film-like production credits. When used as a doorway or window, the open portal allows Lepage to straddle the division between the stage and backstage. Conversing with Horatio, Lepage sits sideways along its lower edge, as though on a windowsill, alternately angling his face out to the audience (as Hamlet) or (as Horatio) slightly behind the monolith. A camera behind the monolith records him and relays his enlarged image onto the front – producing a disconcerting picture of the live Hamlet sitting on the knees of a filmed Horatio three times his size.

Lepage saw the monolith as like another actor, and in this production perhaps more than any other, his idea of the actor as machine and machine as actor came to the fore. Watching, it was at times difficult to decide whether the actor was under the control of the machine or vice-versa: but this also became a provocative reflection on the relationship between Hamlet and the monodrama in which he was engaged. The same could be said of the video; for all that the production became, at one level, a display of the performer's 'acrobatic' virtuosity in working with the technology, at times he seemed to be dominated by the blocking demands of the live recording.

These demands and the ingenious ways in which set and video combined will be illustrated through discussion of a few scenes. The third scene, in which Hamlet encounters Rosencrantz and Guildenstern, exemplifies how video was employed consecutively in different ways. Initially, the monolith is vertical, with the portal open. Hamlet stands in view just behind this, alternately addressing an imagined Rosencrantz

and Guildenstern, as though they are on either side of the portal: all
their dialogue is cut, so that effectively Hamlet delivers a brief monologue, condemning Denmark as a prison and asking them the reasons
for their appearance. Two cameras behind the monolith film him from
either side. The differently angled shots are projected in enlarged
close-ups onto the front panels – creating the effect of him being seen
from the two different points of view of Rosencrantz and
Guildenstern.

As Hamlet recounts his loss of mirth and describes 'this most excel-
lent canopy, the air' as appearing like a 'foul and pestilent congrega-
tion of vapours', a celestial backdrop is projected; standing in the
portal, Hamlet is spun round by the revolving central disc – a literalising image of his *décalage*. Coming to a standstill, he embarks on the
well-known speech:

> What a piece of work is man! How noble in reason! How infinite in faculties! In
> form and moving how express and admirable! ... (*Hamlet*, II.2)

As he delivers this standing side-on in the portal opening, images of a
naked running man flicker across the set – recalling Eadweard
Muybridge's famous 19th-century studies of the human form in
motion that are seen as a precursor of early film. These give way to an
image of Leonardo da Vinci's classic study of human proportions,
known as Vitruvian Man – projected onto the performer. We might see
this as a productively ironic citation of the epitomes of Renaissance
and post-Enlightenment study of the human 'form and moving'; or it
may seem a rather obvious steering of the audience's response to the
speech. Whichever, the video functions here, uncommonly for Lepage,
in choric commentary mode. That Lepage sees it as a significant sym-
bol of Hamlet's story, indicative of a gap between a world of reason
and science and Hamlet's experience of a world out of joint, is suggested by the fact that the image was reproduced in the programme
and publicity leaflets for the production.

Video, abetted by a body double, is used ingeniously in the final
duel scene with Laertes. Again, action mostly occurs behind the monolith, with the open portal providing glimpses of some of it, while video
projection onto the side screens conveys the rest. The scene begins
with a close-up of Laertes rubbing poison onto his foil. Lepage then
fights against a body double who has a micro-camera in the tip of his
foil, so that a very filmic action sequence is created, with shots of
Hamlet's swordplay appearing from the point of view of his opponent.[15]

Figure 33   *Elsinore*

Other cameras capture Lepage as he pauses to deliver the various interjections of Claudius, Gertrude and Laertes. (Here, as throughout the production, digital modification of his miked voice aids the transitions between characters.) When the Queen and Claudius die the video images are frozen on their moments of death – replacing the usual pile of bodies that accumulates at the end of most productions of *Hamlet*.

Inventive combinations of kinetic scenery and video projection are complemented by simple, yet evocative, moments of transformational play with objects, of a kind commonly found in Lepage productions. In particular, his handling of the Mousetrap 'play within the play' makes ingenious use of musical instruments to represent the various figures of the play, and his playing of the Laertes/Claudius interview, with the portal serving as a revolving table, is an effective piece of showmanship.

The continual play with setting and imagery, as well as enabling the piece to be produced as a one-man show did, contrary to some reviewers' assertions, suggest various interpretative avenues, while refraining from expressing a univocal view of the play. The overall conceit of the play as a monodrama played out in Hamlet's mind has already been noted; a picture of Denmark's instability, along with its destabilising effect on Hamlet, also emerged strongly, along with the parallels between the court and a panoptic prison. Closer investigation would also show how themes of incest and what Lepage calls Hamlet's lack of blind passion (with which he identifies) circulate through the production. Furthermore, there is a provocative ambiguity over the extent to which the performer/Hamlet is in charge of the play that he sets in motion or is subject to it.

This tension or oscillation between the performer's (and character's) mastery of the set and his subjection to it does, however, lie behind some of the reservations raised about the production even by critics sympathetic to Lepage's overall approach. The topsy-turvy world of shifting locations and constant role-switching demands great versatility on the performer's part, and this might be seen as emblematic of Hamlet's own situation. But, in effect, particularly when Lepage was performing, the show gradually assumed the air of a magician's display, as one 'trick' was topped by another one. This could then produce a sense that the show increasingly became about Lepage's inventiveness as director/performer, rather than about Hamlet and the Danish court. This does suggest grounds for qualifying Steen and Werry's otherwise convincing arguments that much of the critical response was a reaction against its challenge to the conventional 'authority' (in the Derridean sense) of such a canonical Shakespearian text. They further suggest that it challenges the authority vested in director and actor, and the way dominant critical practice looks for a degree of unification between these three sites of authority. While such an argument is attractive, I am not convinced that the production undermines authority altogether. While the demands of dealing with the challenges of the set and video sometimes make Lepage's mastery of it all quite precarious, his overcoming of the challenges – which, after all, he as director has set himself, only enhances his combined authorship/authority as director and performer, even if he avoids the sort of seamless joint *interpretative* authority of director and actor that they ascribe to productions based on dominant approaches to texts.

Of course, the sense that a production may be more about the performer's encounter with the text, rather than an illustration or fulfilment of the text, is commonly found in postmodern theatre, and we have already seen it as a key aspect of The Wooster Group's work. Lavender makes the point:

The spectator's pleasure really takes wing when the staging itself rather than, solely, the show's over-familiar content becomes available for enjoyment. This is part of the novelty, the excitement, that we seek. … It also defamiliarises the material, another source of pleasure. (Lavender, 2001, 147)[16]

As we have seen in the case of reaction to some of The Wooster Group's work, especially *To You, the Birdie!* and *Brace Up!*, critics often resist this sort of approach to certain 'sacred' texts of the canon.

The Far Side of the Moon

The general response to Lepage's next solo show was more generous, perhaps because it was not 'misusing' a canonical text, perhaps because it seemed more 'personal', and perhaps because it seemed less dominated by flamboyant use of video and other technology – even though it made considerable use of both.

As with previous solo shows, the production's origins lay in Lepage's personal life – his feelings about his mother's death two years previously, but these were refracted through engagement with a broader thematic framework concerning lunar exploration and the space race. The core narrative plays out the reactions of two brothers (both played by Lepage) to the loss of their mother. Philippe, in his early 40s like Lepage, is a perpetual student writing a doctoral thesis on the effects of the Moon landing on the popular imagination. Diffident, unsuccessful in career terms (his thesis is continually rejected), and living an isolated life in a small rented flat, he is contrasted with his gay younger brother, André, a successful television weatherman who lives in an expensive house with his lover. While Philippe is totally shaken by his mother's death, André takes it in his stride and disdains what he sees as his brother's messy life and emotions; he doles out positive thinking mantras and tells him he needs to get out more.

While Lepage does have a brother, Philippe and André cannot simply be mapped onto Lepage and his brother. The tensions shown between them are as much a way of exploring different aspects of Lepage's own character and his own mixed emotions over his mother's death. Moreover, the personal story is complicated by layering it against an exploration of the space race between the US and the Soviet Union. A prologue recounts how the Moon was once thought to be a giant mirror reflecting the Earth, and how its hidden, far side was the object of speculation – until a space probe revealed it to be pockmarked with craters. Taking up the notion of the Moon's hidden disfigured face, and suggesting the American and Soviet space race was the product of narcissistic rivalry rather than a project of scientific enquiry, Lepage draws parallels with the sibling rivalry of two brothers who each 'finds in the face of the other an image of his own disfigurement'.

Incidents in the brothers' lives are interspersed with talks by Philippe about early cosmonauts and a Russian space pioneer, Konstantin Tsiolkovsky, who a century ago developed basic theories of rocket propulsion. Inspired by the Eiffel Tower, Tsiolkovsky also dreamed of an enormous space elevator, which would reach 20,000 miles into space. Attempts to understand and reach the Moon become a metaphor for Philippe's attempt to discover the truth about his mother's death: he is shocked to learn that she may have committed suicide. The weightlessness experienced by astronauts also becomes a metaphor for Philippe's own sense of aimless floating through life. Towards the end, he suggests that Tsiolkovsky's tower-elevator should be built on the far side of the Moon, since from there the Earth would not be seen. He compares the vertigo such an event would induce with the experience of losing one's parents: 'You discover that, although they meant the whole world to you, they were just blocking the view and keeping you from seeing the horizon.'

The idea of hidden sides, whether of the Moon or of people, is reflected in the set and in the way Lepage employs its transformability, along with video, to play with appearance and disappearance. The two principal elements of the set are a rear stage-width wall made up of sliding panels that are used to reconfigure locations, and a similarly sized mirror-wall, which at first reflects the audience back to itself, before being flown into position above the stage, where it later contributes to a visually stunning climax to the performance. As well as representing walls, a blackboard, an elevator door and so on, the rear panels are used for video projection.

Perhaps the most versatile and emblematically significant element of the set is a round glass washing-machine door located in one of the panels. Doubling as a porthole for a space capsule, it provides a literal route between inside and outside and between the domestic and lunar storylines. This is exploited immediately after the prologue, when Philippe piles a basket of clothes into it (these later turn out to have belonged to his dead mother). Filmed from behind the wall and projected onto the panel beside the 'door', an enlarged view of the laundry being inserted appears, as if from inside the 'washing-machine'. As Lepage peers inside, the live relay shows his head. After running the machine for a while, Lepage opens the door again and climbs in. To a soundtrack of cosmonauts conversing, the video projection shows Lepage 'floating' inside the machine, before moving on to show cosmonauts floating weightlessly in a spacecraft. After further images of a rocket being launched, the dirty laundry reappears. Lepage then embarks upon Philippe's Tsiolkovsky lecture, which includes the telling quotation: 'Earth is the cradle of man, but man should not spend his life in a cradle.' (Later, Philippe is shown being 'born' from the porthole as a doll and being carried around by his mother – played by Lepage of course; his subsequent attempts to escape her cradle parallel the attempts of space travellers to escape Earth's cradle.)

The sort of transitions between different elements of set, text, performance, and video seen here foreshadow their fluid interplay throughout the show. They also suggest the characteristic spatial and temporal fluidity of Lepage's filmic storytelling, as locations cross-fade into each other and the brothers' story is depicted through flashbacks. As well as serving again as a washing-machine door, the glass door also becomes the window of an aeroplane, a clock, and a bowl with a (projected) fish swimming around in it. It is further used for projection when Lepage plays a doctor examining the young Philippe. Donning a white coat and spectacles, Lepage arranges an ironing-board so that it resembles the back of a chair, in which the audience is to imagine the young Philippe sitting. As if from Philippe's point of view, the looming face of the doctor peering into the young boy's eyes is seen on the glass door.

Figure 34 *The Far Side of the Moon*

Most of the pre-recorded video consists of clips related to space travel and lunar landings. At one level this serves as quasi-documentary supplement to the narrative, but the way space travel is depicted also informs the spectators' understanding of the characters. Philippe has a romantic view of the Soviet space programme, having as a child heard the first man to walk in space, Aleksei Leonov, speaking about his experiences. At one point Lepage, working with a tailor's dummy and Russian military uniform, adopts the persona of Leonov and describes how he did drawings in space and turned them into paintings on his return to Earth. The contrast between Philippe's appreciation of Leonov's artistic vision of space exploration and André's more pragmatic, scientific way of seeing the world is immediately drawn out, as Lepage transforms into his brother delivering a weather forecast in front of a video image of Earth seen from space.

Although video provides a point of transition here, it is worth noting that in this show Lepage generally does not use video for simple temporal or spatial shifts; he does not, for example, use it to show childhood memories, or to enable scenes between André and Philippe (there are no *Elsinore*-like conversations between stage and screen). Spatial relocations are enacted through theatrical means: he chalks floor numbers onto a panel and it is transformed into a lift; he flips the ironing-board about as various kinds of exercise machine and André is located in a gym; he dons a wig and headscarf and wheels a doll about in a shopping trolley to become his mother at the laundrette.

One very effective use of video recalls his handling of OHPs in *Needles and Opium*. Philippe enters a competition to make a video that will be sent into space to show extraterrestrial beings what life on Earth is like. Wielding a camera, he takes putative spectators on a tour around his flat, while his running commentary reflects the empty life he lives there. No video is in fact shown, and Lepage simply evokes the various elements of the flat in the imagination of the spectators. After an interlude in which he falls back into playing his mother, Philippe returns to making his video. Lepage flips the ironing-board over and squats on it as though it is a motor-scooter. He becomes Philippe riding through the Plains of Abraham, a large park in Québec City, with video projection of parkland scenery rushing by providing a diorama-like background. Recalling being there in 1972, when Apollo 17 landed on the Moon, he remembers feeling that he could see the Moon bleeding and being overcome by his sense of the overwhelming nature of the cosmos. Transported to 1972, he runs home in a panic – while the park scenery transforms expressionistically into dizzying kaleido-scopic imagery. Soon after, when he resumes his documentary, Philippe addresses his potential extraterrestrial audience, commenting,

> You've probably already picked up 50 years of television. You should know that TV offers a distorted image of life on earth ... For me the only thing that could describe the intricacies and subtleties of the human soul is poetry ... there's not much poetry on TV. So I decided to read a poem.

He recites a moving poem by the French Canadian poet Émile Nelligan, *Looking at Two Portraits of my Mother*. At the very moment when Philippe is making a video, he suggests a preference for poetry over the distorting power of the televised image. Similarly, Lepage, for all that he employs video in the show, tends to place greater emphasis on a more general poetry of the theatre to explore his subjects – no more so than in the final sequence of the production. After flying to Moscow to deliver a lecture on Tsiolkovsky, only to discover he is a day late, Philippe speaks to his brother on the phone. André stands in a pool of water in Philippe's flat: their mother's gold-fish, which André was supposed to be caring for, has died. There is a comic pathos behind their mutual attacks on each other's fecklessness. When André opens Philippe's mail and reveals that his PhD thesis has been rejected again, it would seem all is set for a downbeat ending. Then he discovers a letter informing Philippe that he has won the video competition: 'The whole cosmos will see you.' After they agree to meet up soon, Beethoven's Moonlight Sonata is heard playing and Lepage stretches out on a line of chairs and begins to writhe slowly; the floating mirror wall tilts into position to reflect his body out to the audience, looking as if he is floating in space. For all that it is drenched in sentimentality, visually this is a breathtaking moment of resolution, 'a sublime fusion of performance, direction and set design' (O'Brien, 2003). Where in earlier sequences there was a sense that Philippe's aimless floating through life had led to an anxious weightlessness, it as though now he has transcended earth's cradle and is floating free of his past.

The Seven Streams of the River Ota (1994–97)

Created to mark the 50th anniversary of the destruction of Hiroshima and Nagasaki (and presented in Tokyo in 1995), the production is an intricately structured exploration of the interlocking lives of three generations of characters during the half-century following the destruction of Hiroshima. In a brief prologue Jana, a Czech Holocaust survivor who becomes a Buddhist nun in Japan, describes it as being about people 'who came to Hiroshima and found themselves confronted with their own devastation and their own enlightenment. For if Hiroshima is a city of death and destruction, it is also a city of rebirth and survival' (Lepage and Ex Machina, 1996, 1). It developed over a two-year period from a three-hour work in progress into a seven-hour epic, consisting of seven parts (echoing the seven streams whose confluence at Hiroshima forms the River Ota).[17]

The set, simple in appearance, yet complex in operation, is based around the exterior of a long tile-roofed Japanese house, the facade of which consists of seven sliding screens made of rice paper. In front of this are a low wooden porch and a raked stone garden. Although this anchors the play in Hiroshima, where Parts One, Six and Seven are located, the action moves around the world as different screens slide open to 'reveal' other locations: a New York apartment, an Amsterdam library, a concentration camp, a theatre in Osaka, and so on. In keeping with the production's focus on photography, the tightly lit opening and shutting of the screens often resembles a camera shutter revealing snapshots of the characters' lives. At times shadow-play occurs behind the screens or video is projected on to them. A set of mirrors behind them is used to great effect in an evocation of the ghetto at Terezin and a concentration camp. Video is used relatively sparingly, and yet, as often with Lepage, an open theatricality is paradoxically combined with the sort of tight focus shots, cross-fades, lighting effects, music and employment of extra-diegetic inserts that remind us of film.

There is much to do with interculturalism, with comings together and wrenching apart of lives, and with the interweaving of individual lives and historic events. In a show that attempts to harness together Hiroshima, Nazi concentration camps and the AIDS pandemic, a sense of loss is never far away. This is countered by a sense of spiritual or artistic quest on the part of several characters, and, disturbingly for some critics, by gently absurd comic encounters or scenes of an erotic nature. Lepage traces this concern with the reaffirmation of life and sensuality in the face of death and destruction back to his first visit to Hiroshima in 1993, when he discovered that one of the first steps in the reconstruction of the city had been to build 'a Yin bridge and a Yang bridge, one with phallic shapes and the other with vaginal shapes' (Charest, 1997, 90).

Threaded through the complicated narratives of destruction and rebirth is an apparent concern with issues around representation, with the characters including a photographer, an artist, an actor, a television journalist, and a translator. This is also reflected in the diverse representational forms and incidents in the performance: at various points characters rehearse or perform theatre, opera, dance, Bunraku puppetry, and a magic show; characters frequently photograph themselves or each other, and a television documentary is filmed and edited. Implicit links are also drawn between flash photography and the atomic flash that destroyed the inhabitants of Hiroshima while leaving their ghostly images imprinted on the ground.

There is also much play with translation, with English, French, Japanese, German and Czech being spoken – sometimes translated, sometimes not. Drawing links between Lepage's approach to intercultural engagements, representational modes, and physical and linguistic translation, Sherry Simon suggests that the production embodies

> a kind of 'translational culture', one in which idioms are in constant contact and interlap. Lepage's plays enact a kind of code-switching, using varieties of language interaction for specific types of effects. As such, they propose a vision of 'cosmopolitan globalism' as a dialogue among differences. (Simon, 2001, 227)

Following Jana's brief prologue, Part One establishes the axis around which the various lives intersect as it depicts a brief affair between Nozomi, a widowed survivor of Hiroshima, and Luke, a married American Army photographer. The first scene consists of a wordless interplay between video and mime. While an image of the Torii (arch) of Miyajima is projected onto the screens, Luke and a boatman appear in silhouette behind them. They load a camera and tripod into a boat and depart. While video pans across the Bay of Miyajima, Luke takes photographs. Luke is charged with recording the post-Hiroshima landscape – interpreted as the destroyed buildings; Nozomi, whose house he comes to photograph, demands that he photograph her disfigurement also. (The audience is never shown her disfigurement, as she always performs with her back to the audience, or in silhouette.) This introduces an element that recurs throughout the production – the taking of photographs and recording of history. The play becomes an ever more complex picture of the human remains of World War II, as various lives and tales become linked through this initial encounter between conqueror and conquered, photographer and subject.

As Part One sketches a growing relationship between Luke and Nozomi, live scenes at Nozomi's home alternate with brief sequences where video provides a background to mimed or silhouetted action. Three video sequences depict succinctly Luke's movement between the world of American occupation forces and Nozomi's world as a survivor. In Scene Three, for example, a silhouetted soldier mimes painting one of the screens: the computer-generated 'painting' transforms into a video of an American Air Force plane. The soldier 'paints' a semi-naked woman onto its fuselage, and it flies off, with the soldier running after. In Scene Five, video of the Japanese countryside forms a backdrop to a mimed train journey in which Luke gets into a fight with other American soldiers. After a scene in which Luke photographs Nozomi in her wedding kimono but draws back from taking their growing intimacy further, another interlude employs video for what might be seen as a subjective insert. Nozomi's mother-in-law contemplates some old photographs. One, recording a wedding procession, appears on the central screen, before turning into a video as she touches the groom's face. As she kneels, watching the wedding video, the bride and groom clap their hands twice, and

hands clap off stage in synch with the video image, the Mother-in-law tapping with them. The scene freezes on the screen; the Mother-in-law stands up, cries out harshly, and slaps her hands against the screen several times; each time she slaps, the image grows smaller, until it's small enough for her to put her hands on it and 'drag' it into the portfolio, which she closes up and takes off-stage (Lepage, 1996, 10).

The video here provides an imaginative insight into the mother's thoughts as she replays her dead son's wedding in her mind and anticipates her upset over Nozomi's subsequent lovemaking with Luke. A brief and tender scene depicting this is followed by further video of a train, as Luke finally departs – shown again in silhouette.

The nine scenes are very brief, and yet the rhythm provided by the alternation between the Luke/Nozomi scenes and those employing video contributes to a strong sense of a drama unfolding over a period of time; the play with shadow, silhouettes and video create a sense of fleeting action, while the filmic approach to editing and the use of video evoke the atmosphere of classic wartime movies. The impression is of a condensed cross between Puccini's *Madame Butterfly* (an operatic influence acknowledged subsequently when a concentration camp inmate sings an aria from it) and Resnais' 1959 film, *Hiroshima mon amour*, which also centred on a romance pursued in the shadow of the Bomb – between a Japanese man and French woman.

Part Two opens with a video sequence that immediately marks a strong change of mood and location – from the tragedy of Hiroshima to a vibrant New York twenty years later. The video is an extract from an Abbott and Costello routine 'Who's on First', which revolves around confusion over names. Its knockabout nature foreshadows the farcical tone of much of Part Two, in which most of the action is crammed into a bathroom shared by the tenants of an apartment block. The tenants include Luke, who, unseen, lies dying from cancer in a room he shares with his son Jeffrey. In a Menandrian twist, a newly arrived Japanese-American tenant is also called Jeffrey and is later revealed to be the product of Luke's liaison with Nozomi. The two Jeffreys, ignorant of their relationship at first, embark on the Abbott and Costello routine as they discover their shared name. Among their fellow tenants is a Dutchwoman, Ada, whose mother died in a Nazi concentration camp, but not before she had befriended a young Czech girl, Jana – the Buddhist monk of the prologue. Twenty years after this New York meeting, Ada and Jeffrey 2 (along with his Japanese wife, Hanako) attend Jeffrey 1 as he undergoes an assisted death in Amsterdam (having suffered from AIDS). A further twelve years on, Jana, Ada and Hanako gather to dispose of the ashes of Jeffrey 2 in the waters of the River Ota, attended by Hanako's son, David. Also with them is Hanako's boarder Pierre – whose story echoes that of Jeffrey 2 in reverse. He has come from Canada to study Butoh in Japan – where 27 years earlier his actress mother had a brief affair with a Canadian cultural attaché, Walter. In such a tangled tale, it comes as no surprise that David and Pierre become lovers briefly and that at the end it is suggested that Pierre and Hanako make love.

Were it not for their setting, the twists and turns of the plot could easily lend themselves to farce, and Lepage himself nods a wink in this direction both in his handling of life in the New York apartment block and in his framing of Walter's affair with Pierre's mother, Sophie, against the performance of a Feydeau farce in which she was acting. There is also a certain comedy of recognition when, towards the end, Sophie and Pierre, and Walter and Ada encounter each other in the Hiroshima Peace Museum.

While the epic scope of such a production and its concern with technologies of reproduction and representation may have lent themselves to considerable play with video, in practice, its subsequent use is limited to a few scenes in Parts Five and Six.[18] Part Five, set in Osaka in

1970, introduces Walter, his wife Patricia, Sophie and the Feydeau company. On three occasions characters photograph themselves in a station photo booth; each time live video feed provides an enlarged image of their behaviour inside the booth. In one instance Sophie's lover, after a bitter parting with her, is seen striking himself on the face. In another Hanako is shown protecting her face as the camera flashes – while on the centre screen an image of an atomic blast appears. This is quickly replaced, however, by video feed of Jeffrey 2 and Hanako kissing and laughing as they take their photo. The interpolation of the parallel between atomic and photographic flashes seems somewhat facile. It is perhaps more surprising given the subsequent critical use of video in Part Six. Set twenty-five years later, it shows Patricia, now a filmmaker, interviewing Jana about her choice to live in monastery near Hiroshima. After a lightweight interview, Patricia and the camera crew are shown recording reactions shots and room tones, and then editing the tape. Feeling that it needs livening up, Patricia suggests superimposing a shot of the Atomic Bomb Dome onto Jana's bald head.[19] The implicit critique of this handling of such subject matter seems at odds with Lepage's own earlier juxtaposition of the camera and atomic flashes.

This exemplifies potential reservations concerning the production as a whole. The intricacy of its plotting, the inventive theatrical means employed, and the modulation of tone and atmosphere, evoke delight, as so often with Lepage; and it is easy to be seduced by the message of survival and renewal which is threaded through the complicated narrative. Yet it is difficult to escape the feeling that the production sometimes falls into either aestheticising or rendering banal the historical events that provide the springboard for the narrative. As Simon says, 'One would wish for a more nuanced and problematised confrontation of these historical "events"' (Simon, 2001, 224). Equally, the running concern with representation, allied with the interplay between the different nationalities and cultures presented, may be seen as 'metatheatrically emphasising the ways in which representations are culturally produced instead of naturally given' (Harvie, 2001, 123). Yet, as Harvie also argues, 'its critique of those practices is disappointingly limited' (122). In particular, it is difficult to reject the argument that, for all that the production sometimes implicitly critiques the outsiders' attempts to come to terms with Japan, the representation of characters such as Nozomi and Hanako and of Japanese art-forms such as Bunraku and Butoh ends up reinforcing Orientalist views of Japanese culture and behaviour; it appears as an idealised exotic Other, a site of ceremony, spirituality and sensuality – and a feminised one at that, given that no Japanese men are represented. Lepage is a prolific director and the four productions discussed here are not the only ones in which he has employed video, but they do give a representative impression of his approach. For Lepage, video functions for the most part on a par with lighting, music, objects, machines, shadow-play and puppetry, and with his eclectic approach to performance styles: it is a device to be wielded at will as he seeks to create highly atmospheric, cinematically fluid productions. It may be used scenographically, dramatically, subjectively, intertextually, for multiplying the range of characters, and for rhetorical emphases. Most of these approaches have been anticipated in the work of other practitioners, and there is little sense of the sustained exploration of the broader implications of using film or video on the stage found in their work. That said, the constant inventiveness with which he employs video within the governing aesthetic of transformation that informs his productions does mark his work out from much other multimedia work. Although the facility with which he creates his mesmeric stage pictures has sometimes been portrayed as simply postmodern facileness, Lepage's development of a cinematic theatre of attractions has contributed to a growing acknowledgement that theatre may be productively influenced by a cinematic aesthetic without losing a sense of being highly theatrical.

Conclusion

This study started off with questioning the undifferentiating, ahistorical ways in which critics have sometimes responded to so-called multimedia performances. Through illustrating something of the diverse ways in which film and video have been used in theatre, it has argued that the tendency to deploy simplistic binaries around the live versus the mediated in discussing such work can only be misleading. It has aimed to demonstrate that film and/or video can provide extremely versatile means for practitioners to extend their approaches to scenography, dramaturgy and performance in ways that make creative demands on spectators' imaginations. While noting the tendency of such work to exploit visual and performative aspects of theatre more perhaps than much text-based theatre and to often include more simultaneous material, it has rejected easy assumptions that this either disempowers spectators or underestimates their powers of imagination; rather, it suggests that such work often demands a more active, flexible spectatorship which brings to bear strategies for dealing with the material acquired through exposure to theatre, film, television and computer screens.

In Chapter 1 the emergence of three early traditions of working with film was noted: a theatre of attractions approach; an approach that made use of film's capacity to provide images of the 'real' world outside the theatre; and one based on the idea of film being able to access the subjectivity of characters. Much subsequent work has pursued similar paths, while developing them down various byways and using different methods. More recent work has also troubled standard distinctions between the 'real' world and the subjectivity of characters. Moreover, there has been greater use of video to create more overtly intertextual work, and a related tendency to use film or video more self-reflexively to implicitly critique the media themselves.

Beyond reflecting broader trends in postmodern culture, this intertextual, self-reflexive turn also coincides with the rise of video and video art and the way in which this responded to the place of television within contemporary culture. Even as much recent work has largely moved away from working with television monitors, working with video projection instead, much of it still exhibits a strong concern with broader issues of living in a screen culture, where television and video have now been joined by the computer screen. Before moving to some final comments about the significance of work in this area at a time when screen culture has become a cultural dominant, it may be worthwhile to survey briefly some of the key areas of continuity and development that have been traced through from the early experiments of figures such as Méliès and Piscator to the more recent work of companies such as Forkbeard Fantasy and The Builders Association, revisiting a few of the subjects discussed in the Introduction: scenography, dramaturgy and performance.

At one level, scenography is an area where initially one might discern the most continuity in practice; yet even here more recent work has adopted a more radical approach. Earlier scenographic use was essentially a development from the moving diorama of 19th-century spectacular theatre, providing a two-dimensional, but moving, projected background for the performers – whether to represent more fantastic landscapes or to introduce real landscapes, sometimes in very charged ways, as when Piscator used footage of the real October Revolution as background 'scenery' for the fiction of *Tidal Wave*. Much contemporary mainstream multimedia use in opera and drama is similar, although employing more sophisticated equipment for filming, editing and delivery. It is perhaps at its weakest when it simply substitutes three-dimensional settings or painted backdrops with film and relies on the dynamism of editing alone to inject something dynamic into the production. It is at its strongest when the dynamism comes from the interplay between the live performer and the filmic setting; one thinks, for example, of the way Forkbeard Fantasy works with the corridors and vault in *The Fall of the House of Usherettes* or Lepage's handling of Cocteau's acrobatics in *Needles and Opium*. A further dynamic aspect of scenic use is the way subjective or explanatory inserts using POV shots, tracking shots or close-ups may suggest a character's subjective experience of a situation; this may be fairly straightforward, as in much of Svoboda's use, where it contributes to suturing the spectator into the narrative, or it may be played with in a knowing, comic manner, as in much of Forkbeard Fantasy's use of such devices.

An ongoing motivation for much scenic use has been the capacity of film or video to shift location at will and the freedom this allows for narrative leaps or rapid shifts in atmospheres. Such usage often transports the spectator from one fictional scene to another fictional scene, in a way similar to conventional scene-changes or displaced diegetic inserts in cinema. However, from early on, the camera was also used to make the boundaries between the fictional and the real world of the theatre more porous, by showing performers coming from or going to real locales in the vicinity of the theatre. Variants of this device have made frequent appearances in contemporary work, from the highly charged live relay of demonstrators outside the theatre when *Intolerance* was performed, to The Wooster Group's road trip in *Route 1 & 9*, and the way in which Station House Opera's site-specific films show the performers moving about elsewhere in and outside the buildings where they perform. In their different ways such practices draw attention to the way theatrical events take place on a threshold between the fictional and the real and contribute to the greater self-reflexivity about the act of making theatre which much contemporary work evinces. A similar reflexivity informs the metaphoric potential found in their use in productions such as Burian's *Spring Awakening* (with his performers caught up in a projected world), Laterna Magika's *Graffiti*, The Builders Association's *SUPER VISION*, and Station House Opera's *Roadmetal Sweetbread*, where, in different ways, the virtual nature of their projected settings contributes significantly to the spectators' reading of the worlds depicted therein.

Turning to the dramaturgy of work discussed (and again just touching on some key trends), there is a shift from film being initially employed as simply another tool for telling a story to it providing a means of commenting on a story being told, often through presenting further stories, events or information to supplement an onstage story; eventually film and/or video contributes to a dramaturgy that moves away from telling stories of a conventional kind to tell 'impossible' stories or question the way stories and characters are constructed. More directly narrative use may just take for granted the slippages to and fro between media, or it may draw attention to the transitions and play with the different effects of performances that are live or mediated by film or video. Film or video as supplement to a central story may work through dialectical montage in the manner of Piscator, or may form part of a collage of diverse types of material, as in much Wooster Group work. Increasingly, in a way that reflects a channel-hopping approach, shows are made up of interweavings of several stories or situations which are not connected in a narrative way; recall, for example, the multiple stories of productions such as *Jet Lag* and *SUPER VISION*, where what link there is between them is a thematic concern with 'global souls' or living in the datasphere. Companies such as The Wooster Group, Forced Entertainment and Forkbeard Fantasy all play with knowing pastiches of different film or television genres, sometimes playing different genres off against each other and sometimes insinuating a metacommentary on theatre and media through how they handle genres. The simultaneous or interwoven presentation of various sources and genres demands an alert specta-torship ready to read the relationships between different types of material or presentation.

Accompanying all this is an increasing self-reflexive play with per-forming and the creation of character – naturalistic characterisation disappears, and, particularly when using live relay, video is used to draw attention to the performance of identity or construction of char-acter. This can move toward implying a commentary on the nature of identity today as hybrid, cyborgian images are created and images undergo morphing, or as video works to blur the boundaries between real and imaginary behaviours. Whether through devices such as these or through having performers move in and out of the events that are presented onscreen or onstage, or playing with video doubling of their actions, notions of unified, continuous characters are often destabilised.

In Chapter 1 we noted Piscator defending himself against the charge that his fixation with technology and film led him to ignore the acting in his shows, yet admitting that actors did find working with the tech-nology and film difficult. Similar concerns have been raised about the work of subsequent practitioners. Sometimes it is suggested that the intensity and scale of the filmic image can overwhelm the onstage per-former – as it does at times in *The Wonderful Circus*, for example; sometimes it is argued that the interactions with film and technology become merely a display of tricks, detracting from the actor's oppor-tunities to create full-blown characters with whom an audience may feel an emotional bond. In discussing Lepage and The Builders Association it was noted that such charges often take insufficient account of dramaturgies that are not concerned with naturalistic char-acter-driven performance; such critics would not expect to judge a physical theatre piece or a pantomime by the standards of naturalism, so why should they judge intermedial pieces so?

Nevertheless, the way performers act alongside or interact with mediated imagery is an area for continuing experiment. Where film or video is fully integrated into the production, performers recognise that much of what they do depends upon its completion by a mediated image – whether it is literally a completion of their body, as in some examples of hybrid human/screen images, or through live relay of the action, or through their interaction with another, screened performer. It was remarked that in many ways actors are then placed in a similar situation to film or television actors, who rely on the editor to make their piecemeal performances coherent. Yet there is a vital difference: here the actor is performing in front of an audience as well (and the spectators assume the role of editors). While some critics have argued that the presence of the mediated images impairs the possibility of the actor creating the sort of shared relationship with an audience that is often seen as an essential characteristic of live theatre, it has been shown that this is not necessarily the case. Indeed, often it might be argued that the very conjunction of the mediated image with the live performer heightens the spectator's sense of the liveness of the performer. We have also seen how cameras and microphones may extend the range of performance levels – from creating intimate performances in large spaces, as Lepage noted, or playing off the manipulative intimacy of television genres as The Wooster Group and Forced Entertainment do.

Where, as is often the case, a production does not attempt to disguise its mechanics and the performers adopt a presentational style of performance which acknowledges the fact of performing and the presence of the audience, they establish a complicitous relationship in which the audience shares the challenges they face in working with the mediated imagery. Unlike the naturalistic actor who tries to disguise the work of performance, performers in many of the productions studied here lay bare the making of the performance: here Jeff Webster's work on the Richard Dearborn video-diary might be seen as emblematic. Such work implicitly acknowledges the spectators' role in completing the performance – something which applies to all theatre, of course, but which is often ignored. The imagery of the cyborg may also be extended beyond the more literal presentation of hybrid images to include all performances which play off the interaction between live performers and technology – which nowadays includes most theatre, even though many types of performance do not draw attention to the fact. The difference with intermedial theatre is that it draws attention to the mediation involved in performance.

The practitioners discussed here have consistently asserted that theatre needs to embrace advances in technology as they appear, not just for the potential improvements in appeal or efficiency, but also because they recognise the extent to which the nature of experience has changed in the face of the rapid developments in technology, especially visual and communications technologies, over the last century. While for Piscator and Svoboda this had much to do with theatre needing to reflect the pace and dynamism of the modern world, for postmodern practitioners the presence of television monitors, video projection, computer screens and CGI has become a way of not just reflecting but reflecting upon both the literal proliferation of screens in contemporary culture and the implications this has for ways of thinking about existence today. Onstage screens increasingly become a means of playing across the interface between the material and the immaterial that characterises postmodern understandings of reality and identity.

The emergence of theories about cyborgs and hypersurfaces (and their impact on theatrical performance) in recent years has been a response to the way subjectivity and the social and cultural spheres are increasingly shaped by mediatisation, a process which seems to be accelerating exponentially. When Baudrillard was describing the human being as 'now a pure screen, a switching centre for all the networks of influence' (1985, 133), Disneyland provided an important image for his theorising of the way simulation has superseded the real. Today the internet world of Second Life is set to take over as an emblem of the way the virtual and the real have become intermeshed to such an extent that to assume a binary distinction between them is problematic. A development on from chat-rooms and virtual environments such as MUDs and MOOs, Second Life exists as a cyber-world with an ever-growing population of over seven million players/ inhabitants, whose avatars engage in activities which mimic those of the 'real' world to such an extent that many of the players now make a living out of their avatars' virtual jobs on the site. Their avatars offer various services such as estate agency, building, architecture, clothes design, hairdressing and so on, with the Second Life currency being convertible into real dollars. (Over a million dollars is spent every day.) The first 'real-world' millionaire from transactions on the site has now appeared, it has experienced its first 'strike' by some of the providers of services, and, as I write, Sweden has announced that it is opening a virtual embassy on the site, with a real diplomat manning it! Here truly is a screen world.

Yet, of course, just as for Baudrillard Disneyland was not really different from the America that existed beyond its gates, so Second Life, for all that it is presented in the press as an extreme manifestation of cyberculture, is in fact just a more overt manifestation of the way in which many people today function, with fragmented, performative identities, in the space of information and communications technologies which have collapsed classical spatio-temporal distinctions. During an ordinary day, it is not unusual, even for someone who is not a dedicated 'cybernaut', to use the internet to check the news, do some research, make travel arrangements, purchase some goods or download a music-video, chat with distant friends and family on other continents and in different time-zones using a videotelephony system such as Skype, and participate in a chat-room; and then there are sites such as MySpace and YouTube which encourage further types of self-performativity and viewing. When they turn on their television, they will be confronted by the mediatisation of politics and political life and by the inundation of so-called 'reality' shows of one sort or another, in which people are put in some artificial group situation and left to live/perform while viewers/voyeurs get to cast their votes on whether they will survive to the next day or week. Of course, although such shows claim to be reality, audiences and participants are increasingly conscious of the extent to which 'living' merges with performance and editing the daily 'slices of life' shown on television produces heroes and villains and dramatic climaxes.

Given all this, and in the face of some of the hyperbole that characterises the visions of evangelists of the cybersphere, it is perhaps not surprising that sometimes theatremakers may desire a retreat back to some simpler form of art which holds out the hope of authentic, unmediated, embodied performance. Yet, as was seen in the Introduction, there are grounds for scepticism about the feasibility of such a theatre now, or at least question marks over whether such an approach provides a way of engaging with the critical issues surrounding notions of identity and the real in a society so permeated by different media and technologies. Rather than it being a sign of defeat when theatre works with film, video or computer imagery, it may be that it is a sign of a theatre that is willing to engage actively with some of the key forces which shape our experiences of the world today. For all that the practitioners studied here have often happily embraced the various expanded possibilities opened up by their use of screens of one sort or another, we have also seen repeatedly how the work draws attention to the screens that are used (along with other projection surfaces): they have been reshaped, veiled, torn up, cut up, flipped over; they have slid in and out, up and down, to and fro; people have entered and exited through them, dived into them, or merged with the images they contain. All these ways of staging the screen, of destroying the normal cloak of invisibility that is cast over it in cinemas and on television, by extension invite spectators to treat with a critical playfulness the place screen-based media have in their lives.

Notes

Notes to the Introduction: Contamination or Remediation?

1. As discussed in Chapter 3, from the 1960s on artists such as Nam June Paik, Wolf Vostell, Carolee Schneemann and Joan Jonas developed installational work that incorporated video and sometimes performance elements; see Birringer (1998), Goldberg (2001), Kirby (1966), Sayre (1992), Youngblood (1970).
2. Other recent Complicité productions *The Noise of Time* (2000) and *The Elephant Vanishes* (2003) have also used large-scale projection and video.
3. Although Dudley won several awards for his design, it also evoked Lawson-like responses from some; Peter Lathan, for example, asked 'What is the point? Are we trying to beat cinema at its own game?' (www.britishtheatreguide.info/articles/071104.htm)
4. Auslander (1999, 17) illustrates how television sold itself as offering its audiences a 'home theatre', which abolished the demands and discomforts of attending the 'real' theatre, such as having to drive to it, pay parking and admission charges, and so on. Nowadays, of course, advertisers sell us 'home cinema' packages, with digital wide-screens and surround sound.
5. Bolter and Grusin (1996) use the term 'remediate' in the context of computer interfaces adopting conventions from film, television and the visual arts.
6. Picon-Vallin (1999) includes a range of essays on the subject in French.
7. Birringer (1998) in particular, is valuable for the way he grounds his enthusiasm for, and scepticism about, multimedia work in close discussion of various projects in which he has been involved. Though excited by its compositional possibilities and potential critical role, he expresses concern about the risks of such work either succumbing to the seduction of spectacle or contributing further to a tendency to relegate embodied experience in favour of a world based on informational overload.
8. The term 'intermedia' was associated with the Fluxus movement in the 1960s. Gene Youngblood (1970, 365–86) applied the term 'intermedia theatre' to various American experimental events involving film and live

performers during that period. Of course, this begs the question as to whether theatre, film and video individually are not all intermedial art-forms; so for example, theatre may be seen as drawing on literary, visual, musical and performance arts. The remediation of film and video into theatre might then be seen as simply a further extension of theatre's inherent hybridity.

9. Lampert-Gréaux (2005) and Dudley (2004) describe how the 3D effects were achieved. While sometimes static sets such as a drawing room were depicted, exterior shots and sequences such as the onrushing train produced the effect of video, although they were in fact based on animated CGI designs.

10. The term (from 'cybernetic organism') describes a hybrid of mechanical and organic matter: a person fitted with a prosthetic limb may be seen as cyborgian. The notion has come to embrace the idea that human beings today are so implicated with the technologies on which societies depend that we might all be seen as functioning as cyborgs; the cyborg then becomes a metaphor for the idea that there is no such thing as a natural body, but that the body is always a product of material and discursive practices. The allegorical possibilities for theorising relations between nature and culture in contemporary societies, and as a model for a post-modern feminism, were popularised by Donna Haraway's influential 1985 article, 'A Cyborg Manifesto: Science, Technology and Socialist Feminism in the Late Twentieth Century' (Haraway, 1991). Jennifer Parker-Starbuck (2004) develops the idea further in her description of the work of companies such as The Wooster Group as 'cyborg-theatre'.

11. See Kohn (2002).

12. Strictly speaking, it might be argued that most stage performances are also 'virtual', in that the performers and settings are representations or evocations of absent characters and locations.

13. Compare Fredric Jameson's view of postmodern culture's fascination with 'this whole "degraded" landscape of schlock and kitsch, of TV series and Reader's Digest culture, of advertising and motels, of the late show and the grade-B Hollywood film, of so-called para-literature with its airport paperback categories of the gothic and the romance, the popular biography, the murder mystery and science-fiction or fantasy novel' (1991, 2).

14. Critical response to individual productions is often shaped, whether explicitly or implicitly, by disappointed expectations of this relationship of identification. It sometimes appears as if Brecht had never existed, as responses criticise work as unemotional, too intellectual and not exploring fully the characters' lives.

15. See Jameson: 'It is because we have had to learn that culture today is a matter of media that we have finally begun to get it through our heads that culture was always that, and that older forms or genres ... were also in their very different ways media products' (1991, 68).

16. See Jameson, 1991, 67–96.

17. The 'presence' and 'authority' challenged here should not be confused with the sort of charismatic 'presence' we sometimes associate with certain performers, even though the latter sometimes goes along with the kind of theatrical presence being discussed. Copeland (1990) critiques Fuchs' limited application of the term 'presence' and explores a range of other types, including the idea of an 'authentic presence' sought by some post-Artaudian performance work, which again is open to a Derridean deconstruction. Fuchs' limited application is, however, useful in the context here.

18. This focus partly responds to the fact that the majority of the readership for this study will be British or North American; as all the companies studied regularly tour to Europe, and the British companies have occasionally presented their work in the US, there is a reasonable chance that some readers will have seen some of the companies. It also reflects my desire to discuss primarily work which I have witnessed live. Although some of the significant contemporary European work does travel, it has not been seen as widely, and I only make occasional reference to such work. Readers interested in exploring such work further should consult Picon-Vallin (1998) and the bibliography dealing with German productions in Carlson (2003).

Notes to Chapter 1: Magic to Realism

1. See Frazer (1979), 160–2, 172–6; and Sadoul (1985), 166–8, 263–5.
2. It seems apposite that a century later the Châtelet produced José Montalvo's production of Rameau's Baroque opera, *Les Paladins*, whose spectacular use of video Anthony Holden celebrated as 'ushering in a whole new theatrical era' (*Observer*, 6 June, 2004). Holden's praise of its 'technological wizardry' echoes the notion of 'magic' often associated with recorded media in theatre. Rebecca Brite was more sceptical in *Opera Japonica*: 'A three-tiered terrace served as a screen for digital video "décor" mixing animal images, classical statuary and topiary, Pythonesque cartoons, pixel doppelgangers of the singers and dancers, and much, much more. There was no other physical set except for, briefly, a trampoline. The video images and the dancers were in such a frenzy of constant motion that anything else would just have been in the way – as in fact the singers often seemed to be.' (www.operajaponica.org/archives/paris/parisletterpast04.htm)
3. The toppling figure of the horse made a great impression on Sergei Eisenstein. This was the first film he saw, as a child visiting Paris. The horse later reappeared in a famous image, toppling off a bridge in his film *October*. The drive through the heavens in The Builders Association production *Jump Cut (Faust)* clearly pays homage to the Méliès film.
4. See the video *Méliès le cinémagicien* (prod. J. Mény, Paris: Arte Vidéo, 2001).

5. Compare *Round the Alster* in Hamburg in 1911, discussed below. Its use in the work of Forkbeard Fantasy and Station House Opera is discussed in Chapters 7 and 8.

6. The linkage found in several early productions and in Kranich's discussion, between film and revues, cars, planes, trains and so on, i.e. between technology and popular performance, is also found in various Futurist manifestos.

7. The exit through a window or door, only to be followed off by a camera, has become a common trope in contemporary work, appearing in productions by The People Show, Station House Opera, and Forkbeard Fantasy to name but a few. Carlson (2003) discusses similar examples in recent German theatre.

8. Low and Manvell note how early film audiences 'were satisfied to see any simple scene from everyday life reproduced on the screen' (1948, 51). They include railway scenes and waves breaking on the sea-shore amongst favourite subjects for such short actuality films.

9. It is arguable that one factor in the increasing use of video in recent years has been the diminished funding for theatre companies; as companies can afford to employ fewer performers, video sometimes provides a means to expand the scope of what they can depict. In *XTRAVAGANZA*, The Builders Association plays ingeniously with this, using video and computer animation to enable two dancers to create the impression of a Busby Berkeley chorus-line.

10. A 1920 production of Goll's earlier play *The Immortal* also used film and photographic projections.

11. See the videocassette, *Surrealism and Science: the Weird World of Jean Painlevé* (BFI and Argos Films).

12. Goldberg (2001), Kuenzli (1987) and Meltzer (1994) discuss this event.

13. See Seton (1952) and Swallow (1976).

14. Piscator included a Goll play in his proposals for the 1920/21 season of The Proletarian Theatre – although the production did not eventuate. It is curious that in *The Political Theatre* (1980) Piscator makes no mention of Goll when discussing the use of film in theatre.

15. Piscator also regularly mixed with members of the Bauhaus, which espoused a synthesising approach to the arts and an accommodation between the arts and technology. Although Piscator's approach differed from that of the Bauhaus, one of its leading figures, Walter Gropius, designed his apartment and in 1927 produced designs for a new 'Total Theatre', which was intended to incorporate multiple, mobile stages and the technology necessary to surround the audience with film projection.

16. See Rorrison (1980); Pearlman's edition of Toller's text (2000) includes extracts from Piscator's promptbook, detailing the staging of many scenes.

17. In *Twentieth-Century Stage Decoration*, an international survey first published in 1929, W. R. Fuerst and S. J. Hume argued that 'it is extremely difficult, if not impossible, to achieve a unity between the background

with its moving projection and the stage proper, not to mention the actor, who in his living presence, finds himself directly opposed to the phantoms being projected behind his back' (1967, 80–1). Like Kranich, they accepted that 'the non-existent character of the projected stage decorations' might be suitable for 'fantastic plays', but they generally considered such usage 'a return to the old type of stage setting long since abandoned' (114). While acknowledging that the 'ghostly character of the projection' seemed justified for *Storm over Gottland*, they rejected the use in *Tidal Wave* as not offering 'the necessary scenic unity' (81).

18. Bauhaus ideals of a synthesis of the arts were maintained and developed particularly at the Black Mountain College in North Carolina, where Joseph Albers became Director. There, in the summer of 1952, John Cage, Merce Cunningham, Robert Rauschenberg and others mounted a multimedia event, *Theater Piece No. 1*, which is generally seen as the first 'Happening'. (See Goldberg, 2001, and Sandford, 1995.) Its use of film alongside various other media influenced American experiments in intermedia in the 1960s, which in turn informed later work with video in theatre; but, as Mary E. Harris (2002) makes clear, although Cage was influenced by the general cross-disciplinary nature of activities at BMC, his play with chance and arbitrary juxtapositions owed more to his interests in Zen Buddhism, Dadaism, Surrealism and Artaud's writings. These exerted a greater influence than Piscator and the Bauhaus on the nature of North American experiment in this field.

19. Federal Theatre Project, Production Notebook from Seattle production of *Power*. (http://memory.loc.gov/cgi-bin/ampage)

Notes to Chapter 2: Polyscenicness

1. See Burian (2002), 40–58.
2. See Bablet (1970), Burian (1971), and Svoboda (1993).
3. In *The Secret of Theatrical Space* (1993), Svoboda claimed the title of scenographer rather than designer, asserting the scenographer is a key collaborator in production, whose task is more than just providing décor and costumes: it is defining, controlling and transforming space, working in architectural and sculptural ways that function dynamically.
4. Although Svoboda was a major figure of international theatre, whose innovative work made a great impact, little detailed discussion of individual productions with Laterna Magika is available in English. Consequently, my account of productions I have witnessed includes considerable descriptive detail, in order to illustrate significant developments in the company's approach.
5. The production is still in Laterna Magika's repertoire; my account is based on a viewing in 2003. Švankmajer subsequently gained an international reputation for his animated films, including a nightmarishly surreal *Alice in Wonderland* (1987).

6. In the 1980s the company experimented with live relay video projection in two plays writtten and directed by Antonin Máša, *Night Rehearsal* (1981) and *Vivisection* (1987). The latter dealt with a man's response to his wife's death from an illness caused by careless spraying of agricultural chemicals: it was set in a television studio, with filmed documentary material supplemented by live relay video of the man himself. Little detailed information is available about these productions, which proved to be passing experiments by the company and were very much intended for Czech audiences. As in *Intolerance*, Svoboda again used large-scale projection rather than monitors, and it seems to have been more the ability to do live relay and the documentary reporting aspects of television that were of interest.

7. For a full explanation of the Pepper's Ghost apparatus and the optical principles behind it, see Speaight (1989). The effect depends on the strength of the light onto the screen influencing whether it is reflective or transparent at any point.

Notes to Chapter 3: Big Screen to Small Screen

1. Some key figures such as Higgins and Brecht had attended Cage's course on Experimental Composition at the New School in New York between 1957 and 1959. (Piscator had, of course, taught theatre there a decade earlier.) In what follows I am using very broad brushstrokes; as with the Surrealists and Dadaists four decades earlier, different currents of activity led to various denunciations of particular events as not being properly Happenings or in accordance with Fluxus principles, and much was done which claimed to be neither. See Higgins (1976) for links between the Happenings and Fluxus activities; cf. also Sandford (1995) and Schimmel (1998).

2. See Youngblood (1970, 366–71) for Schneemann discussing this and *Night Crawlers* (1967), in which Schneemann and a partner performed live on top of and inside a Volkswagen car stuffed with foam rubber, while *Viet-Flakes* was being projected: 'It was a very intimate and humorous event in front of this horrifying Vietnam film' (367).

3. An excerpt of the video can be seen on YouTube. Although normally she performed solo, Jonas went on to perform with The Wooster Group in *Nayatt School* and *Brace Up!*.

4. See also Baudrillard and James in Podesta (1986), along with counter-arguments by Taubin.

5. *The South Bank Show: The Wooster Group* (dir. Alan Benson, LWT 1987).

Notes to Chapter 4: Postmodern Collage

1. In Callens (2004), Daniel Mufson, Julie Bleha and Ehren Fordyce discuss The Wooster Group's influence on American work. In Britain, Forced

Entertainment, Desperate Optimists, Third Angel, Blast Theory and Clanjamfrie are just a few examples of companies that have clearly been influenced.

2. A detailed account of its early work can be found in David Savran's *Breaking the Rules* (1987), and in Bertens and Natoli's *Postmodernism: The Key Figures* (2002), I discuss its longer-term development and working methods in relation to postmodernism. Cf. also Vanden Heuvel (1992 and 1995), Kaye (1994), Giesekam (2004) and Callens (2004).

3. LeCompte regularly describes their play with different styles, voices and media as adopting 'masks' (e.g. Savran, 1986, 27). Despite Grotowski's influence on The Performance Group, The Wooster Group has rejected the Grotowskian quest for authenticity, with the notion of adopting masks directly contrasting with his idea of performers stripping away social and aesthetic masks. In the light of his comments quoted in the Introduction, it is ironic that the company's 2004 production *Poor Theatre* included a detailed mimicry of video of Grotowski's *Akropolis*.

4. Savran notes that Route 1 and 9 takes the traveller from New York through the urban sprawl of New Jersey and eventually skirts the area where Wilder's fictional Grover's Corners is located.

5. Markham was an African-American comedian whose career spanned fifty years, including touring with Bessie Smith in the 1920s. Although black, he blacked up with burnt cork to do blackface comedy routines for African-American audiences at venues such as Harlem's Apollo Theatre. His 1946 film *House Rent Party* centred on a wildly comic party.

6. LeCompte shot the film before even contemplating *Route 1 & 9*. She decided to include it 'after the fact ... without dovetailing it ... What I did with the footage was cut it in half and run the two parts simultaneously' (Savran, 1986, 41).

7. See Savran (1985) for discussion of how *The Crucible* was used.

8. Susan Letzler Cole (1992, 91–124) provides a fascinating insight into its creation during 1985–86. It went through many developments over several years; my account draws on viewing its 1990 version in Glasgow, a videotape of the show and the text published in The Wooster Group (1996), both of which are very close to the Glasgow version.

9. In 19th-century France the story was adapted by touring theatre troupes and puppet groups, attracted by the opportunities for sensational and erotic action, which could be justified by its 'life of a saint' framing.

10. The show's programme glosses each episode with a summary and extract from Flaubert's text. Episode One is called 'The monologue, in which Frank runs his tape and takes a call from Cubby', while the Flaubert extract is: 'Enfeebled by prolonged fasting, the hermit finds himself unable to concentrate upon holy things. His thoughts wander; memories evoke regrets that his relaxed will can no longer suppress. His fancy leads him upon dangerous ground.'

11. See Arratia (1992, 137–9) for the influence of Barthes' *Empire of Signs* (1982) here, including Valk's comment: 'When we watch Japanese theatre and Japanese movies, we are not trying to reproduce their technique, we are not going to try and walk as they walk in the Noh theatre. We make our own Japan, our own Japanese style because it's culturally removed, it's existing in our heads.'

12. Michael Stumm played Soliony during rehearsals. In some performances, sequences from Godzilla movies were shown as Valk spoke his lines. Stumm's videotaped presence survived in one sequence: where Chekhov calls for a Russian folk song to be played, the monitors showed Stumm playing guitar and singing *Blowing in the Wind*.

13. Their choice of this was decidedly ironic: the film depicts a group of women who leave New York and head out West in the late 19th century, to work as waitresses, a trajectory directly opposite to what the three Prozorov sisters long for.

14. Callens draws parallels between Stein's *Faustus* (whose electric light turned night to day, thus enabling the 24/7 society) and Thomas Edison, a pioneer of both the electric light and cinema, who commissioned the first Frankenstein film and the first American film of the Faustus story (2002, 120).

15. Theramenes is played as Hippolytus' friend, rather than tutor; moreover, although references to Hippolytus' love for Aricia are retained, Aricia does not appear. Hippolytus' character thus resembles more Euripides' Hippolytus, who rejects women's company entirely.

16. Vawter's prolonged illness before his death in 1994 informed aspects of *Saint Antony* and *Fish Story* as well as solo shows he performed in his last years. With many other figures in the New York arts scene similarly affected, Schmidt's shift in metaphor had wider ramifications than his own and The Wooster Group's biography.

17. The Programme distinguishes between Leaming as 'Venus/Referee' and Roche as 'Video Venus'.

Notes to Chapter 5: Third-hand Photocopies

1. Unpublished talk, 'You – The City', given at the ICA, London, July, 1989.

2. Etchells' writings frequently contain traces of key theorists such as Baudrillard, de Certeau, Derrida, Lyotard and Hayden White.

3. Etchells (1999, 94–7) discusses the company's preference for 'old technology'.

4. Both couples were played originally by Fred McVittie and Claire Marshall. Oddey (1994) recounts the early development of the show. It changed radically in its first year; my comments (and quotations) are based on the later version, presented at the National Review of Live Art in 1990.

5. The audience might initially imagine that the interviews employ live relay from behind the scene, but it becomes clear that Mike and Dolores' contributions are all pre-recorded, demanding split-second timing from Robin Arthur as their interlocutor.

6. Between *Some Confusions* and *Emanuelle Enchanted* the company produced *Marina & Lee*, in which Lee Harvey Oswald's widow Marina is shown wandering on foot across a media-scape America encountering situations which pastiche various performance genres: she stumbles across a gibberish opera, a kung fu movie, a Western, a domestic melodrama, and so on – with video occasionally playing a role in their depiction. As in *Some Confusions*, video brings someone back from the dead – as Lee appears on video towards the end of the production and engages in a poignant conversation with Marina.

7. Texts from the production are in Etchells (1999, 142–61). Occasionally, I quote from an unpublished typescript of the production which contains further material. Photographic documentation appears in Lowdon and Etchells (1994).

8. *Goodbye Emmanuelle* was one of a series of French soft-porn movies made in the 1970s. Until the film scene towards the end of the production, there is no other reference to the film and there is no overt link between it and the action of the show. A more metaphoric association may be suggested in the way the performance does, in ways discussed below, partly deal with the pornography and voyeurism involved in performance and media.

9. This might almost be taken as a motto for much of the Forced Entertainment approach to performance; following Meyerhold and others, they often work through playing out the external signs of an emotion until the action seems to produce an affect very much like the emotion.

10. This was still the conventional format for the most part, although around then news programmes began to open out the camera and show more of the studio and the presenters, as if, by so doing, they were opening out the process of the news's creation.

Notes to Chapter 6: Live Films on Stage

1. The company's name derives from Act Three, where the local Builders Association attends the opening ceremony for Solness's fatal building.

2. See Fried (1985). After early experiments in applying cinematic and televisual approaches in his writing, Jesurun used film in *Dog's Eye View* (La Mama, 1983); he then employed television monitors and lip-synch in *Number Minus One*, presented at The Wooster Group's Performing Garage in 1984. Subsequent shows such as *Red House* (1984) and *White Water* (1986) frequently played with interaction between live and videotaped

performers. His earlier texts often incorporated lines from rock and popular music and references to the Second World War and the paranoia of the Cold War.

3. A version published in *PAJ*, 78, 2004, 98–127, formed the basis for a production at the Brooklyn Academy of Music in 2004. Only parts of it were used in The Builders Association productions.

4. Callens (2004, 247–61) discusses both versions, but focuses more on the Swiss version. He notes that 'the early career of Gründgens was inextricably entwined with the rise of Fascism and its ideological appropriation of *Faust*' (253), a fact which feeds into the production's conclusion.

5. This brings out parallels with the myth of Prometheus: both rebels against the gods create conditions for human progress and adventure, but once let loose, such progress is in danger of descending into chaos.

6. French anthropologist Marc Augé applies the term 'non-place' to airports, shopping malls, and motorways: 'spaces of circulation, communication and consumption, where solitudes co-exist without creating any social bond or even a social emotion' (Augé, 1996). The airport exemplifies the excesses of simultaneity of information and events which he associates with 'supermodernity'. He draws analogies between the effects of such non-places and the compression of time and space that results from modern communications technologies.

7. An ongoing thematic line in the company's work concerns over-reaching ambition that proves fatal: from the master builder Solness, through Faust and Dearborn, up to the figures in *XTRAVAGANZA*. Acknowledging that such a pattern emerges, even if it was not an active consideration in making the work, Weems recognises it as 'key in *XTRAVAGANZA* – the whole idea of these four visionary pioneers who held onto their dreams long after it was practicable, and all of them ended up dying in poverty' (Interview, 2003).

8. Fuller held many patents for her work with lighting, pioneering the use of coloured gels and developing new lighting controls. Having begun in burlesque, by the mid-1890s she was the subject of works by Toulouse-Lautrec and Rodin and mixed regularly in French scientific circles, counting Marie Curie amongst her friends.

9. Ziegfeld was ruined by the Stock Market Crash of 1929, Berkeley went insane, and Fuller gradually lost her sight, probably due to the constant exposure to calcium lights in her performances.

10. Weems describes the importance of the NATO computer software: 'Peter Norton who designed the video, went to STEIM in Amsterdam and started working with NATO there. When he came back, he had really found this key element. Because the joke was you have five straggly little downtown performers and they're going to make these fantastic Busby Berkeley spectacles' (Interview, 2003).

11. It has, for example, been involved in design for the Notting Hill Carnival, created a large-scale participatory project for the Tate Modern

gallery, and collaborated with Peter Gabriel on the spectacular opening ceremony of London's Millennium Dome. See Khan (1998) for further discussion.

12. Khan commented: 'For us, as Asians living in London, it was fascinating ... these people felt very empowered by what they were doing, not disempowered. They very clearly saw this as a way of getting economic power' (Wessling, 2002, 32). Note Khan's description of himself and Zaidi: although they, three performers and the composer, Shri, are of South Asian origin, they all live in Britain or the US, thus sharing some of the circumstances of Iyer's 'global souls' and being subject to the ambiguities and tensions surrounding relations between diasporic South Asians and those based in the Indian subcontinent. This perhaps conditioned the extent to which the production focused more on the performing identities aspects of the call-centre operators and the global souls and on the desires circulating around technology, rather than broader political and economic issues surrounding call-centres. For a contrasting performance created in 2003 by Arjun Raina, an Indian actor who had worked as a trainer in one, see www.arjunraina.com/photographsreviews4.htm.

13. The effect employed recently developed motion-sensitive software called DinoVision, which creates the effect of blue-screen filming; the performer's face, which is moving, is captured but the surrounding setting is not. The resulting picture may then be mixed with other video.

14. P. Rae, *Arts Magazine* (online edition), July/August 2003, reviewing the Singapore performance.

15. Mo Angelos also plays the grandmother into a minicam from there. Other cast-members also sit at computers when they are not onstage.

16. Unsurprisingly, given their work, the websites for all these artists contain extensive documentation and illustration, as well as useful bibliographies; see www.stelarc.va.com.au; www.orlan.net; www.srl.org; www.critical-art.net. For Critical Art Ensemble, see also Schneider (2000) and a collection of documents in the same volume of *TDR*.

Notes to Chapter 7: Crossing the Celluloid Divide

1. They were soon joined by lighting designer and filmmaker Robin Thorburn, designer Penny Saunders (since 1980), and performer and sound technician Ed Jobling (since 1987). These remain the core company members. While Tim and Chris Britton lead the development of the shows, the work emerges from close collaboration between these core members.

2. The company website (www.forkbeardfantasy.co.uk) provides a lively picture of activities over the years and includes details of resources available to students, including a DVD of early films.

3. See White (1994).

4. The plot recalls Buster Keaton's silent classic *Sherlock Jr.* (1924), a surreal fantasy about a film projectionist and would-be detective who climbs into a movie and solves a crime. (This influenced Woody Allen's 1985 *Purple Rose of Cairo*, in which a character steps out of the screen to enter the life of a young woman.) In the Keaton movie, however, the narrative 'explains' the transition as a dream. Both films self-reflexively explore how films function as sites of projection and fantasy for cinemagoers.

5. While generally their film sequences are shot on 16mm film, partly out of an attachment to film as a medium, partly because of the better picture quality, for *Frankenstein* they recorded and edited most of the material on digital video, which was then converted into film for projection purposes.

6. Recent developments in digital media have affected viewing conditions, but most commercial films are still filmed on the assumption that they will normally be viewed on a cinema screen; hence the fact that most films are shot in an aspect ratio of 1.85 or 2.35 to 1. Only recently have widescreen television monitors been introduced to cope with such ratios more effectively than earlier monitors, which cropped the film image.

7. Quotations are from a video of the 1996 production. This broadly matches the storyboard version of the text produced by Tim Britton and available from the company.

8. Just before this a rather different example of self-reflexivity occurs; while Jobling fiddles with some sound equipment (dressed as Deirdre, but operating as sound technician), Tim Britton, in the guise of Lucy, drew audience attention to the 'beautiful 78 gramophone' supposedly providing the music; to much laughter from the audience, he then asked Deirdre/Jobling, 'but is it really compatible with that brand spanking new mixing console?'. Assured of its better sound quality, and less flutter and wow, he dropped back into the action.

9. The implication is perhaps clearer in the original comic storyboard version: there a (printed) voice-over comments, 'And so the Empire fell ... swallowed by the abysmal tarn ... never to rise again'; as The End comes up on the screen, the usherettes are shown saying 'Until tomorrow sisters ...'.

10. The bird does indeed echo Klinger's darkly symbolic etching, the last of a series of nine called *The Glove*, featuring a bird that is half bat, half alligator.

11. See Giesekam (2003, and on the Forkbeard Fantasy website).

12. The effect was created using reverse-motion; i.e. a paper monster was filmed being blown by a wind-machine, and the film reversed. This echoed the procedure used to create the composite monster of the first Frankenstein film, made by J. S. Dawley in 1910; W. W. Dixon describes how, 'The use of reverse-motion allows the skeletal form of the monster to assemble out of nothingness', as 'we see flesh compose on the bone, eyes find sockets, limbs take on a human aspect' (Behrendt, 1990, 167).

13. The extensive 'User's Handbook' / Programme for *Frankenstein* includes references to performance artists Stelarc and Orlan, whose work has explored the interface between the body and technology in recent years. It also includes an article by a science historian, Chris Philippides, on continuities between 19th-century ideas concerning electricity and Galvanism and contemporary biotechnology. Its popular comedy surface notwithstanding, this reworking of *Frankenstein* is well grounded in contemporary debates in both performance and science.

14. That said, performances have occasionally stalled due to technical malfunctions, but the relationship the performers create with their audiences, along with their improvisatory skills, allows them to incorporate such glitches into the general atmosphere of the shows.

Notes to Chapter 8: Quantum Theatre

1. For *Snakes and Ladders*, video was in fact projected onto the outside of The Fire Station, with the performers moving about on terraces, balconies and fire escapes; again, there was a blurring of real and projected site, real and projected performers.

2. My discussion here draws on notes of a live viewing in Glasgow's Tramway in March 2002, along with viewing a video of the show's 2001 Zürich performance – which itself involved a drastic editing, since, as it moves to and fro between the two sides, what is shown at any point excludes what was going on simultaneously on the other side of the screen.

3. For further discussion of this and other telematic performances, see Giannachi (2004).

Notes to Chapter 9: Electric Campfires

1. See interviews in Duchesne, Prefontaine, and Beauchemin (1997), Hauer (1992), and Charest (1997, 155–8).

2. Bunzli (2000) applauds this aspect; in contrast, Harvie sees him succumbing 'to the kind of political passivity, and negligence, that postmodern art is so often accused of practising' (2002, 224).

3. Laurie Anderson, with whom Lepage collaborated on *The Far Side of the Moon*, describes her work similarly in her performance *Stories from the Nerve Bible* (1995). In *The Far Side of the Moon* Lepage's alter-ego character Philippe describes television as the modern equivalent of the campfire.

4. The company's website describes it as 'bringing together actors, writers, set designers, technicians, opera singers, puppeteers, computer graphic

designers, video artists, film producers, contortionists and musicians'. (www.exmachina.qc.ca/ENGLISH/ex.asp?page=Machina)

5. Charest's detailed professional chronology (until 1997) illustrates well his prolific output (1997, 179–96).

6. Although Lepage is from a Francophone Québécois family, his parents adopted two Anglophone children. As a bilingual child in a Francophone area, he sometimes encountered hostility from other children.

7. Lepage comments, 'How can you understand the West, the culture of the twentieth century, when you're a Quebecer with virtually no cultural means at your disposal to interpret the world? You need a mirror, and one of my first mirrors was the East' (Charest, 1997, 36). This has brought him in for criticism for having an Orientalist attitude (e.g., Harvie, 2001).

8. We might trace the notion back indeed to Existentialist notions of nausea. Bunzli (1999) discusses the various meanings and implications of décalage more fully.

9. A comparison between Svoboda and Lepage might be fruitfully explored in relation to one of Lepage's recent ventures, KÀ, of which Laterna Magika's A Wonderful Circus seems to be a distant ancestor. Premiered in Las Vegas in February 2005, this $35 million collaboration with Cirque du Soleil is described in the MGM press release: 'KÀ combines martial arts, acrobatics, puppetry, interactive video projections and pyrotechnics to tell the epic saga of Imperial Twins – a boy and a girl – who embark on an adventurous journey to fulfill their destinies .... Lepage describes the story as 'the coming of age of a young man and a young woman through their encounters with love, conflict and the duality of KÀ, the fire that can unite or separate, destroy or illuminate. The Twins' journeys take them through a succession of challenging landscapes and ever-changing performance spaces that conjure an entire empire on stage.'

10. The unpublished text calls this figure 'Robert'. In my discussion, I refer to him as 'Robert' to distinguish him from Lepage the actor performing as Cocteau or Davis.

11. It subsequently toured in 1997 with Peter Darling performing. The account here draws on notes taken during Lepage's 1996 performance and later viewing of video of Darling's performance. See Lavender (2001, 95–153) for the production's evolution.

12. Curtis (1997), Gardner (1996), Gorman (1997), Taylor (1996).

13. Lepage himself called it a rock video version of the play (Gorman, 1997).

14. Ten years later, discussing plans for an operatic version of Orwell's 1984, Lepage referred to Bentham's Panopticon as a visual resource (R. Christiansen, Daily Telegraph, 23 April, 2005). Today, of course, CCTV cameras serve a similar surveillance function.

15. As Hamlet and Laertes both wore fencing masks, the body double, Pierre Bernier, sometimes played Hamlet's movements, allowing Lepage to perform Laertes, Claudius and Gertrude as needed. Bernier worked throughout the show, enabling Lepage to make rapid transitions between roles, while

almost appearing to be in two places at once.

16. Carlson (1985) explores different ways of viewing theatrical production as illustration, translation, or fulfilment of a dramatic text. The various types of pleasure spectators may take in viewing a production, and the way in which the management of their expectations plays a crucial role in such pleasure, are well discussed by Anne Ubersfeld (1982).

17. Although I saw an earlier version in the theatre, my discussion draws primarily on the published script of the 1996 Vienna production and a videotape of the same (Lepage, 1996).

18. Towards the end of Part Two there is also a brief scene in which Jeffrey 1's television shows a laughable 1960s American public education film on how to respond during a nuclear attack.

19. The Atomic Dome was one of the few buildings left standing after the Bomb, although in a skeletal state. It has been preserved as a memorial.

A Selective Bibliography

General

Augé, M. *Non-Places: Introduction to an Anthropology of Supermodernity* (tr. J Howe, London: Verso, 1995).

Augé, M. 'Paris and the Ethnography of the Contemporary World', in *Parisian Fields* (ed. M Sheringham, London: Routledge, 1996), 175–81.

Auslander, P. 'Towards a Concept of the Political in Postmodern Theatre', *Theatre Journal*, 39.1, 1987, 20–34.

Auslander, P. *Presence and Resistance* (Ann Arbor: University of Michigan Press, 1992).

Auslander, P. *From Acting To Performance Essays In Modernism And Postmodernism* (London and New York: Routledge, 1997).

Auslander, P. *Liveness* (London and New York: Routledge, 1999).

Auslander, P. (ed.) *Performance: Critical Concepts in Literary and Cultural Studies*, 4 vols. (London: Routledge, 2003).

Baudrillard, J. 'The Ecstasy of Communication', in *Postmodern Culture* (ed. H. Foster, London: Pluto, 1985), 126–34.

Baudrillard, J. *Baudrillard Live* (ed. M. Gane, London: Routledge, 1993).

Baudrillard, J. *Selected Writings* (ed. M. Poster, Stanford: Stanford University Press, 1998).

Bender, G. and Druckrey, T. *Culture on the Brink: Ideologies of Technology* (Seattle: Bay Press, 1994).

Benjamin, W. *Illuminations* (tr. H. Zohn, London: Fontana, 1973).

Bergman, I. *Four Screenplays* (tr. L. Malstrom and D. Kushner, New York: Simon and Schuster, 1960).

Birringer, J. *Theatre, Theory, Postmodernism* (Bloomington: Indiana University Press, 1991).

Birringer, J. 'This is the Theatre that was to be Expected and Foreseen', *Performance Research*, 1996, 1.1, 32–46.

Birringer, J. *Media & Performance Along The Border* (Baltimore: Johns Hopkins University Press, 1998).

Blossom, R. 'On Filmstage', *Tulane Drama Review*, XI.1, 1966, 68–73.

Bolter, J and Grusin, R. 'Remediation', *Configurations*, 4.3, 1996, 311–58.

Bordowitz, G. 'Tactics Inside and Out: Gregg Bordowitz on Critical Art Ensemble', *Artforum*, September, 2004, 212–17.

Braun, E. *The Theatre of Meyerhold* (London: Eyre Methuen, 1979).

Carlson, M. 'Theatrical Performance – Illustration, Translation, Fulfillment or Supplement?' *Theatre Journal*, 37.1 (1985), 5–11.

Carlson, M. 'Video and Stage Space: Some European Perspectives', *Modern Drama*, 46.4, 2003, 614–27.

Chekhov, A. *Plays* (tr. E. Fen, Harmondsworth: Penguin, 1970).

Copeland, R. 'The Presence of Mediation', *TDR*, 34.4, 1990, 28–44.

De Marinis, M. 'Dramaturgy of the Spectator', *TDR*, 31.2, 1987, 100–14.

Dixon, S. 'Theatre, technology and time', *International Journal of Performance Arts and Digital Media*, 1.1, 2005, 11–29.

Dudley, W. 'Interview with William Dudley' (by J. Potts) in *The Woman in White Education Pack* (no author, London: The Really Useful Group, 2004), 18–22.

Elsaesser, T. (ed.) *Early Cinema: Space, Frame, Narrative* (London: BFI, 1990).

Ezra, E. *Georges Méliès* (Manchester: Manchester University Press, 2000).

Feral, J. 'Performance and Theatricality', *Modern Drama*, 25.1, 1982, 170–81.

Frazer, J. *Artificially Arranged Scenes* (Boston: G. K. Hall, 1979).

Fry, T. *Rua/Tv?: Heidegger and the Televisual* (Bloomington: Indiana University Press, 1993).

Fuchs, E. 'Presence and the Revenge of Writing: Re-Thinking Theatre after Derrida', *PAJ*, 9.2–3, 1985, 163–73.

Giannachi, G. *Virtual Theatres An Introduction* (London: Routledge, 2004).

Giesekam, G. 'A View from the Edge', *Contemporary Theatre Review*, 2.2, 1994, 115–31.

Goldberg, R. *Performance Art* (New York: Thames and Hudson, 2001).

Goll, Y. *Methusalem*, in *Seven Expressionist Plays: Kokoschka to Barlach* (tr. J. M. Ritchie and H. F. Garten, London: Calder, 1980).

Golub, S. *Evreinov, the Theatre of Paradox and Transformation* (Ann Arbor: UMI Research Press, 1984).

Grotowski, J. *Towards a Poor Theatre*, (ed. E. Barba, London: Methuen, 1969).

Hall, D. and Fifer, S. J. (eds) *Illuminating Video* (New York: Aperture, 1990).

Hanhardt, J. (ed.) *Video Culture: A Critical Investigation* (New York: Peregrine Smith, 1986).

Haraway, D. *Simians, Cyborgs and Women: The Reinvention of Nature* (London: Free Association, 1991).

Harris, M. E. *The Arts at Black Mountain College* (Cambridge, MA: MIT Press, 2002).

Hayward, P. *Culture, Technology and Creativity in the late 20th Century* (London: Libbey, 1990).

Higgins, D. 'The Origin of Happenings', *American Speech*, 51.3/4, Autumn–Winter, 1976, 268–71.

Jameson, F. *Postmodernism, or, the Cultural Logic of Late Capitalism* (Durham, NC: Duke University Press, 1991).

Jones, R. E. *The Dramatic Imagination* (New York: Theatre Arts Books, 1941).

Kantor, T. *A Journey Through Other Spaces* (ed. and tr. M. Kobialka, Berkeley: University of California Press, 1993).

Kaye, N. *Postmodernism and Performance* (London: Macmillan (now Palgrave Macmillan), 1994).

Kaye, N. (ed.) 'British Live Art', *Contemporary Theatre Review*, 2.2, 1994.

Kaye, N. *Art into Theatre* (Amsterdam: Harwood, 1996).

Kaye, N. *Site-specific Art* (London: Routledge, 2000).

Kirby, M. 'The Uses of Film in the New Theatre', *Tulane Drama Review*, XI.1, 1966, 49–61.

Klaver, E. 'Spectatorial Theory in the Age of Media Culture', *NTQ*, 11, 1995, 309–21.

Kohn, R. 'Why Mikel Rouse is Becoming an Enduring Master', *Arts4All Newsletter*, 14.20, 2002, www.arts4all.com/newsletter/issue20/kohn20.html

Kozel, S. 'Spacemaker: Experiences of a Virtual Body' *Dance Theater Journal*, 11.3, Autumn, 1994, 12–13.

Kranich, F. *Bühnetechnik der Gegenwart* (Munich and Berlin: Oldenbourg, Vol. I, 1929, II, 1933).

Kuenzli, R. E. *Dada and Surrealist Film* (New York: Willis, Locker and Owens, 1987).

Lampert-Gréaux, E. 'Victorian Secrets: *The Woman In White*', *Live Design* (online journal: www.livedesignonline.com), 1 January 2005.

Low, R. and Manvell, R. *The History of the British Film 1896–1906* (London: Allen & Unwin, 1948).

Marranca, B. 'The Politics of Performance', *Performing Arts Journal*, 6.1, 1981, 54–67.

Meltzer, A. *Dada and Surrealist Performance* (Baltimore and London: Johns Hopkins University Press, 1994).

Minwalla, F. 'Postmodernism, or the Revenge of the Onanists', *Theater*, 23.1, 1992, 6–14.

Morse, M. *Virtualities: Television, Media Art, and Cyberculture* (Bloomington: Indiana University Press, 1998).

Nagler, A. M. *A Source Book in Theatrical History* (New York: Dover, 1952).

Norris, C. *Deconstruction: Theory and Practice* (London: Methuen, 1982).

Paik, N. J. *Video 'n' videology 1959–1973* (Syracuse, NY: Everson Museum of Art, 1974).

Pavis, P. *Theatre at the Crossroads of Culture* (tr. L. Kruger, London: Routledge,1992).

Perrella, S. *Hypersurface Architecture* (London: John Wiley, 1998).

Picon-Vallin, B. (ed.) *Les écrans sur la scène* (Lausanne: L'Age d'Homme, 1998).

Podesta, P. (ed.) *Resolutions: A Critique of Video Art* (Los Angeles: LACE, 1986).

Racine, J. *Iphigeneia / Phaedra / Athaliah* (tr. J. Cairncross, Harmondsworth: Penguin, 1963).

Sadoul, G. *Lumière et Méliès* (Paris: Pierre Lherminier, 1985).
Sandford, M. R. (ed.) *Happenings and Other Acts* (London: Routledge, 1995).
Sayre, H. *The Object of Performance* (Chicago: Chicago University Press, 1992).
Schimmel, P. (ed.) *Out of Actions: Between Performance and the Object, 1949–1979* (London: Thames and Hudson, 1998).
Schneider, R. 'Nomadmedia: On Critical Art Ensemble', *TDR*, 44.4, 2000, 120–31.
Sontag, S. 'Film and Theatre', *Tulane Drama Review*, XI.1, 1966, 62–7.
Stein, G. *Writings and Lectures 1911–1945* (ed. P. Meyerowitz, London: Peter Owen, 1967).
Ubersfeld, A. 'The Pleasure of the Spectator', *Modern Drama*, 25.1 (1982), 127–39.
Vanden Heuvel, M. *Performing Drama / Dramatizing Performance* (Ann Arbor: University of Michigan Press, 1992).
Wirth, A. 'Interculturalism and Iconophilia in the New Theatre', *PAJ*, 33/4, 1989, 185.
Wilder, T. *Our Town* (Harmondsworth: Penguin, 1962).
Youngblood, G. *Expanded Cinema* (Toronto and Vancouver: Clarke, Irwin, 1970).

Piscator

Fuerst, W. R. and Hume, S. J. *Twentieth Century Stage Decoration* (New York: Dover, 1967).
Innes, C. *Erwin Piscator's Political Theatre* (London: Cambridge University Press, 1972).
Kipphardt, H. 'For Erwin Piscator' (tr. A. Vivis), in *Erwin Piscator, Catalogue of an Exhibition by the Archiv der Akademie der Künste* (ed. W. Huder, London: Goethe-Institute, 1979), 10–11.
McAlpine, S. *Visual Aids in the productions of the First Piscator Buhne 1927–8* (Frankfurt am Main: Peter Lang, 1990).
Piscator, E. *The Political Theatre* (tr. H. Rorrison, London: Eyre Methuen, 1980).
Rorrison, H. 'Piscator's Production of *Hoppla, Wir Leben!*, 1927', *TQ*, X.37, 1980, 30–42.
Seton, M. *Sergei M. Eisenstein: A Biography* (London: J. Lane, 1952).
Stoppard, T. *Rosencrantz and Guildenstern Are Dead* (London: Faber, 1967).
Swallow, N. *Eisenstein : A Documentary Portrait* (London: Allen and Unwin, 1976).
Toller, E. *Plays One: Transformation, Masses Man, Hoppla, We're Alive!* (ed. and tr. A. R. Pearlman, London: Oberon, 2000).
Willett, J. *The Theatre of Erwin Piscator* (London: Eyre Methuen, 1978).

Svoboda and Laterna Magika

Bablet, D. *Josef Svoboda* (Lausanne: La Cité, 1970).

Burian, J. M. *The Scenography of Josef Svoboda* (Middletown: Wesleyan University Press, 1971).

Burian, J. M. *Modern Czech Theatre: Reflector and Conscience of A Nation* (Iowa City: University of Iowa Press, 2000).

Burian, J. M. *Leading Creators of Twentieth-Century Czech Theatre* (London: Routledge, 2002).

Day, B. 'Czech Theatre from the National Revival to the Present Day', *NTQ*, II.7, 1986, 250–74.

Speaight, G. 'Professor Pepper's Ghost', *Theatre Notebook*, xliii.1, 1989, 16–24.

Svoboda, J. *The Secret of Theatrical Space* (ed. J. M. Burian, New York: Applause Theatre Books, 1993).

The Wooster Group

Aronson, A. 'The Wooster Group's *L.S.D.* (... *Just the High Points* ...)', *TDR*, 29.2, 1985, 66–77.

Arratia, E. 'Island Hopping: Rehearsing The Wooster Group's *Brace Up!*', *TDR*, 36.4, 1992, 121–42.

Barthes, R. *The Empire of Signs* (tr. R. Howard, New York: Hill and Wang, 1982).

Bertens, H. and Natoli, J. (eds) *Key Figures in Postmodernism* (Oxford: Blackwell, 2002).

Brietzke, Z. 'Review of *The Emperor Jones*', *Theatre Journal*, 50.3, 1995, 382–5.

Callens, J. 'Going Public, Performing Stein', in *Staging a Cultural Paradigm: The Political and the Personal in American Theatre and Drama* (eds B. Ozieblo and M. López-Rodriguez, Brussels: Peter Lang, 2002), 113–30.

Callens, J. (ed.) *The Wooster Group and Its Traditions* (Brussels and Bern: Presses Interuniversitaires Européennes / Peter Lang, 2004).

Cole, S. L. *Directors in Rehearsal* (London and New York: Routledge, 1992).

Fordyce, E. 'House of Stein', *Theatre Forum*, 13, 1998, 29–33.

Fuchs, E. 'End of the Road?', *Village Voice*, 25 October, 1988, 104.

Gardner, L. 'Absolutely Potty', *Guardian*, 9 May, 2002.

Giesekam, G. 'The Wooster Group', in Bertens and Natoli (2002), 327–33.

Giesekam, G. 'What Is This Dancing? The Pleasures of Performance in The Wooster Group's Work', in Callens (2004), 51–62.

Goldmann, L. *The Hidden God: A study of the tragic vision in 'Pensées' of Pascal and the Tragedies of Racine* (tr. P. Thody, London: Routledge, 1964).

LeCompte, E. *A Video Interview with Lin Hixson* (Video Data Bank, 1990).

Lyotard, J-F. *The Postmodern Condition* (tr. G. Bennington and B. Massumi, Manchester: Manchester University Press, 1984).

Mee, S. 'Chekhov's *Three Sisters* and The Wooster Group's *Brace Up!*', *TDR*, 36.4, 1992, 143–53.

Neuman, S. and Nadel, I. B. *Gertrude Stein and the Making of Literature* (Basingstoke: Macmillan (now Palgrave Macmillan), 1988).

Rosten, B. 'The Gesture of Illogic', *American Theatre*, February, 1998, 16–19.

Savran, D. 'The Wooster Group, Arthur Miller and *The Crucible*', *TDR*, 29.2, 1985, 99–109.

Savran, D. 'Adaptation as Clairvoyance: The Wooster Group's *St Anthony*' [sic], *Theater*, 18.1, 1986, 36–41.

Savran, D. *Breaking the Rules* (New York: Theatre Communications Group, 1987).

Savran, D. 'Revolution ... History ... Theater: The politics of The Wooster Group's Second Trilogy', in *The Performance of Power* (eds S.-E. Case and J. Reinelt, Iowa City: University of Iowa Press, 1990), 41–55.

Stein, G. *Everybody's Autobiography* (London: Virago, 1985).

Vanden Heuvel, M. 'The Politics of the Paradigm: a Case Study in Chaos Theory', *New Theatre Quarterly*, IX.35, 1992, 255–66.

Vanden Heuvel, M. 'Waking the Text: Disorderly Order in The Wooster Group's *Route 1 & 9 (the Last Act)*', *Journal of Dramatic Theory and Criticism*, IX.3, Fall, 1995, 59–76.

The Wooster Group. *Frank Dell's The Temptation of Saint Antony*, in *Plays for the End of the Century* (ed. B. Marranca, Baltimore and London: Johns Hopkins University Press, 1996).

The Wooster Group. *House/Lights* (New York: The Wooster Group, 2000).

Forced Entertainment

Etchells. T. 'these are a few of our (half) favourite things', *City Limits*, 9 February, 1989.

Etchells. T. 'Forced Entertainment Theatre Co-operative', *Commissioned Articles* (Glasgow: National Review of Live Art, 1990).

Etchells. T. 'Diverse Assemblies', in *Contemporary British Theatre* (ed. T. Shank, London and Basingstoke: Macmillan (now Palgrave Macmillan), 1994).

Etchells. T. 'A Decade of Forced Entertainment', *Performance Research*, 1.1, 1996, 73–88.

Etchells. T. *Certain Fragments* (London: Routledge, 1999).

Lowdon, R. and Etchells, T. '*Emanuelle Enchanted*: Notes and Documents', *Contemporary Theatre Review*, 2.2, 1994, 9–24.

Malzacher, F. and Helmer, J. (eds) *Not Even A Game Anymore – The Theatre of Forced Entertainment* (Berlin: Alexander, 2004).

Oddey, A. *Devising Theatre* (London and New York: Routledge, 1994).
Quick, A. 'Searching for Redemption with Cardboard Wings: Forced Entertainment', *Contemporary Theatre Review*, 2.2, 1994, 25–37.

The Builders Association

Fried, R. K. 'The Cinematic Theatre of John Jesurun', *Drama Review*, 29.1, 1985, 57–72.
Harries, M. 'Lost in Transnation', *Hunter on-line theater review* (www.hotreview. org/articles/lostintransnation.htm) (2003).
Hutcheon, L. 'The Postmodern Ex-centric: The Center That Will Not Hold', in *Feminism and Institutions* (ed. L. Kauffman, Oxford: Basil Blackwell, 1989), 141–65.
Iyer, P. *Global Soul: Jet Lag, Shopping Malls, and the Search for Home* (London: Bloomsbury, 2000).
Jesurun, J. 'Faust / How I Rose', *PAJ*, 78, 2004, 98–127.
Kaufman, W. (tr. and ed.) *Goethe's Faust* (New York: Anchor, 1963).
Khan, N. 'The Art of the Magician: The Work of Keith Khan', in *A Split Second of Paradise* (eds N. Childs and J. Walwin, London: Rivers Oram, 1998), 136–51.
Parker-Starbuck, J. 'Global Friends: The Builders Association at BAM', *PAJ*, 77, 2004, 96–102.
Weems, M. 'I Dream of Global Genies', *American Theatre*, December, 2003, 24–8.
Weems, M. Interview with G. Giesekam, July, 2003 (unpublished).
Wehle, P. 'The Builders Association and *Jump Cut (Faust)*', *Theatre Forum*, 14, 1999, 4–9.
Wehle, P. 'Live Performance and Technology: The Example of *Jet Lag*', *PAJ*, 70, 2002, 133–9.
Wessling, K. 'dreaming of genies: a conversation with motiroti and the builders association', *(ai) magazine*, Fall, 2002, 30–5.

Forkbeard Fantasy

Behrendt, S. C. (ed.), *Approaches to Teaching Frankenstein* (New York: MLAA, 1990).
Giesekam, G. 'Station House Opera, *Mare's Nest*; Forkbeard Fantasy *Frankenstein*', *Western European Stages*, 15.1, Winter, 2003, 79–84.
White, T. 'The Screen: Looking Through It, Walking Through It', *Contemporary Theatre Review*, 2.2, 1994, 107–14.

Station House Opera

Jones, A. 'Conspiracy on Stage, Screen and in the Audience', *Birmingham Post*, 5 February, 2001.

Kent, S. 'An Act in Several Parts: The Work of Station House Opera', in *A Split Second of Paradise* (eds N. Childs and J. Walwin, London: Rivers Oram), 1998, 117–35.

Lyon, M. 'The Play's Not The Thing', *The Flying Inkpot*, 2006 (Theatre Reviews website at http://inkpot.com/theatre/06reviews/0622,playoneart,ml.html)

Martins, K. and Sohn, P. (eds) *Performance: Another Dimension* (Berlin: Frölich and Kaufmann, 1983).

Peyton Jones, J. 'Review of *Mare's Nest*', *Live Art Magazine*, 38, 2002.

Rogers, S. 'Showing the Wires', *Performance*, 56/7, 1988/89, 9–14.

Robert Lepage

Bernier, E. *The Seven Streams of the River Ota* (ed. K. Fricker, London: Methuen, 1996).

Charest, R. *Robert Lepage: Connecting Flights* (tr. W. R. Taylor, London: Methuen, 1997).

Bunzli, J. 'The Geography of Creation: Décalage as Impulse, Process, and Outcome in the Theatre of Robert Lepage', *TDR*, 43.1, 1999, 79–103.

Bunzli, J. 'Autobiography in the House of Mirrors: The Paradox of Identity Reflected in the Solo Shows of Robert Lepage', in Donohue (2001), 21–42.

Curtis, N. '*Elsinore*', *Evening Standard*, 6 January, 1997.

Donohue, J. I. (ed.) *Theater sans Frontiers: Essays on the Dramatic Universe of Robert Lepage* (East Lansing: Michigan State University Press, 2001).

Duchesne, M., Prefontaine, M. and Beauchemin, L. *The 7 Faces of Robert Lepage* (DVD, Fremantle: Hush Performing Arts Library, 1997).

Dundjerovic, A. *The Cinema of Robert Lepage* (London: Wallflower, 2003).

Eyre, R. 'In Conversation with Robert Lepage', 10 January, 1997, Royal National Theatre, www.nationaltheatre.org.uk/?lid=2627

Foucault, M. *Discipline and Punish: The Birth of the Prison* (New York: Vintage, 1995).

Gardner, L. 'Review of *Elsinore*', *Guardian*, 26 November, 1996.

Gorman, B. 'Elsinore Houses One-Man Wonder', *Ottawa Sun*, 10 September, 1997.

Harvie, J. 'Transnationalism, Orientalism, and Cultural Tourism: *La Trilogie des Dragons* and *The Seven Streams of the River Ota*', in Donohue (2001), 109–25.

Harvie, J. 'Robert Lepage', in *Key Figures in Postmodernism* (eds H. Bertens and J. Natoli, Oxford: Blackwell, 2002), 224–30.

Harvie, J. and Hurley, E. 'States of Play: Locating Québec in the Performances of Robert Lepage, Ex Machina and Cirque du Soleil', *Theatre Journal*, 51.3, 1999, 299–315.

Hauer, D. (dir.) *Who Is This Nobody from Quebec?* (BBC *Omnibus* television programme, 1992).

Hunt, N. 'The Global Voyage of Robert Lepage', *TDR*, 33.2, 1989, 104–18.

Jacobson, L. 'Tectonic States', *American Theatre*, November 1991, 16–22.

Lavender, A. *Hamlet in Pieces: Shakespeare Reworked by Peter Brook, Robert Wilson, Robert Lepage* (New York: Continuum, 2001).

Lepage, R. and Ex Machina. *The Seven Streams of the River Ota* (ed. K. Fricker, London: Methuen, 1996).

O'Brien, H. '*The Far Side of the Moon*', 2003, www.culturevulture.net/Theater6/FarSide.htm

O'Mahony, J. 'Aerial Views', *Guardian*, 23 June, 2001.

Ouzounian, R. 'Lepage's Struggle to Remain Free', *Globe and Mail*, Toronto, 12 August, 1997.

Peter, J. '*Elsinore*', *Sunday Times,* 24 November, 1996.

Spencer, C. '*Elsinore*', *Daily Telegraph*, 22 November, 1996.

St-Hilaire, J. 'Entretien avec Robert Lepage', *Le Soleil*, Québec, 22 January, 2000.

Simon, S. 'Robert Lepage and the Languages of Spectacle', in Donohue (2001), 215–31.

Steen, S. and Werry, M. 'Bodies, Technologies, and Subjectivities: The Production of Authority in Robert Lepage's *Elsinore*', *Essays in Theatre / Études Théâtrales* 16.2, May, 1998, 139–51.

Taylor, P. 'Review of *Elsinore*', *Independent*, 23 November, 1996.

Winsor, C. 'Alas, Poor Robert!: Lepage Is Hoist with His Own Hamlet', *eye Magazine*, 25 April, 1996.

Wolff, T. '*Elsinore*', *Theatre Journal*, 50.2, 1998, 237–40.

Index

277